AF657419

Russia Looks at India

A Spectrum of

Philosophical Views

Research pursuits of

The Institute of Philosophy

Russian Academy of Sciences

Russia Looks at India

A Spectrum of Philosophical Views

EDITED BY
Marietta Stepanyants

Indian Council of Philosophical Research
New Delhi

D.K. Printworld
Publishers of Indian Traditions
New Delhi

Cataloging in Publication Data — DK
[Courtesy: D.K. Agencies (P) Ltd. <docinfo@dkagencies.com>]

Russia looks at India : a spectrum of philosophical views /
edited by Marietta Stepanyants.
p. cm.
Contributed articles.
Includes bibliographical references.
ISBN 13: 9788124605851

1. Philosophy, Indic. 2. Hindu philosophy. I. Stepaniants, M. T. (Marietta Tigranovna) II. Indian Council of Philosophical Research.

DDC 181.4 22

Some articles have been published earlier as *History of Indian Philosophy: A Russian Viewpoint*, edited by Marietta Stepanyants (published by Indian Council of Philosophical Research, New Delhi, 1993).

First published in 2010
© Indian Council of Philosophical Research, New Delhi, 2010
ISBN 13: 978-81-246-0585-1 ISBN 10: 81-246-0585-8

All rights reserved. No part of this publication may be reproduced or transmitted, except brief quotations, in any form or by any means, electronic or mechanical, including photocopying, recording, or any information storage or retrieval system, without prior written permission of the copyright holder, indicated above, and the publishers.

The views and contents of this book are solely of the Author/contributors. While the Author/s of this publication has/have taken all reasonable care to ensure that the contents of this publication do not violate any existing copyright or other intellectual property rights of any person/s or organisation/s in any manner whatsoever, in the event the Author/s has/have been unable to track any source and if any copyright has been inadvertently infringed, please notify the PUBLISHER in writing for corrective action in the subsequent edition.

Published by:
INDIAN COUNCIL OF PHILOSOPHICAL RESEARCH
Darshan Bhawan, 36 Tughlakabad Institutional Area
Mehrauli–Badarpur Road, New Delhi – 110 062

and

D.K. PRINTWORLD (P) LTD.
Regd. Office: 'Srikunj', F-52, Bali Nagar
Ramesh Nagar Metro Station, New Delhi – 110 015
Phones: (011) 2545 3975; 2546 6019; *Fax*: (011) 2546 5926
E-mail: indology@dkprintworld.com *Website*: www.dkprintworld.com

Typeset by: Printo Graphic Systems, New Delhi.

Printed by: D.K. Printworld (P) Ltd., New Delhi.

Foreword

THE deep interest shown in the philosophy and culture of one country by the scholars of another country is as old as the hills. The practice of scholars travelling to far-off countries in search of knowledge and wisdom existed in the ancient world just as widely as it exists in today's world. This phenomenon, named by some scholars of modern times as "inter-culturality," is an outstanding feature of many classical civilisations. Inter-culturality is an intellectual sign of the recognition on the part of one civilisation that values, similar to their own, exist in other civilisations and cultures. Thus inter-culturality is itself a high watermark of a culture and a measure of its high respect for "the other."

Among many ancient civilisations, classical India was very well known far and wide, and, just as Indian traders and scholars visited other countries and cultures, traders and scholars from other cultures also visited India. The subcontinent of India became so wealthy in ancient times that it went on attracting through centuries a series of invaders, the last of them being the British who colonised India for close to two and a half centuries. One of the positive aspects of this colonisation was that it attracted many competent British scholars to make a detailed and deep study of languages, religions, arts and cultures of India. This resulted in India becoming well known among scholars of the world for its rich classical heritage.

While the British empire was busy colonising India, and even more so during post-independent days, many scholars from Europe and other parts of Asia also visited India and developed an inter-cultural interest in our subcontinent amongst whom the Russian scholars have definitely been in the forefront. The Russian interest in India has a long history, and the present book *Russia Looks at India: A Spectrum of Philosophical Views,* edited by Professor Marietta Stepanyants, is a remarkable attempt by a number of excellent Russian scholars at portraying their pursuits of, and interests in, India's tradition and Indian philosophy. As pointed out above, this tradition of Russia's interest in India is not something new or of recent origin; it has been coming down from an illustrious past very well known through a celebrated galaxy of scholars like Fyodor Stcherbatsky, Sergei Oldenburg with their colleagues and pupils. One of the glowing features of this book is its consistent attempt to overcome many of the difficulties which Western students encounter in studying Indian philosophy and also to remove many misunderstandings about it, such as that it is all illogical mysticism, that it is based upon some supernatural intuition, that it has no logical or contemporary relevance, and so on.

In many ways, this book addresses fresh issues in Indian philosophy and is a definite source of authentic information on modern researches relating to Indian philosophical issues. A good balance in the treatment of the religious/theological aspects as well as epistemological/metaphysical aspects of different schools on an almost equal footing is found uniformly throughout the volume. Considering the multi-author character of this book, it naturally has its own built-in limitations that are not always easy to avoid. Howsoever, the editor has made a successful attempt to effect a balance between the philosophical contents from the most traditional systems of Indian thinking like Vaiśeṣikas and Sāṁkhya up to the most modern thinkers like Maulana Azad and Satchidananda Murty, and that is indeed a surprisingly welcome feature.

Conforming to the standardised pattern of exposition of the tenets of each school, explaining the basic as well as peculiar tenets of those schools, and critically analysing problems not addressed so far, this volume will be a fresh and welcome addition to the literature on Indian philosophy. Every essay in this volume has been written by a scholar who has admirable expertise in the system he/she is dealing with. This makes the book bristle not only with critical analysis but also with vigorous authenticity and citations of original texts, especially in all matters concerning the special points in expositions.

Looking at "the other" is never like looking at oneself. A person hardly perceives his/her own defects while he/she perceives most easily the defects in others. But here we have a very different case. The book mirrors the greatness of "the other" in relation to Russia, and this "other" is India, her invaluable philosophical tradition. The book reflects on "the other" with the admiration it deserves. This is the model for a book that cements the cultures of nations instead of raising the wall of differences on the basis of petty considerations, thus opening the doors of philosophical creativity for others to emulate.

One peculiar and delightful feature of this book is that in each chapter one finds a very new analysis and new turns of thought which add to the freshness of the existing Indian thinking instead of being just a repetition of old tenets. Other special features of the book are the comprehensive range of topics from Cārvāka to Maulana Azad, and its thorough discussions of the orthodox schools of Indian thought reaching right up to the most modern authors. More than all this, I admire the involvement and interest of the scholars who are critically doing Indian studies in Russia. All the essays reflect the neatness, precision, and critical thinking which are found in the pages of this book containing rare references and meticulous analysis.

It was with much more than a customary sense of pleasure and privilege that I received Professor Stepanyants' request to write a Foreword to this collection of essays. On behalf of ICPR, I congratulate Professor Marietta Stepanyants whose genuine efforts and involvement have brought India and Russia much closer together, and we expect to have many more volumes from her and her colleagues to open up the world transcending the man-made boundaries and unite us in the realm of thinking.

If scholars from other countries bring together similar analyses and presentations of Indian philosophy from their own unique perspectives, we will be equally delighted to consider publishing them by the Council.

Vasantapancami, 2010 **Godabarisha Mishra**
Member Secretary

Preface

It was in the 1980s that the academic exchanges and co-operation between Indian and Russian philosophers received a really strong impetus. The reasons were both objective and subjective. The former were primarily connected with the political changes in Russia, which had brought radical changes in all spheres of public life, including the academic. As to the latter, one should keep in mind the personal efforts of a number prominent Indian philosophers who demonstrated a keen interest in the development of Indo-Russian co-operation. Professors K. Satchidananda Murty, D.P. Chattopadhyaya, Daya Krishna and Bhuvan Chandel deserve special mention in this context.

One of the tangible results of those efforts was the publication of *History of Indian Philosophy: A Russian Viewpoint* by the Indian Council of Philosophical Research (1993).

About 15 years have passed since the publication of the above-mentioned collection of articles. Though it is a very short period historically, still much has happened during those years in the field of research on Indian philosophy. In fact, so much has happened that one can say that it has been the most fruitful period for the Russian studies in Indian philosophy. Allow me to point out the most important proofs of the above statement:

1. Never before so many translations have been made with highly qualitative commentaries within just a few years. Because of them, the Russian readers have, for the first time, a chance to read the basic texts representing practically all the other *darśana*s besides Mīmāṁsā. All these texts have been translated from Sanskrit.
2. The history of Russian Studies in the field of Indian philosophy does not know any other instance when in 15 years so many fundamental works were published. Most of them are in the series "History of Eastern Philosophies" which was founded by the Institute of Philosophy, Russian Academy of Sciences in 1993.
3. The tradition of comparative studies initiated by Fyodor Stcherbatsky has been revived and developed. The launching of this tradition was initiated by two international symposiums which were held in Moscow. Their proceedings were published in 1993: *God–Man–Society in Traditional Cultures of the East* and *Feminism: East-West-Russia*. In 2000, the series *Comparative Philosophy* (ed. M. Stepanyants) was founded by the Institute of Philosophy. Three volumes have so far been published under this series. The first volume introduces to the Russian readers the history of comparative philosophy; the second volume is compiled from the articles contributed by the participants of the First Moscow International Conference on Comparative Studies "Comparative Ethics in a Global Age"; the third volume consists of the proceedings of the Second Moscow International Conference on Comparative Philosophy "Knowledge and Belief: Different Cultural Approaches." In each case, the Indian approach to the discussed problems is compared with the Chinese, the Arab-Muslim and the Western views.

4. Russia did not include serious courses on either the history of Indian philosophy or on other philosophies of the East. For the first time, the systematic teaching of Indian philosophy along with Sanskrit classes was introduced when, in 1999, Mahatma Gandhi Chair of Indian Philosophy was established at the Institute of Philosophy in Moscow. Consequently, the first Russian manuals and textbooks on Indian philosophy have been composed and published.
5. Significant achievements in the field of Russian philosophical Indology made it possible to bring radical changes in encyclopedic publications. The most stunning examples of that are the *New Philosophical Encyclopedia* (Moscow, 2001) which includes about 350 articles on Indian philosophical schools, categories, notions, personalities, etc., and an impressive volume (of about 1000 pages) titled *Indian Philosophy: Encyclopedia* (ed. M. Stepanyants, Moscow, 2009).

The publication of *Russia Looks at India: A Spectrum of Philosophical Views* has been initiated by ICPR. The proposal has received very enthusiastic welcome by Russian scholars. In this edition, six new articles have been added to all the other articles published earlier. It has been done due to the following reasons. First, Mahatma Gandhi's teaching of non-violence has been radically re-evaluated in recent years. Gandhi's views are justly assessed as relevant to the contemporary life of humanity. Second, the Russian scholars have started taking Indian philosophy as a vibrant tradition. Their high respect for the contributions of the leading contemporary Indian thinkers was clearly demonstrated by the publication of the book *Alive Tradition: Towards 75th Anniversary of the Indian Philosophical Congress* (Moscow, 2000). Two articles in which tributes are paid to K. Satchidananda Murty and D.P. Chattopadhyaya are included in this edition. Third, there is a new generation of scholars in the field of Indian philosophy who are yet unknown outside Russia. Hence the writings by Natalya Kanaeva and Ruzana Pskhu are presented to the readers. Fourth, by concluding the volume with the article by Sergey Serebriany we wish to invite the readers to look into the prospects and limits of the dialogue of cultures. The "encounter" of Leo Tolstoy and Sri Ramakrishna proves that the assumption like the well-known dictum that "all great minds meet" should not be understood too literally. Great minds do differ quite often, especially if they belong to different cultures and to different traditions. It is also a fact that the differences between great minds are no less interesting and enlightening than their meeting points.

In conclusion, I would like to express profound gratitude to the ICPR, and in particular, to Professors K. Ramakrishna Rao and Godabarisha Mishra, who kindly suggested and also made all preparations for bringing out this volume.

The electronic version of the manuscript has been prepared by Lev Titlin, a Ph.D. student who represents the youngest generation of philosophical Indology in Russia.

Marietta Stepanyants

Contents

CHAPTER ONE

Jaigīṣavya Branch of the Ancient Sāṁkhya-Yoga Tradition

VLADIMIR SHOKHIN

ANYBODY who is familiar with the history of Sanskritology should be aware of the progress achieved in the field of academic studies concerning the six classical *darśana*s. However, these results are based mainly on the study of "ready" material recorded in the canonical texts of these systems (in the first place, in the *sūtra*s) and their principal commentaries. The genesis of the *darśana*s and their relation to the preceding periods of each of these traditions have been investigated considerably less. This is due to the fact that these systems are looked upon as certain standards, the ultimate goals of all preceding periods of the development of corresponding traditions, while in reality they are nothing more than a historical form of the dogmatisation of the latter. Therefore, in order to correctly interpret the *darśana*s one should not proceed from them to the ancient schools, but vice versa — beginning from these schools, one should try to analyse their functioning in the systematised *darśana*s. A good opportunity for this is provided by studying the history of Yoga.

Jaigīṣavya (literally "a descendant of Jigiṣu — one striving for victory") was one of the ancient Yoga teachers to whom classical Yoga ascribes a treatise *On the Dhāraṇā*. The tract is concerned with the sixth stage of normative Yoga. Though his authorship is doubtful, it is important to understand Jaigīṣavya's place in the tradition as we shall see later, the title of this tract corresponds to the actual practice of the teacher. As an ancient sage he is frequently mentioned together with the celebrated teacher Asita Devala, as for instance in the 222nd chapter of the "Mokṣadharma" (*Mahābhārata,* XII below, crit. edn.), which explains his teaching, in *Harivaṁśa,* in the ninth book of the *Bhāgavata Purāṇa,* and in the *Bṛhat-Saṁhitā* of Varāhamihira. He is called one of the greatest *yogin*s by the famous Sāṁkhya-Yoga teacher Ārāḍa Kālāma in the 12th chapter of Aśvaghoṣa's *Buddhacarita* and is correlated to "the old man Parāśara," an authority who appears also in the *Majjhima-Nikāya.* Jaigīṣavya's views are referred to twice in Vyāsa's commentary on the *Yogasūtras* and in the sub-commentary of Vācaspati Miśra. In the epic list of Sāṁkhya teachers Jaigīṣavya appears as the first (again with Asita Devala — *Mahābhārata,* XII.306.57). The indicated chapter on "Mokṣadharma" describes him as "the wise one" and "one who has come to know all traditions of *dharma*s," but above all as "one who does not experience anger and exultation" (it is this very trait which attracted Asita Devala to him). The legend about his dialogue with Āvaṭya (see below) testifies to the fact that tradition ascribes to Jaigīṣavya such a distinguished characteristic of *yogin*s as the ability to remember past births during the previous *kalpa*s (cf. *Sāṁkhyatattvakaumudī,* 5).

Despite his significance in the history of the Yoga tradition, textual evidence concerning Jaigīṣavya has not attracted, as far as we know, any special attention of scholars. As a rule, scholarly papers note his relation to Yoga and date the period of his life (for unknown reasons) as late as the first century CE (see, for instance, R. Garbe and A. Keith[1]), though it can obviously be dated some centuries

1. R. Garbe, *Die Sāṁkhya-Philosophie,* Leipzig, 1894, S. 36. A.B. Keith, *The Sāṁkhya System,* Calcutta, 1949, p. 54.

back. The only scholar who has touched the heritage of this teacher is E. Johnston. A detailed analysis of the three sources — the epics, the poem of Aśvaghoṣa and the commentary of Vyāsa — led him to the conclusion that all these texts consistently relate to one and the same tradition which is reliable.[2]

Therefore we are going to turn to the study of the heritage of this ancient tradition from the starting point. We shall begin where E. Johnston has stopped — that is, with a comparison of the related sources.

The main place in the teaching connected with the name of Jaigīṣavya belongs to soteriology, which includes ethics (a system of prescriptions leading to "right conduct") and *yoga* proper, the advanced discipline leading to the attainment of "that place of *Brahman* which is superior to the *prakṛti* and is solid" (*Mahābhārata,* XIII.222.23). Characteristic of Jaigīṣavya's practical teaching is a clear distinction between ethics and *yoga*, as between the first and the second storeys of one spiritual building. That is just what the epic chapter testifies to, where verse 22, concluding the recommendations on ethics, sums them up by stating that the wise one who observes this law prospers, which means one can stop at this stage, while the next verse introduces a new topic, i.e. control over the *indriyāṇī* and the *manas* (that is, *yoga* proper), which helps to attain a higher state — that of *mokṣa.* The same idea is articulated more clearly in the poem of Aśvaghoṣa, where Ārāḍa Kālāma, claiming to expound Jaigīṣavya's views, prefaces the description of the four *dhyāna*s by exposition of the 'behavioural' preparation, i.e. *śīla* (cf. verses 46-47, 48-65).

While, as a whole, the ethics of this teacher can be compared to the first storey of the ascetic building, the foundation of it is one central virtue — that is, the cultivation

2. E. Johnston, *Early Sāṁkhya,* Delhi, 1974, pp. 8-9.

of a balance of mind which nothing can disturb. The main means for achieving this is the elimination of exultation when one is praised or of discontent when one is blamed. It is the first virtue (*Mahābhārata,* XIII.222), the essence of the discipline of speech (verse 14) and the only solid base for interaction with people (verses 18-19). The absolute development of this virtue makes a mendicant aspire towards being blamed and scorned:

> Let him who knows the truth receive blame as the drink of immortality and fear elevation as a poison: a blamed one sleeps sweetly here as yonder and in both worlds together delivered from any evil — it is an offender who is tied.
>
> — verses 20-21

However, indifference to praise or scorn is not an aim in itself and is not sufficient for conquering the self. Other virtues are required from a mendicant: to conceal one's good deeds in order to hinder pride (verse 8); to suppress rage by action, word and thought (verses 12, 15); not to give way to envy and suffering because of other people's success (verse 13). But the struggle with vices alone is not enough — one should also develop good emotions. The most important "positive virtues are permanent satisfaction with everything that happens both in the inner and outer worlds" (verses 10, 16) and the sympathetic feelings of a man "who hasn't any relative who isn't a relative of all other men and any foe who isn't a foe of somebody else" (verse 16).

The position of Jaigīṣavya in asceticism or *yoga* proper can be concluded from Vyāsa's commentary on Patañjali's *sūtra* II.55, which is dedicated to "the victory over the senses" (*vaśyatā indriyāṇām*) and is given in the context of comparison of several ancient authorities on this topic. As the view of Jaigīṣavya can be correctly understood and appreciated only in comparison with that of others it would be expedient to expound all these views one by one.

The first view: Suppression of the *indriyāṇī* can be achieved by cessation of their inclination to objects.

The second: One ought to suppress only "illegal" perceptions, "legal" ones can be admitted.

The third: To stop the very inclination to objects one ought to permit the *indriyāṇī* to contact them at will.

The fourth: The suppression of the *indriyāṇī* can be attained through suppressing the greed or hatred for objects; in these cases the feelings of happiness or suffering are absent.

The fifth: that of Jaigīṣavya. Suppression of the *indriyāṇī* can be reached only on one strict condition — "single-mindedness" (*cittaikāgrya*). This view is also spelled out in the epic chapter, where a *yogin* is recommended by Jaigīṣavya to "gather all his thoughts or aims together" (*samāhṛtya kartum*) and only thereafter to "suppress the *indriyāṇī*" (*Mahābhārata,* XII.222.23). It is noteworthy that classical Yoga — i.e. both Vyāsa and Vācaspati Miśra — considers the position of Jaigīṣavya the most competent and correct of all. The result of the suppression of the senses through "singlemindedness" is estrangement (*kaivalya*). In comparison with it the highest euphoria seems to be nothing but suffering. Jaigīṣavya makes one reservation, which is more evident in the epic chapter, namely the highest states can be attained only by a person working through relative *yoga*-practice — which is impossible for gods and other supernatural beings (*Mahābhārata,* XII.222.24).

Though practical teaching occupies the main place in the legacy of Jaigīṣavya, a detailed analysis of textual evidences helps to reveal some of his cosmological views as well. The account of his talk with Āvaṭya (*Yogasūtra-bhāṣya,* III.18), which, although cannot be regarded as a genuine document, still most possibly contains quite a real version of the Jaigīṣavya school of teaching, which gives an opportunity to make such an analysis.

This dialogue reveals above all Jaigīṣavya's understanding of all of cosmos as a constant, non-interrupted flux of rebirths of all beings who incorporate one body after another and inhabit various worlds (gods are born the same way as men do). Characteristic of the existence of all these beings is suffering. Suffering may vary as to its degree, but it is completely universal. What is more, the notion of suffering is used as a basic one for the hierarchical description of the cosmos: each lower stratum (level) of life is looked upon as a suffering compared to the higher one. Existence in hells and in animal wombs is considered as the lowest level, whereas the bliss of the *yogin*, who has not yet attained complete *kaivalya*, is considered the highest. In the Sāṁkhya tradition this motive seems to be present from the very beginning permanently. One can observe it already in the model of Arāḍa Kālāma: *saṁsāra-duḥkha* (*Buddhacarita*, XIII.32, 37), while *Mahābhārata*, XII.290, alongside many other epic passages, testifies to the alleged ability of the Sāṁkhyas to behold, like Jaigīṣavya, their previous lives (births) as well as suffering in hells and animal wombs and the frailty of happiness of *svarga*-inhabitants. Add to this the evidences of the *Maitrī Upaniṣad* already saturated with Sāṁkhya ideas, particularly the tremendous picture of the decay of all living beings in the introductory chapter of this text (I.3-4).

Let us make an attempt now to sum up the results obtained both from the study of the evidences on Jaigīṣavya's personality and from an analysis of his teaching.

1. Although the texts related to Jaigīṣavya's person (as also those of other ancient Indian teachers) are full of literary clichés, there is no doubt concerning the historical existence of this ancient school and, quite possibly, of a person bearing this name, whose teaching appears as being individual, which is

stressed in some important sources (e.g. Vyāsa and Vācaspati Miśra). The school of Jaigīṣavya played an important role both in the Sāṁkhya and Yoga traditions.

2. The presence of the name of Jaigīṣavya in epic and post-epic literature as well as Vyāsa's records on the "philosophical" dialogue testify to an important connection of this school with the trends of Sāṁkhya. One can draw a line connecting the school of Jaigīṣavya with those associated in ancient Indian lore with the names of Ārāḍa Kālāma and Asita Devala. A special study of the history of ancient Sāṁkhya conducted by us (the results are published elsewhere) showed that this was one of its leading lines (alongside Kapila's and Pañcaśikhā's lines). Being unanimous with other schools of ancient Sāṁkhya in the attempt to describe the "flux-of-being," in stressing the ontological aspect of suffering and in seeing the main aim as elimination of suffering, the Jaigīṣavya school differs from them in that it does not strive to train "laymen" but confines itself to mendicants only.[3]
3. As to the role of the Jaigīṣavya school in the tradition of Yoga, one ought to stress that its practical teaching, as in some other ancient traditions mentioned by Aśvaghoṣa, is characterised by distinctions drawn between ethics and asceticism — these being two stages of self-perfection: initial and advanced. The goal of ethical training is achieving a stability of mind under favourable as well as unfavourable circumstances. This is followed by

3. To appreciate the suffering doctrine in ancient Sāṁkhya one should explore, for example, the passages connected with the tradition of Pañcaśikhā, especially *Mahābhārata*, XII.212, 367.

suppression of vices and cultivating the "balanced state" and "sympathetic" attitudes. Stability of mind, leading to the state of *kaivalya,* is fully achieved in the ascetic stage of psycho-technics — in the fulfilment of the sense-repression strategy. What is specific to the Jaigīṣavya school is not only its firmness in resolving the *indriyajaya* question. It is also more sophisticated than the other Yoga schools mentioned by Vyāsa. It puts forward the task of eliminating the mind's fluctuations whereupon the senses are suppressed automatically, rather than direct control of the senses.

4. The evidences we have so far analysed are of importance for solving the problem of the genesis of the classical *darśana*s from the ancient teachers' traditions. One can see that classical Yoga has dogmatised the succession of stages in the adepts' advance, one being ethical (in two directions, i.e. suppression of bad and cultivation of good dispositions — cf. *yama* and *niyama*), and the other yogic proper, and a strict position in solving the *indriyajaya* problem. These views were introduced by several ancient traditions of *yoga* ascetics, one of which was that of Jaigīṣavya and some schools close to it.[4] Moreover, Vyāsa's comparison of the views of the *yoga* authorities clearly demonstrates that the Yoga-Darśana was established and standardized (perhaps by the nearest surroundings of its *sūtrakāra*) through debates between the *yoga* traditions, which resulted in the adoption of the views of one of them.

5. The above-mentioned facts throw light on the

4. Cf. a strict view of Pārāśarīya Brāhmaṇa on the *indriya* restriction problem — *Majjhima-Nikāya,* III.298-302 (cf. *Mahābhārata,* XII.308.24).

complicated problem of the typological relations of the Sāṁkhya-Yoga tradition with other trends of ancient thought. There is in the Sanskritology of today a definite ignorance of the achievements in the studies on Sāṁkhya-Buddhistic parallels (which are represented mainly by the works of R. Garbe, H. Jacobi, Th. Stcherbatsky and some other scholars of the past). However, an investigation of the ancient Sāṁkhya schools claims the revision of contemporary views on the "pure Brāhmanical" features of Sāṁkhya. One of the most striking similarities between the traditions of the Sāṁkhyas and the Buddhists is connected with the development of the doctrine of suffering, including its ontological dimensions and some peculiarities of the *saṁsāra-duḥkha* model (the doctrine which is initially exponent for the Sāṁkhyas and not only for the *Sāṁkhya-Kārikā* as many scholars assert). Also significant is the idea of man's superiority to gods. This idea, although it has some parallels in the Hindu thought, is expressed in the most clear-cut terms by the Buddhists and Jainas. The question of typological relations between Yoga and other religious traditions is also quite important because of the popularity in modern studies of religions of the quasi-scientific views that are represented mainly by numerous authors. In their writings the "universal soteriological core" of all religions (which indeed is mythical) is identified with some kind of *yoga*-like practice. To solve the problem correctly one ought to carefully study the main principles of the practical conception of Yoga. This kind of "salvation" as the classical variant of the self-redemption soteriology is the standard of the whole of ancient Indian spirituality (Hindu, Buddhist and Jaina), but it is not universal.[5]

Yoga's significance cannot be considered in the context of the Indian culture alone. Yoga's presumptions are very similar to those of late Hellenistic gnostics, neo-Pythagoreans, and neo-Platonists (first of all of Plotinus and Porphyry). Ethics for them too was nothing more than a preliminary training permitting an adept to get to meditative practice. Both Indian and Hellenistic esoterics, in elaborating the "machinery" of self-redemption, considered that it is quite possible to eliminate the misfortune of the "heritage" of transmigration (which has no beginning in time) by one's own efforts (in spite of the evident logical shortcomings of this position). These fundamental parallels must be differentiated from the superficial (but popular with students of religion) correlations which can be found in any religious tradition with no account given of their peculiarities. Of this kind are the semblances between yogic elimination of the mind's fluctuations and "the pacification of mind" of Christian ascetics, semblances which only stress the fundamental differences between the two traditions. Fluctuations of mind, whose restriction by a "self-redeeming" *yogin* is the first task of *yoga*-practice (cf. the strategy of the *Yogasūtras* from the very beginning of the text), are looked upon in patristic soteriology as only one consequence of much more complicated processes which have affected the utmost depths of the human inner structure as a result of man's fall. Thus, the authentic "pacification of mind" from the Christian point of view

5. Although these traditions allow for the existence of the traditional polytheistic gods, the part of the latter in salvation is negligible, being nothing more than that of the most humble satellites of the advanced adept (cf. the life of the Buddha).

requires a fundamental rehabilitation of the whole personality, and first of all of its injured spiritual centre. Such a rehabilitation is not possible through any method of self-redemption, however perfect in itself, including meditative practices, stoical virtues and "sympathetic" feelings (like those developed by Jaigīṣavya and other yoga teachers), although the importance of man's personal efforts is by no means neglected. Clearly, the appreciation of the significance of ancient Sāṁkhya-Yoga needs careful investigation of all the ancient Indian trends of thought in their interactions (first of all of the so-called "orthodox" and "unorthodox" trends) and a differentiation between various types of religions based upon a study of their theoretical principles and the facts of their real history as well.

CHAPTER TWO

The Atomistic Theory of Vaiśeṣika
Problems of Interpretation

VICTORIA LYSENKO

WHILE the doctrine of *mahābhūtās* (great elements) which we find in Vaiśeṣika can be traced back to the Upaniṣads and to the ancient Indian epics, the atomistic view of the structure of the universe hardly had any precedent in the Vedic literature.[1]

It is more or less generally accepted that Indian atomism appeared in the doctrines of Jainism, Buddhism and Ājīvika (around the third century BCE) as it is attested in a number of texts pertaining to these heterodox philosophical

* The revised version of the first publication (1993). Since that time the author published the following papers on the same subject: "Atomistic Mode of Thinking as Exemplified by the Vaiśeṣika Philosophy of Number" in *Asiatische Studien*, XLVIII, 2, 1994, pp. 781-806; "Atomistic Formulations in Indian Thought", in Victoria Lysenko and Michel Hulin's, *Classical Indian Philosophy Reinterpreted*, New Delhi: Decent Books, 2007, pp. 9-26.

1. See H. Jacobi, *Studies in the History of Indian Philosophy*, Calcutta, 1978, p. 132. B. Barua, however, finds elements of an atomistic conception in the teaching of Uddālaka Āruṇi, a sage mentioned in the Upaniṣads: "By propounding the theory of combination and separation of particles, Uddālaka anticipated the atomistic theory of Kaṇāda." (B. Barua, *A History of Pre-Buddhistic Indian Philosophy*, Delhi, 1970, pp. 137-38.)

traditions.[2] Which school was the first to formulate the atomistic principles and whether this school influenced Vaiśeṣika or not remains unclear. One way or the other, I agree with scholars who believe the Jaina form of atomism to be the most ancient.[3]

Here a question arises — whether the Indian concept of the atom coincides with the meaning suggested by the etymology of the Greek term *atomos*, "indivisible." The Sanskrit terms for "atom" are *aṇu* ("small," "fine") and *paramāṇu* ("least", "finest").[4] In Nyāya-Vaiśeṣika the term *aṇu* has at least two meanings — it denotes (i) substance (*dravya*) and (ii) size (*parimāṇa*), the latter being regarded as a quality (*guṇa*) of substance. In the first case it refers exclusively to the atom as a material particle, and in the second case, to the size of a single atom as well as of a dyad (*dvyaṇuka*). The term *paramāṇu* denotes only an atom. The etymology of these terms may seem to express a different vision of the atom than the one based upon the opposition of divisible/indivisible as accepted in the Greek tradition. The Sanskrit term implies the dichotomy of fine/gross (*sūkṣma-sthūla*), which is frequent enough in Indian philosophy, especially in Jainism and Sāṁkhya. But fineness

2. The fundamentals of the Buddhist atomism were first enunciated by Dharmaśrī (in the *Abhidharma-Hṛdaya-Śāstra*, 220-206 BCE). The earliest Jaina atomistic conceptions are found in the *Sūtrakṛtānga* (approximately third century BCE). Tamil sources ascribe atomism to Pakudha Kātyāyana (fourth century BCE). See M. Gangopadhyaya, *Indian Atomism: History and Sources*, Calcutta, 1980, pp. 39-54.

3. It should be noted, however, that the ancient character of the Jaina atomism as compared with other atomistic doctrines may simply be due to a greater conservatism of this school.

4. The term *kaṇa* (atom) is a part of the name of Kaṇāda, and the term *pīlu* is used in the expression *pīlu-pāka-vāda*.

does not necessarily imply indivisibility (for example, *tanmātra* or subtle elements constitutive of gross elements of Sāṁkhya are fine but not atomic).

Nevertheless, the history of Indian atomism testifies that the notion of indivisibility is invariably connected, directly or indirectly, with the other qualities of the Vaiśeṣikas' *paramāṇu,* and, particularly, with their eternal (*nitya*) character. The eternity implies the absence of causes from which these *paramāṇu* may be produced as well as parts into which they may disintegrate or be divided (physically or mentally). In the course of its evolution, the Vaiśeṣika atomism attaches ever increasing importance to the notion of indivisibility, which finally comes to be regarded as a key property of *paramāṇu.*

The Jaina concept of *paramāṇu* is the closest to the etymology of the Sanskrit term: it is defined as the finest particle of matter, which possesses every property of macro-objects, but in a non-manifest way (*avyakta*). Some *paramāṇu* (atoms of kārmic matter) are so fine that they cease to be impenetrable. Hence the idea of the Jaina philosopher Umāsvāti that an unlimited number of *paramāṇu* can be concentrated in one point of space, just as an infinite number of light beams could intersect at one and the same point of space.[5]

Neither the *Vaiśeṣika-sūtra* (*c.* first-second century CE), nor the *Bhāṣya* of Praśastapāda (*c.* sixth century CE), the most important of the Vaiśeṣika texts, contains any section specially devoted to atoms. *Paramāṇu* and their characteristics are touched upon only in passing and almost always as a secondary issue with regard to some more important topics. It may seem that the authors of these texts are not still aware of problems connected with the atomistic theory. The evidence contained in the *Vaiśeṣika-sūtra,*

5. Umāsvāti, *Tattvārthādhigamasūtra,* Arrah, 1920, p. 114.

fragmentary as it is, suggests that by the time this work was composed (perhaps in the first century CE), atomism had already been developed into a more or less coherent view but still not into a systematic doctrine. The *Vaiśeṣika-sūtra* presents the existence of atoms as a corollary of the world's existence, lists atom's properties, pointing out that the properties of earth atoms can change if exposed to fire (*pīlu-pāka-vāda*), and so on — it is an outline of the doctrine to be further elaborated in the commentaries.

Praśastapāda uses the atomistic principle to explain the emergence and destruction of the world; he dwells at length on the *pīlu-pāka* (atom-baking), introduces the concept of atomic compounds — the dyads and triads and describes the ways in which macro-objects are formed from the tiniest imperceptible particles. All these ideas are developed and specified in the commentaries on the *Praśastapādabhāṣya:* Vyomaśiva's (*c.* 948-72 CE) *Vyomavatī*, Śrīdhara's (*c.* 950-1000) *Nyāyakandalī* and Udayana's (*c.* 1050-1100) *Kiraṇāvalī* — of the three commentaries it is Srīdhara's *Nyāyakandalī* that is the most circumstantial presentation of Vaiśeṣika's atomistic theory.[6]

It is quite possible that the notion of indivisibility was originally adopted by the Vaiśeṣika authors as something self-evident. But as soon as it became imperative to defend the atomistic doctrine against the Mahāyāna Buddhist's criticism, this notion acquired a paramount importance. This is obvious from some Nyāya texts which developed a logical substantiation of the Vaiśeṣika's atomistic system.

The two main arguments used by the critics of atomism to refute the *paramāṇu*'s indivisibility refer to the

6. Śrīdhara argues that the process of "diminishing the degree of smallness" (*aṇu-parimāṇa-tāratamya*) stops when it reaches the atom. Later, this judgement became one of the most popular in Vaiśeṣika. (See M. Gangopadhyaya, op. cit., p. 159.)

characteristics of the atom put forward by the Vaiśeṣikas. The first one is the limited size of *paramāṇu*; the criticism is based on the idea that any substantial entity of a limited size is characterised by having a certain place in space. Vasubandhu, for instance, states that the atom's spatial divisions corresponding to the cardinal points structure and hence make it divisible. The other objection challenges the attribution to *paramāṇu* of some touch, arguing on the basis of the observation that an object of touch normally has a certain spatial extension and is thus divisible.

In response to these objections, the Nyāya authors Gautama (?) and Vātsyāyana (*c.* 450-500) contend that the atoms cannot be compared to the composed substances, of which they are the building bricks. Constituting not a product (*kārya*), but only a cause (*kāraṇa*), the atoms by their very nature cannot be composite, as composite things have to be products and not causes. Furthermore, assuming that the *paramāṇu* are divisible would lead to the infinite regression (*anavasthā*). This reasoning deserves to be examined in greater detail.

In the *Nyāya-sūtra* (hereafter *NS*), three possibilities of the division of a whole into its parts are suggested. The first possibility is that objects are divided until they are reduced to total destruction (*pralaya*), hence, which would mean that they consist of nothing and therefore do not exist (*NS* IV.2.15 and commentaries). The second possibility is that the division of a whole has no limit and goes on infinitely, which would mean that any object has a set of infinite components (*NS* IV.2.17 and commentaries). Were it so, there would be no distinction in size and weight, and the whole and part would paradoxically comprise an equal number of elements. As Uddyotakara (*c.* 550-610) and Vācaspati Miśra (*c.* 900-80) point out, there would be no difference between a mustard seed and Mount Meru.[7] Hence the third possibility: the divisibility of the whole has a terminal point, which has to be definitely small — the atom (*NS* IV.2.25). That is why we disagree with H. Jacobi, B. Faddegon and other scholars who define *paramāṇu* as "indefinitely small."[8] *Paramāṇu*, therefore, is, on the one hand, a limit to prevent a "lapse into infinity," a minimum of everything in the most general sense, and on the other hand, a minimal quantity of substance, and not "nothing." Thus, to avoid logical paradoxes, the atomistic outlook must be based on indivisibility as the atom's key characteristic.

How individual atoms are getting connected with one another is a problem fundamental to any atomistic teaching. According to Jainism, there are two causes for the combination of atoms: motion, which makes them collide, and their properties of "viscidity" (potential attraction) and "dryness" (potential repulsion) which make them stick together. Only atoms that possess either opposite properties or the same properties, but in different degrees, are regarded as having the ability to enter into combinations. These combinations, therefore, are conditioned by the activity and intrinsic properties of the atoms themselves.

The Vaiśeṣikas' explanation is totally different. Atoms are motionless unless there is an external impetus. During the emergence of the universe the role of such impetus had been played by the *adṛṣṭa* (unseen kārmic forces accumulated in the souls of living beings). Once the material universe is

---

7. See *Encyclopedia of Indian Philosophies*, vol. 2. *The Tradition of Nyāya-Vaiśeṣika up to Gaṅgeśa*, Karl Potter ed., Princeton: Princeton University Press, and Delhi: Motilal Banarsidass, p. 322; M. Gangopadhyaya, op. cit., p. 30.

8. *Encyclopedia of Religions and Ethics*, edited by J. Hastings, vol. 13, New York, 1951, pp. 199-202; B. Faddegon, *The Vaiśeṣika System*, Wiesbaden, 1969, p. 13.

established the motion of atoms is due to some external mechanical impacts. There are two types of atomic compounds — permanent and not permanent. These types embrace homogeneous (made of the atoms of one and the same element: earth, water, fire or wind) and heterogeneous "moleculars" made of atoms belonging to different elements, correspondingly. Śaṅkara Miśra (fifthth-sixteenth century CE) describes the first type as productive (*ārambhaka*), i.e. capable of producing a substance, and the second type as unproductive (*anārambhaka*). Combination of atoms, therefore, is conditioned by some external stimuli. During the cosmic night (*pralaya*), when such mechanical forces are inactive, atoms do not enter into combinations and remain separate.

Another problem raised by the Buddhist opponents concerns the possibility of a continuous transition from the imperceptible atoms to the perceptible macro-objects. In fact, it is a problem of the size or mass of atoms as productive of the magnitude of gross things.

The problem of the atom's size or the atom's mass is one of the most serious trials for any form of philosophical atomism. In the history of European atomism, two different options were developed — mathematical atomism (the atom is a non-dimensional mathematical point) and physical atomism (the atom is a physical particle). These terms were also extensively used by scholars in their interpretation of the Vaiśeṣika atomistic doctrine. I shall try to show, however, that the point-or-particle dilemma hardly received any concrete solution in this philosophy.

The problem of the atom's size in Vaiśeṣika is closely connected with its general concept of dimension (*parimāṇa*). The Sanskrit term *parimāṇa* is usually translated as "dimension," "size," "measure," "magnitude," etc., but none of these words conveys all the connotations of this term.

Etymologically, *parimāṇa* (Greek *perimetros*) is a derivative of the root *mā* (to measure) and the prefix *pari* (around); it signifies "measuring," "embracing," "wholeness." It would be more precise therefore to translate it as "volume" or "a three-dimensional magnitude." There are, besides, at least, two more shades of meaning of *parimāṇa* which are connected with measurement. *Parimāṇa* is (i) a standard scale of measure, and (ii) a process of taking measurement; in other words, *parimāṇa* is not only an object, and an instrument of measurement, but also the process of measurement itself, i.e. the counting of units of measurement. This pragmatical explication of *parimāṇa* is corroborated by the following statement of Praśastapāda: "*Parimāṇa* is the cause (i.e. the basis — *V.L.*) of the practice of measurement (*parimāṇam mānavyavahārakāraṇam*). Praśastapāda divides *parimāṇa* into four classes: the volumetric measures *aṇu* (small) and *mahat* (large), and the linear measures *dīrgha* (long) and *hrasva* (short). The first two, in turn, fall into two types — the *nitya* (eternal) and the *anitya* (non-eternal). The large eternal size (*nitya-mahat*) belongs to such eternal and all-pervading substances as *ākāśa* (space), *diś* (direction), *kāla* (time) and *ātman* (soul); these substances, due to their extreme extensiveness, cannot be perceived by the senses. All the other perceptible objects pertain, according to Praśastapāda, to "the large non-eternal size" (*anitya-mahat*). Opposed to the *nitya-mahat* is the *nitya-aṇu*, "the small eternal size," imperceptible due to its utmost diminutiveness (*aṇutva*). There is in Vaiśeṣika a special term *parimaṇḍala* ("round," "spherical," "globular") to denote the *nitya-aṇu*. *Parimaṇḍala* constitutes technical terms for the size of atom (*aṇu, paramāṇu*), whereas the *anitya-aṇu* presents the size of two atoms combined in a dyad.

Considering the correlation between this classification of *parimāṇa* and the process of measurement, the Vaiśeṣikas' subdivision of the *mahat* and the *aṇu* into the sub-classes of eternal and non-eternal sizes can be rendered as a distinction between the absolute and relative reference systems, in which the *nitya-mahat* and the *parimāṇa* constitute, correspondingly, the absolute maximum and absolute minimum of the dimensional data, and all other sizes may be interpreted as referring to the relative reference system, in which a unit of measure is conventional and dependent on practical needs. Praśastapāda emphasises that the size of any perceptible object due to the very fact of its perceptibility belongs to the category of "large" (*mahat*) but being measured in comparison with some other conventionally selected object, it may be regarded as small:

> Though such things as the water-lily, the myrobalan fruit, the bel and the like, are spoken of as minute and large, yet the idea of minuteness can be applied to these only indirectly, being based upon the existence in them of greater or lesser dimension as compared with something else.
>
> — *PB*, tr. G. Jha, p. 285

As an absolute unit of dimension, the *parimaṇḍala* is an indispensable precondition and a basis of any measurement. The *parimaṇḍala* itself cannot be measured either by any other or by its own dimension (as otherwise one would arrive at the tautology "1=1"). This reasoning suggests that the size of atom is not to be measured by anything but *parimaṇḍala*.

Concerning this problem, David Burke writes:

> As for *parimaṇḍala* being translated as "perfect sphere", that translation is justified only in a poetic sense. Just as the circle has been considered cross-culturally to be a perfect shape and to be imbued with mystical qualities, so the Vaiśeṣikas may have applied *parimaṇḍala* to the atom.

In his view, *parimaṇḍala* is a non-spatial category which "cannot truly be construed as being circular."[9]

This conclusion does not seem convincing to me. It is doubtful that the Vaiśeṣikas would use a poetic metaphor in such a strictly logical classification. They mean precisely what they say: atoms have their own measure in the "metrical system," and this measure is *parimaṇḍala*. The image of a "perfect sphere" is fundamental, as *parimaṇḍala* has the minimum volumetric form. If we take *parimaṇḍala* as the basic unit of measure, the very question of its size would not be justified, as there are no other units to measure it. The reason why the Vaiśeṣikas never raised this question, I believe, was that it may lead to the infinite regression.

The *parimaṇḍala*'s role as a basic unit of measure becomes more evident if we examine the ways in which, according to Praśastapāda, objects are made up from their parts. There are three of them: (1) addition of parts' magnitudes, (2) free combination (*pracaya*) of parts, and (3) increasing the number (*saṁkhyā*) of parts. To illustrate this, the *bhāṣyakāra* offers the following example: two pieces of fabric are compared and their sizes made equal (1) by an equal length of threads composing them, (2) by equal free spaces between the threads, or (3) by the number of threads. In the formation of objects of perceptible size (*mahat*) all three ways are engaged either simultaneously or alternately. For the objects of absolute small size (*aṇu*), only the third one is admissible to the Vaiśeṣikas. Within the Vaiśeṣika group of numerical qualities (number, dimension, separateness, conjunction, disjunction, remoteness, nearness), the *parimaṇḍala* corresponds to the number "one" (*eka*); the most elementary atomic compound — the dyad (*dvyāṇuka*) — to number "two." According to Praśastapāda,

9. B.D. Burke, "On the Measure 'Parimaṇḍala'" *Philosophy: East and West*, vol. 33, no. 3,1983, p. 282.

both *parimāṇa* and the number "one" are qualities (*guṇa*) possessed by all substances without exception. But, in contrast to colour, smell and other sense-qualities, the number is *apekṣābuddhi* (dependent upon *intellect*). During *sṛṣṭi* (the emergence of the universe), as there was no intelligent being apart from *Īśvara* it is through the agency of His *buddhi* that the numbers "two" and "three" contributed to making dyads, triads, etc. productive of perceptible size and length of the gross things.

Since perceptible size and length result not from atoms (the cause) but from the agency of *Īśvara*'s *buddhi,* doesn't that mean that the qualities of macro-objects (e.g. triads) have no continuity with those qualities of atoms?[10] If so, there is a gap between the properties of atoms and objects (i.e. combinations of atoms) beginning with the triad (the dyad will be discussed below). Objects are characterised by extension, form, colour and other qualities not attested in the atoms.

But, then, what does the imperceptibility of atoms mean? Why do the Vaiśeṣikas insist upon it? Would it not be more reasonable to define the atoms as the tiniest perceptible particles?

In the Indian tradition, a perceptible thing is always associated with something transient, liable to birth and destruction, whereas eternal entities are considered to be necessarily beyond direct observation. The Vaiśeṣika's commitment to the imperceptibility of atoms creates many difficulties in their atomistic doctrine, making it relatively difficult to justify, a fact many of the Vaiśeṣika's opponents took advantage of. How may imperceptible particles form perceptible objects, which possess colour, smell, etc.? According to the *Vaiśeṣika-sūtras,* the qualities of an effect

---

10. This argument was later used to prove the existence of God.

arise from the qualities of its cause. It follows then that imperceptible atoms must constitute objects equally imperceptible as they have to impart to them their own imperceptibility. The problem would be easy to solve if it were possible to justify the imperceptibility of atoms by their tiny size. This explanation was adopted by the Jainas, Ājīvikas and Buddhists, who believed that atoms, due to their diminutive size, can be perceived not separately but only in large accumulations, just as a thin hair can only be observable among other hairs.

But the Vaiśeṣikas did not accept this explanation, at least as early as Praśastapāda. He believes that the atoms form regular "moleculars": two atoms make up a dyad, two dyads a triad, etc. What is most important here is that the atoms, as well as the omnipresent substances (*ākāśa, diś, kāla, ātman*) are held by the Vaiśeṣikas to be a sort of *absolute entities*, existing transcendentally and beyond sense perception. So, the atoms seem to be imperceptible not because they are too tiny for the limited capacity of our sense organs (and this limitation can, in principle, be overcome with the help of instruments, such as a microscope), but because the atoms' very nature is transcendental and for this reason accessible only to the extrasensory yogic experience (*yogipratyakṣa*).

J.C. Chatterji was among the first scholars to take notice of the metaphysical character of the imperceptibility proper to the Vaiśeṣika's atoms.[11] From this he concluded that atoms are without extension, like mathematical points. An even more radical interpretation was suggested by the

11. "They are super-sensible, rather, in the sense, that they can *never* be perceived by the senses, *not* even with the aid of the most perfect instruments imaginable." J.C. Chatterji, *Hindu Realism Being an Introduction to the Metaphysics of the Nyāya-Vaiśeṣika System of Philosphy*, Delhi, 1975, p. 33.

French scholar P. Masson-Oursel, who regarded atoms and souls as two types of Absolute which, in the final analysis, are identical.

> The idea of a principle without form, extension and magnitude . . . is nothing but a duplicate of *ātman* or *Brahman* that is imperceptible since it is a condition for the existence of perceptible phenomena.[12]

Masson-Oursel gets at the very root of the problem: the Vaiśeṣika atoms belong to the type of absolute objects. Certainly, no sign of equality can be put between *ātman-Brahman* and atoms, since the former is one and infinite while the latter are multitudinous and finite. At the same time, their belonging to one and the same type of transcendental realities which overpass all normal measures of things can be traced back to the Upaniṣads, where *Brahman* is interpreted as the original cause of the universe: "there is either nothing greater or smaller than it (*Brahman* — V.L.)," it is "smaller than the small and greater than the great."

These and other similar formulae in the Upaniṣads were meant to demonstrate *Brahman*'s unique nature, which is beyond human comprehension. The dichotomies of small/supersmall and great/supergreat (i.e. the opposition between what is perceived by the senses and what is revealed in a yogic trance), seem to be assimilated in the Vaiśeṣika oppositions of the *nitya-aṇu/anitya-aṇu* and the *nitya-mahat/anitya-mahat*.

The smallness (*aṇutva*) of the atoms and the greatness (*mahattva*) of the objects are not just different degrees of the same quality of measure (*parimāṇa*), but two different qualities. This idea, first outlined by Praśastapāda, is dwelt

12. P. Masson-Oursel, "L'atomisme indien", *Revue Philosophique*, no. 99, Paris, 1925, p. 368.

on at length in Śrīdhara's *Nyāyakandalī.* Śrīdhara holds that smallness can only result in a quality of the same type — in a greater degree of smallness. It means that combination of two or more *aṇus*, similar to the addition of negative numbers, produces not a *mahat*, but still greater smallness (*aṇutva*). Since the *aṇu* size of an atom (*parimaṇḍala*) is already the smallest and cannot be diminished, the dyad keeps it intact. The great size of gross objects, Śrīdhara concludes, does not stem from the size of atoms, but from their number (from number "two" onwards).[13]

There is an obvious discontinuity between the imperceptible atoms and the perceptible macro-objects. The atoms do not possess any internal activity or motion necessary for their self-organisation into structured objects. It is *Īśvara*'s *buddhi* which gives the universe its structure through some numerical schematisations. After giving the world its measures, *Īśvara* withdrew into the background. From this moment onwards, the sizes of objects are formed not only by increasing the number of their parts, but also in two other ways — by summation of sizes and free combination of these parts. Interestingly, the tiniest building brick of the visible material universe is not an atom, and not even a dyad, but a triad.

According to Śrīdhara, who develops Praśastapāda's reasoning, separate atoms could produce neither dyad nor triad or other macro objects. As maintained by Śrīdhara, a single atom cannot be productive, because if it could, it would produce its effects eternally and these effects would be indestructible. Nor could the combination of three atoms be regarded as productive, because being perceptible and thus made up of parts, a triad has to be equally made up of constitutive parts which are, in their turn, effects. Therefore,

13. See B. Faddegon, *The Vaiśeṣika System*, op. cit., pp. 367-68.

its parts are dyads (substances-effects), but not three single atoms (substances-causes). And finally, two dyads cannot produce perceptible things because it is not the number "two," but the number "three" which for Praśastapāda is productive of the magnitude of things.

It appears that the genesis of the things starts from the second stage, the dyad, while the first stage, the atom, proves to be superfluous. But without this first stage, the whole atomistic scheme of the world's creation would be incomplete. In Vaiśeṣika, the role of "the missing link" is played by *Īśvara*'s *apekṣābuddhi.* Evidently, *Īśvara* was introduced to justify the atomic combinations in the given numerical order. Were there no dyads and triads, there would be no need for *Īśvara*'s *apekṣābuddhi.* Had the Vaiśeṣikas accepted the Jaina point of view that atoms form molecules due to their own physical properties ("viscidity" and "dryness"), or had they adopted the Buddhist concept of atoms as a simple mass, these problems would never have arisen.

We have so far examined the atomistic formulations in Vaiśeṣika and Nyāya. Now it is necessary to summarise these elements. The main characteristics of the atom are as follows:

1. having no cause, the atom is itself the intrinsic cause of the universe;
2. it is eternal;
3. it is the logical limit of division of a whole into parts;
4. it is not composite;
5. it has no within or without;
6. it is the unit of measure (*parimāṇa*);
7. it possesses *parimaṇḍala;*
8. it is the minimum of the four elements, hence the four types of atoms plus the atoms of *manas;*
9. it is passive, motion is imparted to it through the agency of *Īśvara*'s at the beginning of the world cycle and mechanical impacts;

10. it possesses ultimate "individualising" characteristics (*anityaviśeṣa*);
11. it is imperceptible to the five senses;
12. it is supersensorily perceived by the *yogipratyakṣa*;
13. it is always in combination with *ākāśa*; and
14. by contrast with macro-objects the atom has no magnitude (*mahattva*).

Taken together, these characteristics produce somehow a contradictory, even a paradoxical image of the Vaiśeṣika atom: it is the minutest of substances; it bears the qualities of the physical elements (smell, taste, colour, touch); it gets closely (through the relation of inherence — *samavāya*) combined with other atoms of the same kind (earth atoms with earth atoms, water atoms with water atoms, etc.). At the same time, it is an ideal object, to which qualities of metaphysical character are attributed — eternity, non-composite character, supersensory perceptibility, ultimate individualising characteristics, minimum magnitude, etc. An important, if not the principal, cause of the logical incompatibility of the atom's physical and metaphysical characteristics is correctly accounted for by B.D. Burke.

> By applying the term of measurement (*parimāṇa*—V.L.) to the imperceptible atoms, the Vaiśeṣikas run into a dilemma, namely either the measure of the atoms: (a) yields the measure of their perceptible product, or (b) it does not. If it (a) yields the measure, then (since the *guṇa*s of the effect are similar to the *guṇa*s of the cause) the atom should also be perceptible, if our senses were acute enough. But if this is the case, then the Vaiśeṣika doctrine that atoms are absolutely imperceptible to the five senses is in error. If it (b) does not yield the measure, then either: (b_1) the principle that the *guṇa*s of the effect are similar to the *guṇa*s of the cause has been violated, or (b_2) the objects of perception

> must have some basis other than the atomic one. In either case, the Vaiśeṣikas are in error.[14]

It appears to us that both the dilemma formulated by Burke and the paradoxical nature of the atom's characteristics originate from the essential incompatibility of the two explanatory schemes that underlie the atomistic doctrine of Vaiśeṣika — the physical approach based on philosophy of nature, and the metaphysical logico-epistemological analysis.

The physical scheme presents the atoms as micro-bodies, *minima* of the elemental substances, which hand down to their appropriate macro-objects their qualities in such a way that the whole qualitative diversity of the world can be reduced to the different qualities of the atoms. The challenge from the opponents' logical criticism calls for a postulation of the atom's indivisibility, eternality, non-compositeness, impartible character, its uncreated and non-spatial nature, etc.

Scholars are trying to get rid of this incompatibility on various grounds. As a rule, they relate the physical explanatory scheme with spatial intuition, and the metaphysical scheme to the concept of the atom as a non-spatial entity. A. Keith, for instance, wrote:

> Nor are atoms absolutely without magnitude; the minute is opposed to magnitude, but in the same genus (*parimāṇa* — V.L.); it is not true that the measures of the atoms being added cannot create any magnitude, for in fact three triads consisting of binary atoms make up a thing with magnitude; the atoms are not non-spatial, but devoid of parts, and for the same reason, not because they are non-spatial, they have no within or without. The atoms are indeed supersensible, but that is admittedly due to their small size.[15]

14. B.D. Burke, op. cit., p. 274.
15. A. Keith, *Indian Logic and Atomism: An Exposition of the Nyāya and Vaiśeṣika Systems*, Oxford, 1921, pp. 218-19.

Some scholars (J. C. Chatterji, B. Faddegon, U. Mishra, Th. Stcherbatsky) regarded the Vaiśeṣikas' atom as an infinitesimal point.[16] Faddegon assimilated atoms to mathematical points, thus indefinitely small (*aṇu*). Chatterji draws a Platonic analogy between the atom and the geometrical point, which allows one to compare a dyad to a straight line and a triad to a three-dimensional object.[17] Mishra interprets the line as a point in motion.[18]

We fall in line with Burke, who wrote:

> Although the analogy with geometry may be somewhat useful for the purposes of visualisation, it is not in keeping with the Vaiśeṣika conception of what an atom is and how it behaves. As a philosophical analogy it surely fails and can only serve to confound the issue; once rooted in the mind of the reader it becomes hard to dislodge.[19]

It should be noted, however, that Burke's own interpretation is also based on a negation of the atom's spatial magnitude.

I believe that the disagreement among scholars about the atom's spatial extension arises from their attempts to treat the Vaiśeṣika's atomism as one logically consistent theory, which surely, it is not, as its propositions are often at variance with one another. Whenever there was a necessity to introduce the atom, the Vaiśeṣikas did it in different ways, depending on the problem they were dealing with. The atoms were regarded as being substantial and

---

16. See J.C. Chatterji, op. cit., p. 33; B. Faddegon, op. cit., p. 13; *Studies in the History of Science in India*, ed. Debiprasad Chattopadhyaya, vol. 1, Delhi, 1982.
17. J.C. Chatterji, op. cit, p. 29.
18. U. Mishra, *Conception of Matter According to Nyāya-Vaiśeṣika*, Allahabad, 1936, p. 71.
19. B.D. Burke, op. cit., p. 275.

corporeal when the Vaiśeṣikas discussed the structure and the qualities of the "great elements." When the problem of the arising of the perceptible macro-objects from the imperceptible corpusculars was there, they tried to adjust the atomistic doctrine to some basic principles of their schools. The principle of continuity between qualities of effects and qualities of their constitutive causes made it difficult, if not impossible, to account for a qualitative leap from the imperceptibility of atoms to the perceptibility of things made up of them. Therefore, Praśastapāda speculates about unseen kārmic forces, numbers and *Īśvara*'s *apekṣābuddhi*. This kind of *ad hoc* conceptualisations seem to be due to the polemics as the main stimulus in the development of the Vaiśeṣika's atomism. The most debated concepts of this doctrine became also the most scholastic ones. As very often the opponents argued against atomism in a purely formal way, the defensive formalism of many atomistic propositions is easy to explain. In the heat of the philosophical disputes the Vaiśeṣikas gave little thought to match various characteristics of the atom into a coherent system. The atoms as such were for them but an instrument for establishing ontological pluralism and differentiation, multiplicity and variety of the universe. Being essentially axiomatic and declarative, the Vaiśeṣika's atomism, as I have shown above, readily accepted any *ad hoc* hypothesis to tackle problems created by its own restrictive presuppositions.

The evolution of the Vaiśeṣika's atomism from a naturalistic concept *par excellence* to a metaphysical system seems to be most evident in the development of its idea of the atom's nature. In the early Vaiśeṣika, the atoms were, above all, the structural constituents of natural elements, i.e. physical micro-bodies. We may find a confirmation of this hypothesis in the materialistic and atheistic version of the Vaiśeṣika which was the main object of Śaṅkara's criticism. Śaṅkara presents the arising of the atomistic doctrine in a quite common-sense way.

> We see that all ordinary substances which consist of parts as, for instance, pieces of cloth originate from the substances connected with them by the relation of inherence, conjunction, co-operating with the parts as, for instance threads. We hence draw the general conclusion that whatever consists of parts has originated from those substances with which it is connected by the relation of inherence, conjunction, co-operating. That thing now at which the distinction of the whole and parts stops and which marks the limit of division into lesser parts is the atom. This whole world, with its mountains, oceans, and so on, is composed of parts — it has a beginning and an end; an effect could not be assumed without a cause; therefore the atoms are the cause of the world.
>
> — Śaṅkara's *Brahmasūtra Bhāṣya*, II.2.12 tr. G. Thibaut

As we see, in this exposition of the atomistic doctrine, that is generally held to belong to some earlier version of Vaiśeṣika, the accent is on the impossibility of further division of some small parts into ever smaller parts. It looks as if it is a physical division which is meant here; there is no talk of the imperceptibility of atoms or of mediating role of the "moleculars." Later on, the cosmological function of atoms as the material cause of the universe has gradually lost its ground, and the logical and metaphysical aspects, that is the atom's function as a logical barrier to the regress into infinity, have come to the fore. Hence, the indivisibility of atoms, justifying its ontological status as an absolute entity, has become their key characteristic. It is not impossible that this changeover was brought about by the opponents' questions aimed at clarifying the logical possibility of attributing diverse qualities to the atom, which required a reconsideration of some original natural-philosophical propositions.

If one examines the atomistic doctrines that originated in other cultures in different historical periods, one will certainly notice that all of them were built on rather loose premises.

Indeed, if an atom is regarded as a physical body, the notion of its indivisibility is always challengeable; and if it is held to be a point without extension, how could it give rise to extensive objects? The atom is torn, as it were, between the necessity to be a physical body (since the division's limit for material bodies must be a material body itself) — and the impossibility to be so (since any such body is divisible).

Thomas Mann expressed this situation through the words of one of his heroes:

> The molecule was composed of atoms, and the atom was nowhere large enough even to be spoken of as extraordinarily small. It was so small, such a tiny, early, transitional mass, a coagulation of the unsubstantial, of the not-yet-substantial and yet substance-like, of energy, that it was scarcely possible yet — or, if it had been, was no longer possible — to think of it as material, but rather as mean and borderline between material and immaterial.[20]

20. Thomas Mann, "The Magic Mountain", in *Collected Works,* Alfred A. Knopf, 1927, vol. 1, p. 359.

References

Nyāyadarśanam with Vātsyāyana's Bhāṣya, Uddyotakara's Vārttika, Vācaspati Miśra's Tātparyaṭīkā, and Viṣvanātha's Vṛtti, ed. Taranatha Nyaya–Tarkatirtha and Amarendramohan Tarkatirtha, 2nd edn., New Delhi: Munshiram Manoharlal, 1985.

Vaiśeṣika Sūtras of Kaṇāda with the Commentary of Candrānanda, ed. Muni Sri Jambuvijayaji, GOS 136, Baroda: Oriental Institute, 1961.

Word Index to the Praśastapādabhāṣya: A Complete Word Index to the Printed Editions of the Praśastapāda, ed. J. Bronkhorst and Yves Ramseier, Delhi: Motilal Banarsidass, 1994.

Praśastapādabhāṣyam with the Commentary Nyāyakandalī of Śrīdhara, ed. Vindhyesvarī Prasad Dvivedin, Delhi: Sri Satguru Publications, 1895 (rpt. 1984).

The Nyāya-sūtras of Gautama: With the Bhāṣya of Vātsyāyana and the Vārttika of Uddyotakara, vol. IV, translated into English, with notes from Vācaspati Miśra's *Nyāya-vārtika-tatparyaṭīkā;* Udayana's *Pariśuddhi*, and Raghūttama's *Bhāṣyacandra*, by Ganganatha Jha, Delhi: Motilal Banarsidass, etc.

Padārthadharmasaṁgraha of Praśastapāda, tr. into English by G. Jha. CO 4. Delhi–Varanasi (rpt. from *Pandit* 1903-15).

Chapter Three

Syncretic Nyāya-Vaiśeṣika in Annam Bhaṭṭa's Tarkasaṁgraha and Tarkadīpikā

YELENA OSTROVSKAYA

THIS article attempts to describe the last period in the history of Nyāya-Vaiśeṣika, a leading school of Indian philosophical realism, through an analysis of two treatises by Annam Bhaṭṭa, namely *Tarkasaṁgraha* (*Compendium of Logic*) and *Tarkadīpikā*, the latter being a commentary on the former. In European Indology there have been many different interpretations of these texts, which are believed to date back to the seventeenth century. *Tarkasaṁgraha*, a refined philosophical miniature, has become widely known and has been published 46 times and translated into 14 European languages. *Tarkadīpikā*, a lengthy treatise intended to elucidate the meaning of *Tarkasaṁgraha*, had not been translated into any European language until recently.[1]

The concise and clear form of narration and the conceptual completeness of *Tarkasaṁgraha*, as well as the possibility, upon examining this treatise, of proceeding to the analysis of more sophisticated philosophical texts, have made the work one of the most popular among traditional philosophical literature in Sanskrit.

Tarkadīpikā, unlike *Tarkasaṁgraha*, has generally been regarded as complicated and scholastic, and for that reason

---

1. The author of this article translated *Tarkadīpikā* into Russian in 1985.

it has scarcely attracted any interest. Nevertheless these two texts cannot be correctly interpreted if viewed separately; a study of both is essential for the purpose of this article.

Syncretic Nyāya-Vaiśeṣika holds a special place in the history of Indian philosophy. Formed under the strong influence of Brāhmanical orthodoxy, it consistently propounded the principle of substantiality, justifying it from the standpoint of philosophical realism. It evolved in an atmosphere of conflict between the traditional Brāhmanical mainstream and the non-Brāhmanical (primarily Buddhist) trends. The development of Nyāya-Vaiśeṣika is conventionally divided into periods as follows.

Historians of Indian philosophy relate the first period (until the fifth century BCE) to the writing of the basic texts — the principal *sūtras* of Nyāya and Vaiśeṣika, Vātsyāyana's commentary on the *Nyāya-sūtras* and Praśastapāda's commentary on the *Vaiśeṣika-sūtras*.

The second period is usually identified with the rivalry between Nyāya-Vaiśeṣika and the school of Diṅnāga (the fifth to the twelfth centuries CE). At this time Nyāya-Vaiśeṣika was upheld and developed by such remarkable thinkers as Uddyotakara, Vācaspati Miśra, Udayana and Śrīdhara. Their opponents were Diṅnāga, Dharmakīrti, Dharmottara, Śāntarakṣita, Kamalaśīla and Ratnakīrti — eminent representatives of classical Buddhism. Nyāya-Vaiśeṣika took the lead amongst the realistic philosophico-religious Brāhmanical schools in their antagonistic dialogue with Buddhism.

The last (post-Buddhist) period in the evolution of the syncretic school began in the thirteenth century. At that stage an important role was played by Navya-Nyāya (New Nyāya), which dealt chiefly with logical and epistemological problems. In most historical reviews of Indian philosophy this period is regarded as one of stagnation and conceptual degeneration of the syncretic school. This point of view stems from the notion of Buddhism having had a stimulating influence upon the origin and development of the realistic systems.

On the whole, relevant scholarly works look upon syncretic Nyāya-Vaiśeṣika as a new philosophico-religious school based on the two earlier systems which were different in subject matter but similar in their philosophical orientations. These were the logical realism of Nyāya and the atomistic pluralism of Vaiśeṣika. When the two schools merged, they continued to concentrate on different kinds of problems. Adherents of Vaiśeṣika developed the positive and constructive aspects of the newborn doctrine, whereas those of Nyāya applied their efforts to elaborating logical and dialectical methods and devices in order to substantiate the doctrine and defend it against the opponents' criticism.

There exists also an entirely different view on the history of these two schools.[2] Some scholars maintain that the integrity of Nyāya-Vaiśeṣika can be acknowledged but with many reservations, and that it is more appropriate to speak of a common realistic orientation of the two schools. The *Praśastapādabhāṣya* is reckoned as belonging entirely to Vaiśeṣika. The advocates of this view divide the Nyāya system into Old Nyāya and New Nyāya (which, incidentally, is in accordance with the Indian tradition), and link the origin of Navya-Nyāya with Gaṅgeśa.[3]

Annam Bhaṭṭa's treatises (including *Tarkasaṁgraha*) have been traditionally dated back to the seventeenth century by Y.V. Athalye and M.R. Bodas and this view has been shared by most scholars today. According to the above

---

2. See Bimal K. Matilal, *Nyāya-Vaiśeṣika*, Weisbaden, 1977.
3. See D.H. Ingalls, *Materials for the Study of Navya-Nyāya Logic*, London, 1951, pp. 1-3.

chronology, these treatises have to be placed in the latest synchronic "cross-section" of the school's history. By that time the Buddhist influence on Indian philosophy at large had subsided. The opinion that the post-Buddhist period was a time of stagnation in syncretic Nyāya-Vaiśeṣika leads one to the conclusion that the writings of Annam Bhaṭṭa were a summary of the philosophical knowledge accumulated by the school, epitomising Nyāya-Vaiśeṣika at the final stage of its development.

Tarkasaṁgraha has been considered, as a rule, to belong to the literature of Navya-Nyāya. Even Bimal Matilal, a prominent expert in the epistemology of Indian realism, views Annam Bhaṭṭa as a follower of the Mithilā school of Navya-Nyāya.[4] This, however, is easily refuted if we turn to the *Tarkasaṁgraha* itself: its concluding section says that the scholar Annam Bhaṭṭa compiled *Tarkasaṁgraha*[5] in order to give the beginners an exhaustive explanation of the teachings of Kaṇāda and Nyāya.

Evidently, the last period in the history of the syncretic school was marked by Annam Bhaṭṭa's philosophical activity. This means that the post-Buddhist period lasted as long as five centuries, and throughout this period syncretic Nyāya-Vaiśeṣika possessed spiritual resources sufficient for self-sustenance. Apparently, ideological struggle stimulated the school's progress and was more than a mere polemic with the Buddhist trends in Indian philosophy. We think that at the last stage of its history the school turned to discussing new subjects with new opponents. Otherwise we would have to conclude that these 500 years in Indian philosophy were marked by nothing but stagnation.

To answer the question whether Annam Bhaṭṭa's

4. See B.K. Matilal, *Nyāya-Vaiśeṣika*, p. 107.
5. See *Tarkasaṁgraha* of Annam Bhaṭṭa, a new edition with all extant commentaries by S.C. Śāstrigal, Madras, 1920, p. 79.

treatises really belong to Mithilā literature, it is essential to rely on relevant criteria. Annam Bhaṭṭa's own statement to this effect should be examined from more general historical and philosophical positions. This can be done only through a comparative study of the subject and of various approaches to it. The final solution is still a matter of the future.

There is, however, some evidence that gives an insight into certain aspects of this problem. Raghunātha Śiromaṇi (about 1475-1550), one of the most original representatives of Navya-Nyāya, subjected to criticism the conventional system of seven referents (the underlying concepts of the syncretic school) and offered his own list of referents. If the generally accepted view that Annam Bhaṭṭa's work dates back to the seventeenth century is correct, there can be no doubt that he was familiar with Raghunātha's theory of referents.

Indeed, *Tarkadīpikā* contains a discussion on the number of referents, but Annam Bhaṭṭa strictly abides by the conventional system. This shows that Annam Bhaṭṭa was no follower of Raghunātha, who was a coryphaeus of the Mithilā school.

Regarding a number of other philosophical issues, Annam Bhaṭṭa considered the positions of both Old and New Nyāya without showing any preference. The examination of *Tarkasaṁgraha* and *Tarkadīpikā* from this angle has dissuaded us from attributing these texts to Navya-Nyāya. We confine ourselves to looking upon Annam Bhaṭṭa as a representative of the syncretic school.

Evidently, Annam Bhaṭṭa had perfect mastery over the conceptual apparatus of both Nyāyas and applied it to subjects traditionally dealt with in Vaiśeṣika. This is testified to by the fact that not only do these subjects come up in both treatises, but more importantly, the author tries to extend the principles of Vaiśeṣika to the problems of Nyāya proper, e.g. to philosophico-linguistic problems.

At the time of appearance of *Tarkasaṁgraha* and *Tarkadīpikā* syncretic Nyāya-Vaiśeṣika was a combined religio-philosophical doctrine based on Brāhmanical ideology. Most of its exponents professed Śaivism. Judging by the introductory sections of the two treatises, Annam Bhaṭṭa too was a Śaivite. It should be noted that Brāhmanism as a religious doctrine contains cosmogonal and cosmological teachings. Without taking account of this fact it is hardly possible to proceed to a historical and philosophical investigation of Nyāya-Vaiśeṣika, since it was greatly influenced by matters of cosmology, although it did not discuss them explicitly in logical writings.

Brāhmanical dogma maintains that the empirical world is a gradual unfolding of *ātman* (the supreme spiritual entity). The *Viṣṇu Purāṇa,* one of the most authoritative Purāṇas, proves that there were several cosmological schemes to this process. One of these schemes, for instance, presents the *ātman* as unfolding through the manifestations of the four elements (earth, water, fire and wind). Apparently, this model had a decisive influence first on Vaiśeṣika and later on the syncretic school during their formative periods.

Being the chief code of the doctrinal pragmatism of orthodox philosophy, Brāhmanism never became external to any system that evolved in its bosom, including Nyāya-Vaiśeṣika.

Ātman is regarded as all-pervasive and eternal. Being connected in the process of unfolding with the bodies of living beings, supreme *ātman* is individualised into multitudinous psychic entities. Doctrinal pragmatism prescribed that "the illusion of subjectivity" could be overcome through identification with supreme *ātman,* by gradually freeing one's consciousness from false identification with the body, individual features and personal emotions.

The state of identity with supreme *ātman* was held to be the ultimate religious ideal of *mokṣa* (emancipation), while philosophy was assigned the role of a logico-discursive propaedeutics aimed at putting this ideal into practice. Clearly, ontological theory was not only a philosophical but also a religious-ideological matter. According to Brāhmanical doctrine, the supreme spiritual entity is the basis of the world's existence, and this is not subject to discussion in a logical discourse on how one should proceed from ordinary perception of things to "true knowledge," essential to the realisation of the ideal of *mokṣa*.

Mokṣa means restructuring of individual consciousness. Accordingly, we must look upon *ātman,* on which the whole process of attaining *mokṣa* is based, as a psycho-cosmos. Philosophical discourses transform the concept of the psycho-cosmos into a description of the empirical world in terms of "true knowledge" (i.e. the kind of knowledge that is characteristic of those followers of the system who have attained *mokṣa,* the highest value). This implies formation, on the logico-discursive plane, of a certain descriptive terminology which corresponds to the transition from transformed states of consciousness (*mokṣa*) to ordinary perception of things.

The empirical world, emerging as the unfolding of supreme *ātman,* contains a plurality of individual *ātmans.* Each individual *ātman* taken separately is capable of self-realisation as the supreme *ātman* through the correct description of things which are elevated to the state of abstraction of the seven referents (substance, quality, action, the common, the individual, intrinsicality, and absence). We regard this system of referents in relation to ontology as meta-psychology.

Scholarly works dealing with the history and teachings of Nyāya-Vaiśeṣika usually disregard the religious doctrine while concentrating on the system's logico-discursive aspects. Hence the frequent misinterpretation of meta-psychology as metaphysics with an emphasis upon its specifically Indian approach — seeming indifference to the question of the relationship between thinking and being. This false conception, however, can be easily disregarded if one approaches Nyāya-Vaiśeṣika as a polymorphous ideology, which discusses ontology in religious (doctrinal) and not in logical treatises. This view evidently allows one to treat the fundamental question of philosophy with due regard for the historical context.

Apart from the religious-doctrinal and logico-discursive aspects, syncretic Nyāya-Vaiśeṣika was characterised by a third aspect, which we term "psychotechnical." Achievement of *mokṣa* seen as a process of stage-by-stage transformation of consciousness implied the inclusion of individual spiritual effort in the framework of the system. This meant ritualism, restrictions in everyday life, as well as purely mental practice — *yoga* aimed at self-regulation of the mind.

Stemming from the centuries-old tradition of monastic asceticism which flourished in India in antiquity and the early Middle Ages, this practice of mental refinement, as prescribed by the doctrine, was highly elaborated. It was based on the empirical knowledge of psychic processes, which were studied by methods of traditional science.

Yogic practice should by no means be disregarded, as that would render some of the school's important epistemological propositions totally unintelligible to us. On the other hand, it would be premature to specify how one should analyse the technique of traditional psychic exercise proceeding from the known logical treatises, since this problem requires specialised investigation, the more so because the use in these treatises of terms pertaining specifically to the system's psychotechnical aspect demands serious attention.

To support our judgement concerning the polymorphous character of syncretic Nyāya-Vaiśeṣika, let us examine the passage of *Tarkadīpikā* that comments on the concluding section of *Tarkasaṁgraha*. Annam Bhaṭṭa writes that the ultimate purpose of knowing the referents is emancipation. To cite one example: truly, *ātman* is that which ought to be seen, heard, meditated upon, deeply concentrated upon — this is how Śruti explains the grasping of *ātman* through the teacher's instructions. The value of meditation, which takes the shape of conceptual analysis, is asserted on the basis of Śruti (*ātman* is not identical with the body and other things) and by discarding anything that is not a source of genuine knowledge. Therefore, the Śāstra itself, through the study of the referents, also serves the purpose of attaining *mokṣa*.

The next stage is a deep concentration of the mind, achieved by using the methods of contemplation as prescribed by Śruti. Upon realising that *ātman* is not identical with the body and other things (i.e. upon overcoming the false egocentric conviction that it is the body and other things), all purposeful activity ceases since the psyche becomes "undefected." According to Annam Bhaṭṭa, only true knowledge can eliminate false knowledge, and it alone is a way to *mokṣa*.

All this shows that the polymorphous three-level religio-philosophical structure of Nyāya-Vaiśeṣika at the final stage of its evolution was quite clear to Annam Bhaṭṭa, the last of the school's original thinkers. Although abiding by the orthodox Brāhmanical system of values, Annam Bhaṭṭa was not a mystic or an ascetic. On the contrary, he was a rationalist and had due respect for logic, being fully aware of its capacities.

We find it necessary at this point to touch upon another important aspect of the school — its historico-philosophical qualification. Why has this school been traditionally regarded as realistic?

Syncretic Nyāya-Vaiśeṣika recognises the ontological status of universals. In the system of the seven referents, being (*sattā*) is included under the referent "the common" (*sāmānya*), the highest degree of abstraction, which comprises everything, all being, i.e. supreme *ātman* in its cosmological unfolding. The other universals are less general and are, therefore, interpreted dialectically, by comparison with each other.

The world's objects are seen from the standpoint of their ontological status, since the first six referents (substance, quality, agency, the common, the individual, intrinsicality), describing the objects' structure, were united by a common relation of abstraction — the quality of possessing being (*bhāvatva*). The seventh referent reflects the nature of absence (*abhāvatva*) and describes the relationship between the absence of an object and its locus, and relations of specification.

The seven referents are complemented by the basic principles of substantiality (*dravyatva*), non-identity of part and whole, and non-identity of an object and its quality.

According to Annam Bhaṭṭa, the principle of substantiality means that reality (*sattā*), which pertains to the first three referents in an absolute way, is defined with regard to substance through a relation of specificity, i.e. non-identity with quality and agency. In other words, this principle postulates unadulterated substance.

The principle is premised upon the doctrine which asserts as the ultimate religious value the identification with supreme *ātman*, eternal and without quality. The concept of heterogeneous reality is typical of philosophical realism in general and of European realism, fathered by Plato, in particular. The fact that the same concept is contained in Nyāya-Vaiśeṣika is indicative of the school's typological affinity with the European realistic systems.

It should be kept in mind, however, that in terms of epistemology, the interpretation of this principle is that substantiality, like any other universal, is cognisable through perception. According to Nyāya-Vaiśeṣika, cognition of the universals should be unmediated.

The principle of non-identity of part and whole (*avayava-avayavī-bheda*) originally served to substantiate the school's atomistic theory. The non-identity of a whole and its components (also different from each other) constitutes the conceptual essence of this principle, which yielded a "discrete" mode of reasoning.[6] Being consistent in applying this principle, Annam Bhaṭṭa extended it to analysing the meaning of utterances, a problem traditionally dealt with in Nyāya. Conceived in Vaiśeṣika, the principle is a fundamental characteristic of the syncretic school's system of reasoning.

The last principle — non-identity of a quality and its bearer (*dharma-dharmi-bheda*) — is regarded by specialists in the history of Indian philosophy as the cornerstone of Nyāya-Vaiśeṣika's realism. An object and its quality are essentially different. Original, "pure" substance is different from derivative, qualitatively determinate substance in that qualitative determinance, being an entity by itself, is

6. This conclusion is drawn by the Russian Indologist Victoria Lysenko from an analysis of Vaiśeṣika's atomistic theory. See "The Atomism of Vaiśeṣika and the Atomism of Democretus (A Comparative Study)", in *Ancient India*, M., 1982, pp. 187-201 (Russian edn.).

connected with "pure" substance through an assymmetrical relation of specification. The nature of this relation is described by the referent of *intrinsicality*. Qualities and agency, in turn, are regarded as possessing two universal characteristics — *qualitativeness* and the *quality of being agency*. Here, too, the connection is realised through intrinsicality.

The system of syncretic Nyāya-Vaiśeṣika thus arrives at an extreme yet most consistent form of philosophical realism, reflected in the idea of the essential sameness of an object as such and a specified object. This could be accepted only because the school always remained uncompromisingly faithful to the chief principle of realism — the non-identity of an object and its quality. The idea of essential sameness is more than a logical theorem, it has a broader philosophical meaning. Incidentally, it was rejected by such distinctly different schools as Vedānta and the Buddhist epistemological systems.

In Vedānta, the "pure bearer of qualities" (*dharmin*) alone was acknowledged as an independent entity, since the doctrinal declaration of the identity of *ātman* and *Brahman* was interpreted in the spirit of absolute idealism.

The Buddhists, rejecting the Vedic authority, denied the existence of *ātman;* that is why there was no room in their descriptive idiom for the term *dharmin*.

Obviously, the principles of non-identity of part and whole and of a quality and its vehicle are a distinctive feature of the syncretic school's mode of reasoning. The two principles conceptually correlate: any whole is presentable as an object with a wealth of specifications, the latter being identified with parts. In other words, intrinsicality, i.e. the relationship between a part and whole, between a quality and its object, was presented in syncretic Nyāya-Vaiśeṣika as a universal relation, and this relation alone determined the "discrete" mode of reasoning.

At the time when Annam Bhaṭṭa wrote his treatises, the syncretic philosophy of Nyāya-Vaiśeṣika was a consistent system of extreme realism oriented towards "discrete" reasoning. Accordingly, the subject-object relationship was treated by its exponents in a realistic light: the subject and object, regarded as two aspects of the same reality, were assigned an equal role. This is obvious from the list of nine substances as distinguished by the syncretic school: earth, water, fire, wind, time, space, *ākāśa*, *ātman*, and *manas*. All these substances are equally important in the sense that they are a logico-discursive interpretation of one of the doctrinal schemes of the *ātman* unfolding.

Annam Bhaṭṭa's *Tarkasaṁgraha* and *Tarkadīpikā* faithfully express the basic realistic ideas of syncretic Nyāya-Vaiśeṣika at the final stage of its development, being an excellent synthesis of the achievements of Old and New Nyāya (i.e. moderate Nyāya, not the radical Mithilā school) and Vaiśeṣika. This synthesis underlies the syncretic school's system of reasoning.

Let us now examine *Tarkadīpikā*, the author's commentary on *Tarkasaṁgraha*. The commentary is about five times as long as the basic text and contains a lot of valuable information on later Nyāya-Vaiśeṣika. It would seem appropriate to begin our historico-philosophical analysis with determining the genre of *Tarkadīpikā*. Annam Bhaṭṭa himself qualifies it as a *ṭīkā*, which implies consistent explanation of the basic text. For the time being, hardly anything more definite can be added about the genre since the subject of traditional genres of scientific treatises in Sanskrit has scarcely been studied as yet. We cannot, therefore, pass any judgement as to the correctness of Annam Bhaṭṭa's statement.

Nevertheless, we feel free to analyse that genre proceeding from the text of *Tarkadīpikā* and by comparing it with *Tarkasaṁgraha*. Based on the presumption that *Tarkadīpikā* was, in its time, a typical specimen of this genre, our approach to the problem proves quite relevant, since it sheds light on the genre's evolution if used in diachronic extrapolations and in drawing synchronic parallels.

We have tried to clarify the following questions:

(1) Whether the basic text and the commentary differ in conceptual complexity or merely in abundance of detail.
(2) What specific historico-philosophical information is to be found in *Tarkadīpikā*.
(3) Whether the text is intelligible without reference to the commentary.

Answers to these key problems are essential for reconstructing the synchronic version of syncretic Nyāya-Vaiśeṣika proceeding from the text of *Tarkasaṁgraha*. The text as it is can be regarded a cultural relic of the past. But placed in a certain exegetic system, it becomes a historical and philosophical document. Since we are interested in a historico-philosophical analysis rather than a source study, it is important to examine the two treatises in historical perspective.

The commentary shows two distinct approaches to *Tarkasaṁgraha:* conceptual and structural. On the conceptual plane, *Tarkadīpikā* is an extensive elaboration of *Tarkasaṁgraha*'s descriptive terminology. We mean here those sections of the commentary that contain: explanations of the terms and their philosophical connotations; presentation of the opponents' views as expressed in the discussions cited by Annam Bhaṭṭa; Annam Bhaṭṭa's own ideas; summaries of Nyāya-Vaiśeṣika theories, e.g. the atomistic theory; the teaching on the sources and criteria of true knowledge; etc. We speak of an extensive elaboration of the descriptive idiom because the commentary is terminologically by far more sophisticated than the basic text, which deals with the same conceptual subject matter quite laconically.

On the structural-analytical plane *Tarkadīpikā* examines *Tarkasaṁgraha* by applying methods and criteria of formal logic. The structural approach is connected with the introduction of a new specific descriptive "language," in relation to which philosophical meaning acquires the capacity of an "object-language."

The structure of the basic text is interpreted as follows. Annam Bhaṭṭa chooses a passage of the text and divides it into smaller fragments, each "marked" with a certain specific term. The commentary explains each key-term, not semantically, but in relation to the corresponding logical operation found in the fragment of the basic text (definition, classification, etc.).

In the third fragment, Annam Bhaṭṭa introduces the criterion of correct definition, and in so doing he uses special logical terms which in *Tarkasaṁgraha* are listed in a separate section dedicated to the theory of logical conclusion.

Clearly, the structural analysis of the basic text involves a more complex conceptual apparatus than that found in the sections of *Tarkasaṁgraha* preceding the section on logical conclusion. This nuance is indicative of the greater conceptual complexity of *Tarkadīpikā* as compared with *Tarkasaṁgraha*.

Accordingly, the *ṭīkā*, being a consistent explanation of the basic text, was regarded by the author as a much more sophisticated treatise, to which one should switch over only upon a thorough study of *Tarkasaṁgraha* and the mastering of the whole of its conceptual and terminological system.

Let us now try to analyse *Tarkadīpikā* as a specimen of the *ṭīkā* genre, i.e. from the angle of the historico-philosophical information contained in it. It is essential to bring out, with the help of a comparative analysis of the two exegetic approaches described above, some other significant aspects of the text. The structural and conceptual aspects complement each other in describing syncretic Nyāya-Vaiśeṣika. Apart from that, however, the conceptual aspect of the analysis includes, as mentioned above, citations of discussions with the school's opponents. Some opponents and their schools are named directly, others can be identified only by examining their philosophical views as presented in *Tarkadīpikā*. Annam Bhaṭṭa cites the discussions as a pretext to express his own views. The historian of Indian philosophy can use this material for synchronic comparisons and also in order to investigate how the adherents of Nyāya-Vaiśeṣika "anatomised" the theories of the opponent schools.

Tarkadīpikā does not describe any Buddhist school. Evidently, by the time the two treatises were written, the polemic with the Buddhists had become a thing of the past, and was of little relevance to Annam Bhaṭṭa's work. It was the Brāhmanical systems, which upheld the Vedas, that became the subject of philosophical dispute. The origin of the world through creation or otherwise, and Īśvaravāda (the teachings on *Īśvara*, the Ruler of the Universe) were not discussed. Instead, the polemic focused on linguistic-philosophical problems and criteria of true knowledge.

But these problems, it should be observed, played only an auxiliary role, especially linguistic-philosophical, since linguistic philosophy was basically a logico-discursive embodiment of the doctrinal principles of Brāhmanism. By virtue of this, a comparative study of the linguistic-philosophical differences of the systems, that rested on an essentially uniform doctrine, would enable us to elucidate the religious-ideological determinants of philosophy proper;

Tarkadīpikā contains sufficient material for a detailed study of this kind.

Tarkadīpikā can be used not only as a source of information on syncretic Nyāya-Vaiśeṣika. It also contains information for a synchronic comparative analysis of the logico-discursive aspects of the different systems described in the commentary and enables the scholar to see how these aspects were examined in the religious doctrine of Brāhmanism. Consequently, *Tarkasaṁgraha* can be fully grasped only with the help of the commentary, which defines the place of syncretic Nyāya-Vaiśeṣika amongst the other Brāhmanical schools of the time.

As mentioned above, *Tarkasaṁgraha* has been extremely popular with specialists engaged in the study of Indian philosophy for its highly intelligible and concise compendium of philosophical ideas. Things begin to appear in a different light, however, when *Tarkasaṁgraha* is studied together with *Tarkadīpikā*. *Tarkasaṁgraha* does include an inventory of the basic terms and definitions of the syncretic school and describes the conceptual structure of its teaching, but it does not explain the choice of notions and terms, and therefore may be compared to a statement out of context.

Any attempt to interpret *Tarkasaṁgraha* historically and philosophically without turning to the commentary comes up against the important problem of the philosophical background against which it should be studied. The semantics of its basic terms should be analysed in the broader context of some other relevant text. To choose for this purpose the classical commentary of Praśastapāda would mean to ignore the school's historical development during the period separating these two texts. Such an approach could only be based on the assumption that *Tarkasaṁgraha* is an epitome of Praśastapāda's own philosophical views, which in exegetic terms would lead to uncritical diachronic extrapolations.

A synchronic comparative analysis, if it does not include the commentary, is unlikely to yield any positive results. As the connotations of the terms will remain unknown, any interpretation of them will be arbitrary, and the whole analysis inauthentic.

All this shows that *Tarkasaṁgraha* cannot be correctly interpreted without an analysis of the commentary. An original philosophical miniature, *Tarkasaṁgraha* has a distinct functional purpose. It certainly is not a summary of the entire tradition of syncretic Nyāya-Vaiśeṣika. Figuratively speaking, the relationship between *Tarkasaṁgraha* and *Tarkadīpikā* is the same as between a methodological plan and a monograph, the plan's concrete realisation.

CHAPTER FOUR

On the Correlation of the Philosophical and Ritualistic Aspects of Mīmāṁsā

ALEXEI PIMENOV

OF the various philosophical schools which developed in India in antiquity and the Middle Ages, Pūrva-Mīmāṁsā, as if to justify its name, appears to be "the first" in many respects. Thus, out of the six *darśanas* it is undoubtedly most intimately connected with the ritualistic practices of Hinduism.[1] But when one turns to relevant publications, one finds that Mīmāṁsā is perhaps the least studied Indian philosophical system which very seldom has attracted the attention of scholars.[2] It should also be noted that the works analysing Mīmāṁsā deal mostly with its medieval version, represented by Kumārila Bhaṭṭa, Prabhākara and their many followers, whereas its early versions have barely been studied both textually and theoretically.

All these factors contribute to the contradictory views expressed on Mīmāṁsā, particularly in some works on the history of Indian philosophy.

One important question over which opinions differ is whether it is at all permissible to refer to Mīmāṁsā as a

---

1. A. Jha, *The Prābhākara School of Pūrva-Mīmāṁsā*, Delhi, 1978, pp. 2-4.
2. See Nilola Abagnano, *Dictionario de filosofia*, La Habana, 1963, p. 305.

philosophical system in the strict sense of the word. Many answer this question negatively, believing (as F. Max Müller does in his famous book *Six Systems of Indian Philosophy*) that Mīmāṁsā can be regarded as a philosophical school, but with certain reservations, and then only out of respect for the Indian tradition.[3]

This view will alter, however, if one peruses a number of specialised works on Mīmāṁsā, which convincingly show that this system contains very interesting philosophical generalisations, the two most significant being the theory of the sources of knowledge (*pramāṇas*) and the philosophico-linguistic conception connected with it.

A number of relevant publications (particularly the works by E. Frauwallner and F. Zangenberg) distinguish two periods in the development of Mīmāṁsā. At the early stage it was an exegetic teaching and dealt exclusively with problems of ritualism. The second period was marked by a shift to philosophical, in the first place to epistemological, problems.[4] This was largely due to the polemics between exponents of Mīmāṁsā and representatives of other schools, which required a logical substantiation of the fundamentals of Mīmāṁsā and brought about an interest in epistemology. An analysis of the early Mīmāṁsā texts (particularly of *Mīmāṁsā-sūtra-bhāṣyam*, I.1.1-5) leaves no doubt as to the great formative impact that the sharp discussions with Buddhists had on *pramāṇa* teaching, which developed into

3. Characteristically, Karl H. Potter's *Bibliography* makes no mention of the early Mīmāṁsā texts. See F. Max Müller, *Collected Works*, London, 1859, Vol. XIX, pp. 210-11.

4. E. Frauwallner, *Mīmāṁsārasataraṇī*, I, 1,623, *Weiner Zeitschrift für die Kunde Süd und Gestasiens*, Bd. 5, 1961, S. 124; F. Zangenberg, *Sabara und seine philosophische Quellen, Wiener Zeitschrift für die Kunde Süd und Gestasiens*, Bd. 6, 1962, S. 60-77.

a confrontation with the Buddhist doctrine of Anātmavāda.[5]

Whenever the question of the correlation of the philosophical and the ritualistic in Mīmāṁsā was raised, the topics discussed were the conceptions propounded by adherents of Mīmāṁsā, the parables that interested the followers of Jaimini, and the influence of other philosophical trends on Mīmāṁsā. Another important aspect of the problem was usually disregarded.

It happens quite often that a cultural phenomenon becomes known outside a narrow circle of specialists because of a certain peculiar feature, not necessarily the most significant one. Mīmāṁsā is undoubtedly such a phenomenon in Indian philosophy. No interpretation of this doctrine — be it a specialised study, a chapter containing a historical review of Indian philosophy, or a dictionary entry — is ever undertaken without mentioning the Vedic ritualism of Mīmāṁsā, its relationship with the Brāhmanic ritual and the Dharmasūtra tradition, and its ritualistic and legal impact on Hinduism. There are no grounds for objection to this. But it is nonetheless necessary to define the place of Mīmāṁsā in the philosophical and religious tradition of India and its distinctive features as compared to other ancient and medieval ideological trends.

Naturally, it is beyond the scope of this article to answer these questions exhaustively. Our purpose here is only to raise the problem and make some preliminary remarks.

It would be appropriate to begin with finding out what Mīmāṁsā actually deals with, a task that is not simple. The Mīmāṁsā-sūtras begin with an explanation of the school's main task — the study of *dharma* (*dharmajijñāsā*). *Dharma* is regarded here as a complex of obligatory rituals. Another fundamental principle is that the one and only authority

5. E. Frauwallner, *Materialien zur ältesten Erkenntnis lehre der Karma-Mīmāṁsā*, Wien, 1968, SS. 50-60.

on *dharma* is the text of the Vedas, which is eternal, anonymous (*apauruṣeya*) and infallible.[6]

Thus, the complex of Mīmāṁsā's problems is essentially ambivalent — it is at once ritualistic (i.e. explaining the technique of sacrifice) and exegetic (i.e. defining rules for interpreting texts).

It is well known, however, that exegetics and ritualism are also characteristic of some other Indian philosophical schools. The tasks of Mīmāṁsā, therefore, are not specifically ritualistic or exegetic. As Mohan Lal Sandal notes in his Foreword to the *Mīmāṁsā-sūtras of Jaimini,* Mīmāṁsā is neither an etymology (*nirukta*), nor a theory of ritual (*kalpa*).[7] What is it then?

Max Müller wrote: "Ranking Mīmāṁsā among the six systems of Indian philosophy I was governed . . . by the fact that it has always been considered a philosophical system from the Indian point of view. . . ."[8] In his analysis of Mīmāṁsā he proceeded from the following original sources: the renowned *Sarvadarśanasaṁgraha* (The Compendium of All Philosophies), *Arthasaṁgraha,* written by the seventeenth-century scholar Laugākṣi Bhāskara, and *Jaiminīya Nyāyamālāvistara,* a guide to Mīmāṁsā written by Madhva, founder of one of the Vedānta versions. In *Sarvadarśana-saṁgraha* and some other texts (e.g. the medieval compendium known as Haribhadra's *Ṣaḍdarśana-samuccaya*) Mīmāṁsā is classed as a philosophical school.[9]

6. E. Frauwallner, op. cit., S. 10.
7. Mohan Lal Sandal, *Mīmāṁsā-sūtras of Jaimini,* Delhi, 1980, pp. 3-4.
8. F. Max Müller, op. cit., p. 211.
9. Haribhadra, *Ṣaḍdarśana-samuccayaḥ,* text and translation into English with notes by K. Satchidananda Murty, Tenali, 1958, p. 151.

But this point of view was not unanimously accepted in the Indian tradition. Texts like *Arthaśāstra*, Rājaśekhara's treatise on poetics, entitled *Kāvyamīmāṁsā*, etc. do not regard Mīmāṁsā as a philosophy.[10] It is understandable, for it is well known that Indian authors were not agreed about the number of current philosophical systems and often differed in regarding one or another doctrine as philosophical.

Far more significant seems the fact that some texts describe Mīmāṁsā as a special science and a fundamental component of Brāhmanical education. *Kāvyamīmāṁsā* opens with a classification of man-invented sciences (*pauruṣeya*), followed by *ānvīkṣikas* (philosophies), as well as Purāṇas and Smṛtis.[11]

This view of Mīmāṁsā can be traced back to the ancient period of Indian culture. In the Brāhmaṇas and the Upaniṣads, Mīmāṁsā is mentioned as a "ritualistic discipline"[12] of the same type as the ancestors' cult (*pitṛja*), *itihāsa* and the "science of numbers" (*rāśi*).[13]

Prasthānabheda, a text ascribed to Madhusūdana Sarasvatī, a seventeenth-century brāhmaṇa and Advaita-Vedānta proponent, is noted for the fact that although written in the late Middle Ages, it shares the same attitude to Mīmāṁsā, ranking it among the four subsidiary disciplines (*upāṅga*), the three others being the Purāṇas, Nyāya and the Dharmaśāstras. Madhusūdana explains the classification: just as the Upapurāṇas are parts of other Purāṇas, so Vaiśeṣika includes Nyāya, Vedānta includes Mīmāṁsā, and the *Mahābhārata* includes the *Rāmāyaṇa*. In

10. *La Kāvyamīmāṁsā de Rājaśekhara tract de Sanskrit de N. Stshoupak*, L. Renou, Paris, 1946, pp. 36-37.

11. Ibid.

12. A.B. Keith, The *Karma-Mīmāṁsā*, London, 1921, p. l.

13. Ibid.

exactly the same way, the conceptions of the exponents of Sāṁkhya, of the followers of Patañjali, the Pāśupatikas (Śaivites), Viṣṇuites and others contain the Dharmaśāstras. As a result, Madhusūdana's fourteen sciences *aṅga* are seen as a complex unity.[14]

It is noteworthy that Mīmāṁsā was both an independent philosophical trend and an ancillary discipline. Madhva relates a legend about a discussion between Śaṅkara and the famous Mīmāṁsaka Kumārila Bhaṭṭa, which was won by the latter (see *Śabaravidvijaya*, pp. 61-119). But Madhva is also believed to be the author of the aforementioned text, *Jaiminīya Nyāyamālā-vistara*, a commentary in verse on the *Sūtras* of Jaimini.

Evidently, there existed different attitudes to the status of Mīmāṁsā. Some texts present it as a science of ritual, others as a philosophy. In the first case Mīmāṁsā peacefully coexists with other disciplines, while in the second case it is often sharply criticised. Consequently, for defining the status of Mīmāṁsā the answers to the following two questions are essential. First — what is the subject of Mīmāṁsā as a science and how does it differ from other sciences? Second — why is Mīmāṁsā as an autonomous ideological trend opposed to other trends? For answering these questions it is not enough to study only indirect sources, while disregarding the Mīmāṁsā tradition proper.

The task is complicated by the fact that the sole commentary of the early, exegetic period of Mīmāṁsā's tradition is Śabarasvāmi's *Mīmāṁsā-sūtra-bhāṣyam*. The evidence about Śabarasvāmi's precursors is very scarce, as their works are unknown. We are, therefore, bound to resort to using indirect evidence.

---

14. P. Deussen, *Allgemeine Geschischte der Philosophie, Philosophie der Upanishads*, Leipzig, 1907, SS. 44-64.

Śaṅkara talks about Upavarṣa, one of the first commentators on Jaimini's *Sūtras*. This is a most valuable piece of evidence. To the question why Upavarṣa in his *commentary* on the *Mīmāṁsā-sūtras* does not examine the problem of the existence of *ātman,* the founder of Advaita-Vedānta replies that Upavarṣa deals with it in his commentary on the *Brahmasūtras.*[15] This proves that *ātman* was studied by Mīmāṁsakas long before *Mīmāṁsā-sūtra-bhāṣyam* — a fact that should be taken into account while examining the evolution of Mīmāṁsā. As to the problem of its status, at a certain stage of Mīmāṁsā's development the followers of Jaimini did not form any isolated trend, since the *Sūtras* of Bādarāyaṇa, along with the *Sūtras* of Jaimini, were liable to their commentary.

Quite different is the evidence contained in *Pramāṇa-samuccayaḥ,* written by the Buddhist philosopher Diṅnāga, who talks about the Mīmāṁsaka Vṛttikāra (the author of a *vṛtti*) identified with Bhavadāsa, another representative of early Mīmāṁsā.[16] The discussion between Diṅnāga and Vṛttikāra is over epistemological issues. One refutes the statements of the other on the *pramāṇas* in general and on sense perception (*pratyakṣam*) in particular. Diṅnāga criticises the theory of perception as formulated by Bhavadāsa in his commentary on *sūtra* 1.1.5, which Vṛttikāra interprets as a definition of perception. Bhavadāsa's outlook, which can be reconstructed thanks to *Pramāṇa-samuccayaḥ,* interests us for a number of reasons, and above all, as a stage in the evolution of the theory of the *pramāṇas,* which is a component of Mīmāṁsā. This stage preceded the period reflected in the *Mīmāṁsā-sūtra-bhāṣyam.*

Concerning the status of Mīmāṁsā, *Pramāṇa-*

---

15. E. Frauwallner, op. cit., S. 110.

16. Ibid., S. 107.

samuccayaḥ is relevant for two reasons. First, Diṅnāga regards Mīmāṁsā as an *individual doctrine,* although conceptually not fully independent and consistent. He quotes some of Bhavadāsa's statements, but does not analyse them because, as he writes, they were borrowed from other philosophical systems, already refuted in other parts of *Pramāṇa-samuccayaḥ*. Second, it is important that the issue discussed is the theory of the *pramāṇas* — a domain in which Mīmāṁsā for the first time stands out as an autonomous trend.

The *Mīmāṁsā-sūtra-bhāṣyam* contains evidence which is particularly valuable for defining Mīmāṁsā's status and studying the factors of its evolution. It is noteworthy that here Mīmāṁsā is presented both as a science and an ideological trend. Śabarasvāmi's commentary contains fragments of an unknown *vṛtti,* whose author is referred to as Vṛttikāra in the *Mīmāṁsā-sūtra-bhāṣyam*. His real name is unknown. The interpolation and the parts of the commentary ascribed to Śabarasvāmi are different in many respects. Vṛttikāra's complex theory of the *pramāṇas* is epistemologically far more mature than Bhavadāsa's theorising. The former was adapted and developed by the two medieval Mīmāṁsakas, Kumārila and Prabhākara, and their followers.

The *bhāṣya* itself is of little interest both historically and philosophically; its author scarcely goes beyond the exegetic framework.

Another major difference between the main body of the *Mīmāṁsā-sūtra bhāṣyam* and the interpolation lies in the portrayal of the opponent. Śabarasvāmi's opponent is a purely symbolic figure, he asks too many questions and raises objections at the slightest pretext, while Vṛttikāra's opponent argues from a consistently Buddhist standpoint.

To define the subject of Mīmāṁsā, it would be expedient to examine Śabarasvāmi's commentary on Jaimini's first *sūtra,* which defines the main task of Mīmāṁsā as the study of *dharma* (*dharma-jijñāsā*).[17]

Commenting on this *sūtra*, Śabarasvāmi dwells on a number of problems. He analyses the temporal relationship between the study of *dharma* and another ritual obligation — the ablutions (*snāna*) — and makes the basic statement (which is further developed and concretised) that a study of *dharma* is to be founded on a perusal of the Vedas.

In discussing these problems, Śabarasvāmi quotes the instructions of the *Dharmasūtras* (e.g. *Baudhāyana*) as to the completion of the study of the Vedas and the performance of ablutions, but he is very arbitrary in doing so. To prove that the completion of a study of the Vedas need not necessarily be followed by ablutions, he allows an infringement of the instructions as long as they impede the study of *dharma,* and does so on the grounds that the Vedas are meaningful only as an instruction in mastering *dharma* and a guide to ritual action.

The commentator explains not only when and how *dharma* should be studied, and why the Vedas are the unique source of knowledge about *dharma,* but also why it is necessary to study *dharma* at all.

In the words of the opponent, "*dharma* is neither known nor unknown. If it is known, it ought to be explored. The more so if it is unknown."[18] Śabarasvāmi replies to this that there are different opinions on *dharma*. Some call one thing *dharma,* others another. If a person takes some definition of *dharma* on trust, he may come to grief. It is therefore necessary to explore *dharma,* for the study of *dharma* is for the good of man.[19]

Dharma itself is defined in the next *sūtra* (1.1.2): "*Dharma*

---

17. E. Frauwallner, op. cit., S. 10.
18. Ibid., SS. 14-16.
19. Ibid., S. 16.

is something (*artha*) characterised by an impulse to action (*codanā*)." Commenting on this *sūtra*, Śabarasvāmi dwells at length, on the meaning of the polysemantic term *artha* and gives it a dual definition depending upon the context. In our opinion, at the beginning, when the distinctive quality (*lakṣaṇa*) of *dharma* is defined, *artha* signifies "a thing" or "an object." However, when the discussion touches upon the necessity to study *dharma*, Śabarasvāmi accentuates the *benefit* of this pursuit, and the word *artha* connotes "something useful or beneficial."

Śabarasvāmi specifies why the *sūtra* is an expression of these two theses: (i) the distinctive quality of *dharma* is an impulse to action (an imperative), and (ii) *dharma* is something beneficial rather than deleterious. These explanations constitute a very significant part of the discussion. The usefulness of *dharma* follows from its immanent relationship with the idea of sacrifice (*yajña*). One who makes sacrifices is called "a cook" or "a reaper." *Dharma*, for that reason, is that which is beneficial to man. In the Vedas, as in everyday life, the idea of sacrifice is denoted by the term *dharma*. In corroboration of this idea Śabarasvāmi quotes from *Taittirīya Saṁhitā:* "As a sacrifice, the gods sacrificed a sacrificed. Those were the first *dharmas*" (3.5; I.1.5).[20]

But, the opponent objects, an instruction (*upadeśa*) in the form of an imperative verbal utterance may also call for evil things, not only good ones. There are sacrifices that pursue a good aim, and one of them is Jyotiṣṭoma. There are also sacrifices that cause evil and destruction. The *bhāṣya* cites as examples of the second type the sacrifices connected with the ceremonies of Śyena, Vajra and Iṣu. The term *artha*, in the sense of "usefulness," is adopted in order to avoid

20. E. Frauwallner, op. cit., S. 20.

denoting the evil type with the term *dharma*. But it may seem then that the Vedas prescribe wrong doing. Śabarasvāmi argues that it is a misconception:

> Sacrifice as performed in the Śyena and similar ceremonies is not imposed as an action that it is compulsory to perform. The instruction contains this idea: "For one who wishes to do harm, it is a means." For it was said: "One who invokes evil makes a sacrifice in the Śyena ceremony," but not "It is necessary to invoke evil."[21]

All this elucidates the tasks that Mīmāṁsā dealt with as an ancillary discipline or a science of ritual. As obvious from the denominations attached to this system (viz. Pūrva-Mīmāṁsā, Karma-Mīmāṁsā), its adherents analysed, interpreted and classified various ritual actions.

As Max Müller wrote,

> In what way can brāhmaṇas be correlated both with each other as well as with the existing family and with the local customs, in what way can we find in Brāhmaṇas a meaning to meet the demands of any new generation? This was achieved by Mīmāṁsā. . . .[22]

In our opinion, however, the quoted excerpts testify to the fact that Mīmāṁsā's task was not only to analyse the diverse types of sacrifice in order to co-ordinate them and remove contradictions between them. There was something more to that: its exegetic function was to ethically systematise the ritual instructions of Śruti and to define *dharma* in such a way as to make clear the contrariety of *dharma* and *adharma*, thus proving the necessity to conform to *dharma*, to follow the useful prescriptions and not to make harmful sacrifices despite the fact that they are mentioned in Śruti.

---

21. E. Frauwallner, op. cit., S. 20.
22. F. Max Müller, op. cit., p. 198.

The discussion also touches upon the problem of the *pramāṇas*, but the approach to it is purely interpretational. Śabarasvāmi points out that the nature and hierarchy of the *pramāṇas* lie outside the subject of the discussion.

The problems contained in the fragments of the *vṛtti*, which comment on *sūtras* I.4-5, are essentially different from those discussed in other parts of the *Mīmāṁsā-sūtra-bhāṣyam*. They contain a peculiar theory of sense perception (*pratyakṣam*). Perception, according to Diṅnāga, is regarded as the prerequisite for logical conclusion (*anumāna*) and comparison (*upamāna*), as well as postulation (*arthāpatti*) and negation (*abhāva*), which pertain specifically to Mīmāṁsā. Vṛttikāra provides a detailed substantiation of Jaimini's thesis on verbal communication (*śabda*) that serves as the basis for the underlying principle of the Mīmāṁsā ideology — the presentation of the Vedic text (which is a totality of verbal communications) as the sole and *absolutely authentic* source of knowledge about *dharma*.[23]

The difference in subject matter between the *vṛtti* and the rest of the *bhāṣya* (Vṛttikāra's reformulation of *sūtra* I.1.4) as well as the greater "philosophicality" of the interpolation, compared with the main body of the *Mīmāṁsā-sūtra-bhāṣyam*, have led a number of scholars to the conclusion that Vṛttikāra was a "pure" philosopher and had nothing to do with Mīmāṁsā's ritualistic interests, while Śabara was a strict ritualist innocent of any philosophical thinking. We consider this opinion to be tendentious and at variance with the essential meaning of the *vṛtti*. Apart from discussing perception and the other *pramāṇas*, the *vṛtti* contains an extremely interesting fragment devoted to proving the existence of *ātman*. The controversy over this topic, being part of the general polemics, is reminiscent of the analysis

23. E. Frauwallner, op. cit., SS. 26-32, 38-48.

of perception in other fragments of the *vṛtti;* this fact is relevant to revealing the genesis of the perception theory.

In the context, special notice should be taken of the following. The problem of *ātman* arises not in the commentary on the *Brahmasūtras,* which would be traditional, but in the commentary on the *Mīmāṁsā-sūtras.* In examining the evolution of Mīmāṁsā's status the combination of the analysis of *ātman* and the epistemological ideas in the *vṛtti* is particularly helpful. The fragments of the *vṛtti* are partly similar in content to what is known about Bhavadāsa's *vṛtti,* where, as already mentioned, the epistemological aspect of Mīmāṁsā is presented more consistently than by Diṅnāga's opponent. The theory of the *pramāṇas,* which makes Diṅnāga regard Mīmāṁsā as a separate philosophical trend, is further developed in these fragments. At the same time, they explain more manifestly the reason for such a vigorous study of epistemological problems — it was necessitated by the controversy with the Buddhists over *ātman,* a matter of fundamental significance for both sides.

Relevant to the problems raised in this article is also the fact that the discussion on *ātman* is prompted by the need for a more sound substantiation of the *sūtras* of Jaimini. The principal question here is: who is responsible for conformity to *dharma?* The discussion on the subject of ritual actions brings about the need to confirm the existence in man of a certain element that finally "tastes the fruits" of both *dharma* and *adharma.* The psychological analysis of the subject of ritual actions in the context of anti-Buddhist polemics leads to a discussion on the nature of the subject of perception and cognition as a whole.

Mīmāṁsā is thus transformed from a science of ritual into a philosophical system. It is not only a shift from ritual rules to a philosophical system. It is in fact a change of status: a subsidiary science (*aṅga*) coexistent with the other *aṅgas* of the Brāhmanic complex turns into an individual philosophical trend which is opposed to and which criticises other schools. This helps comprehend medieval Mīmāṁsā as represented by Kumārila and Prabhākara who had disputes with both Buddhists and adherents of the orthodox schools of Vedānta and Nyāya-Vaiśeṣika.

As, in the late Middle Ages, Advaita-Vedānta, due to its growing role in India's spiritual and intellectual life, began to assimilate the other *darśanas*, Mīmāṁsā reverted to its former position of a subsidiary discipline. This reversion is reflected in *Prasthānabheda* and in *Kāvyamīmāṁsā*. From then on Mīmāṁsā's status has remained unchanged to this day.

CHAPTER FIVE

Śaṅkara's Commentary on the Brahmasūtras

NATALYA ISAEVA

UNLIKE Pūrva-Mīmāṁsā, which also declared its direct relationship with the sacred texts, the philosophico-religious school of Vedānta does not explain the ritual rules as prescribed by the scriptures. Instead, it propounds an integral theory based on the Revelation (Śruti). Within the framework of Vedānta, philosophical trends vary from Śaṅkara's monism to Rāmānuja's teaching, which presents the world and souls as parts of attributes of eternal *Brahman*, and to Madhva's theistic dualism, in which *Brahman* is contrasted with nature and living beings.

The three canonical sources (*prasthāna-trayī*) of Vedānta are the Upaniṣads, the *Bhagavad-Gītā* and the *Brahmasūtras*. The *Sūtras* of Bādarāyaṇa, being one of Vedānta's acknowledged theoretical sources, are at the same time not so important as the subsequent commentaries on them.

Śaṅkara's *Bhāṣya* is the earliest extant commentary on Bādarāyaṇa's work dating from the ninth century. Of all the commentaries, it had the greatest influence on the following development of Vedānta. Charles Eliot rightly pointed out that, as it quite often happens in India, the commentary "outgrew" and excelled the commented text[1]

1. Charles Eliot, *Hinduism and Buddhism*, vol. 2, London, 1959, p. 48.

and became in turn the source of further interpretations. In the ninth century Vācaspati Miśra wrote a Vedāntic commentary, entitled *Bhāmatī,* on Śaṅkara's *Bhāṣya.* In the thirteenth century a sub-commentary was written by Ānandajñāna, and in the sixteenth century another by Govindānanda. Padmapāda, Śaṅkara's disciple, wrote his famous *Pañca-pādikā,* a commentary on the first four *sūtras* of Śaṅkara's commentary on Bādarāyaṇa's work (around CE 820). *Pañca-pādikā* became the subject of Prakāśātman's sub-commentary entitled *Pañca-pādikā-vivaraṇa* (around CE 1200).[2]

Śaṅkara's teaching is called Advaita-Vedānta (non-dualism). Its aim is to preach eternal *Brahman* as the supreme and only reality. *Brahman* is one whole; "from the viewpoint of the ultimate truth" (*pāramārthikam*) it has never undergone any transformations, and all the diversity of the phenomenal world unfolds through its creative force — *māyā. Māyā* conceals *Brahman*'s real nature like a veil or magical illusion; it manifests itself as *avidyā,* which means unawareness — not mere ignorance or false knowledge, but the only way to perception and at the same time the node of the profane world's existence.

It is *māyā-avidyā* that yields the characteristics of every individual soul. Each of the infinite number of souls has "a bright core"— genuine consciousness or knowledge, attributeless *ātman,* whose nature originally is identical to *Brahman.* The mystical act of diffusion in *Brahman,* where all distinctions between object, subject and cognition are obliterated, is the only possible realisation of this unity, the end of the illusory evolution of the phenomenal world.

2. See the review of these and other commentaries in Surendranath Dasgupta, *A History of Indian Philosophy,* vol. II, Delhi, 1956, p. 48.

How does a common man become aware of his inner nature? According to Śaṅkara, every man feels *ātman* within himself, it is the primary reality for everyone, not unlike Descartes' *cogito.* It is impossible to deny *ātman,* writes Śaṅkara, for one who tries to deny *ātman* is *ātman* (Commentary on *Brahmasūtras* I.1.4 and II.111.7).

The fusion of *ātman* and *Brahman* is held in the Revelation to be the only way to escape *saṁsāra,* the cycle of reincarnation.

The reading of the sacred texts (which are accessible only to the twice-born, i.e. those belonging to the three highest *varṇas*) results in an unquenchable desire to attain or cognise *Brahman,* for *Brahman,* according to Śaṅkara, is Knowledge.

This path is not easy. In Śaṅkara's view, neither by spiritual or religious merits, nor abidance of ritual instructions, nor the worship of the personalised god *Īśvara* leads to *Brahman.* Accumulation of pious merit is only a prerequisite, essential but insufficient. One who shows ascetic discipline, piety, or love, only receives *bhāga,* a recompense in the next life. This is nothing but a "reference-point" in the world of *karma,* and does not lead one beyond *karma* to ultimate emancipation. "These rites and practices, wearing a sacred cord, etc. are detached from the realisation of unity with supreme *ātman"* (Śaṅkara, *Upadeśasāhasrī,* I.30). Individual intellectual effort and accumulation of knowledge do not lead to *Brahman* either. "There are six *pramāṇas*; they belong to what is called the sphere of phenomenal (*Sarvadarśana-siddhānta-saṁgraha,* XII.85-86). In this context the *pramāṇas* are the so-called sources of true knowledge. The *pramāṇas* include Śruti, sense perception, logical conclusion and others.

According to Śaṅkara, it is impossible to teach *ātman* since every word becomes false and lifeless as soon as one tries to give a strict definition to the supreme reality. *Ātman* is the basis of consciousness, and therefore it cannot become its own object. Any knowledge (and any individual consciousness) is something haphazard and replaceable. To use Śaṅkara's words, it only temporarily *overlaps* (*adhyāsyate*) with *ātman*. The idea of *disproportion* (*apramāṇatva*) between *Brahman* and the rest of the universe is central to all of Śaṅkara's writings.

Advaita points out a means which helps to follow the right path and come closer to this elusive reality, although it does not guarantee that the destination will be reached. Of all the *pramāṇas*, the "instruments" of cognition, one has a special role to play. The evidence of the Revelation (Āgama) is not a mere promise, it shows the correct life-path. The sacred texts do not lead to *ātman*, but they bring one closer to it, overcoming one by one all the temporary characteristics.

In Śaṅkara's view, the dicta or Śruti are not of equal worth; they form a hierarchy according to their proximity to the centre for which these dicta function.

It was Bādarāyaṇa who first exposed the discrepancies between the sacred texts and distinguished between the dicta of the Revelation, relating to supreme *Brahman*, and other dicta, which prescribed ritual observances or meditation on the various stages of reality. The lower dicta or Śruti, according to Bādarāyaṇa, should be understood cither contextually (*prakaraṇāt ca;* I.II.10), or in connection with other texts of the Upaniṣads (*vākyānvayāt;* I.IV.19). This concept was further developed by Śaṅkara, who differentiated two levels of reality: *paramārtha* (the ultimate truth) and *vyavahāra* (phenomenal practice), and respectively, two types of dicta.

The special part that the Revelation plays in Advaita and the very possibility of estimating the proximity of the sacred texts to *ātman* are due to a special approach to language. Indeed, it is impossible, in Śaṅkara's words, to see the seer of a vision ". . . or to think of that which permeates thought" (Commentary on *Bṛhadāraṇyaka Upaniṣad*, III.IV.2). Yet there is something in the nature of language that enables it to reveal reality without directly naming it and to speak about things without categorising them, although categories may help to keep closer to the Supreme. We have not been told and are therefore incapable of knowing everything. That is why, Śaṅkara holds, we seek to grasp the essence of being from fragments of words, which are but an echo of the True Word, unspoken and unspeakable.[3] Hence the general propensity of the Indian tradition (Śaṅkara is no exception) to metaphor, parables and etymology-suggested interpretations. The modern scholar is likely to condescendingly smile at an etymology like this: Upaniṣad = *upa* (near) + *ni* (quite) + *ṣad* (to weaken, to approach, to destroy); in other words, the Upaniṣads are that which loosen the trammels of birth, old age and death, allows one to approach *Brahman* and destroy *saṁsāra* (Śaṅkara, *Upadeśasāhasrī*, I.25). In this regard it is more appropriate to speak of "popular etymology," which explains words not on the basis of their historical origin, but by phonetic parallelism. The grouping of words into lexical clusters not only by meaning but also by phonetic

3. It is appropriate to mention in this connection *the hypothesis* of the ungrammatical composition of the Vedic hymns, first suggested by Ferdinand de Saussure and later by V. Toporov. According to this hypothesis, the said type of composition is universal to all Indo-European poetry. "The key-word . . . is usually absent from the text and is implied by the whole of its phonetic structure." "All the lines of the hymn produce reflections *sui generis* of the key-word."— V.V. Ivanov, *Essays on the History of Semiotics in the USSR* (Russian edn.), Moscow, 1976, pp. 254-56.

parallelism results in what B. Eihenbaum termed "side-connotations" in relation to poetic language.

In European philosophy a similar concept of language is found in the late works of Heidegger, who advocated the advantages of the etymological approach over the scientific. His study of Greek etymology (especially in the book *On the Way to Language*) gave rise to the fundamental thesis: "The word is an indication, not a mere designative sign."

Language is an arrow pointed at eternally evading being, but not a label that provides a monosemantic definition.[4] Heidegger's interpretation of language as not a mere denotation of objects and phenomena but also a self-revelation of reality (language is the only thing that really speaks, and it alone speaks), requires that man — both poet and philosopher — should learn to give heed to what his language prompts.[5]

This view on language has analogies in the Indian tradition. Kumārila, an exponent of Pūrva-Mīmāṁsā, who had a noticeable influence on Śaṅkara, believed (this concept was further developed by Padmapāda, Śaṅkara's closest disciple) that the letters and sounds of Revelation (Āgama) in their textual order were eternal. They are the "seeds" or "embryos" from which the phenomenal world evolves at the beginning of each cosmic cycle.

Besides its significance for Advaita, this problem is also of practical importance to the translator. It is essential to preserve Śaṅkara's derivative series and phonetic

4. Martin Heidegger, *Unterwegs zur Sprache*, Pfullingen-Neske, 1959, S. 119.

5. "Any man is only capable of speaking in so far as he belongs to a language and listens to it in order to be able to utter a word."— M. Heidegger, op. cit., S. 266. (In the German text there is an intentional play on words: "gehörend — auf sie hört".)

parallelism. Unfortunately, this is still far from being achieved.

The following pages of this article present an analysis of the commentary on Bādarāyaṇa's fourth *sūtra*. It has to do above all with Śaṅkara's polemic with the proponents of Pūrva-Mīmāṁsā on the interpretation of the Revelation (Śruti).

On the one hand, Śaṅkara agrees with the Pūrva-Mīmāṁsā thesis on the indisputable importance of the Vedas as the "root" of all other human knowledge (the concept of *Veda-mūlatva* as first formulated in Jaimini's *Mīmāṁsā-sūtras*). On the other hand, he is opposed to Pūrva-Mīmāṁsā in interpreting the message of the Vedas and the correlation between its parts. Jaimini, Prabhākara and Kumārila regard as being of principal value those dicta that induce the adherent to action — the specific instructions (*vidhi*) usually connected with the ritual. The other sections of the Vedas, especially the so-called *arthavāda* sections, according to the Mīmāṁsakas, have a subsidiary, propaedeutic role. The impractical, chiefly explanatory and superfluous propositions of the Upaniṣads (and it is mostly these propositions that fall under the definition of *arthavāda*) are addressed to the spiritually immature adherent, who is yet unprepared to accept the austere scheme of things propounded by Mīmāṁsā, in which there is no room for God or for absolute unity of *ātman*, and which speaks only of religious duty (*dharma*), seen as faithful performance of the ritual.

Mīmāṁsā took shape on the crest of developing Brāhmanism, a religion of sacrifice, and literally became its "philosophical identity." According to Mīmāṁsā's world vision, the whole universe is manifest in space-time relations; it is in no way an external "shell" that conceals the essence and justification of the world.

Cosmos, seen broadly as nature, embraces gods, people and other living beings, and rests on nothing but itself and its own order. To quote R. Panikkar, "this ultimate structure is not to be regarded as 'another' or 'deeper' 'thing' or substance; it is in fact sacrifice, which is precisely the internal dynamism of the universe, universal *ṛta*, cosmic order itself. . . . Sacrifice is the act that makes the universe."[6] At the same time, the ritual action (*yāga*) symbolises supreme significance and order to the individual absorbed in habitual everyday life, to which it imparts meaning and vigour. As Francis d'Sa writes: "Sacrifice is not so much a rite as an act of cosmic union which creates and sustains cosmos as a community."[7]

Every individual's *dharma* (following the instructions) is, in Śabara's opinion, "a meaning which gives man a clue to Supreme Goodness" (*Śābara-bhāṣya*, 16.11-12). "Supreme Goodness" (*niḥśreyasa*), or "man's aim" (*puruṣārtha*), is interpreted in Pūrva-Mīmāṁsā as the source of eternal happiness, usually identified with heaven (*svarga*).

Theoretically, man does not need any persuasion to pursue happiness, as the very idea of happiness spurs him on, arousing in him an "eager desire" (*lipsā*). Supreme Goodness, however, is more evasive and problematic, it is a prospect of the remote future and does not immediately ensue from performing the ritual duties. The indisputable dependence of bliss upon action is stated in the additional definition of *dharma* as that which "is ensured by the relationship between *dharma* and the scriptures."

Jaimini and Śabara term the dicta of the sacred tradition (*vedavacana*) as *codanā* (inducement). The Mīmāṁsakas apply

6. Raimundo Panikkar, *The Vedic Experience*, Darton, Longman and Todd, London, 1977, p. 352.

7. F.X. D'Sa, *Śabdaprāmāṇyam im śabara und Kumārila*, Vienna, 1980, p. 20.

this term both to direct instructions and taboos and to explanations meant to elucidate the purpose of various actions. Kumārila identifies *codanā* with the scriptures (*śabda*) (*Śloka-vārttika, Codanā-sūtra,* 7), which allows him not only to relate the instructions with the Vedas, but also to frame the general concept of the word in Pūrva-Mīmāṁsā.

As mentioned above, Mīmāṁsā considers *vidhi* (instructions in the imperative mood) to be of the highest value, amongst the Vedic dicta. This follows from the notion of the active character of the word, which influences the listener, thanks to the so-called energy of formation (*bhāvanā*).

In the Indian tradition any utterance carries a semantic charge which exceeds the sum total of the meanings of the separate words it involves. Most of this energy evolves in the verb, the nucleus of the sentence, and manifests itself in three ways: as *ākāṅkṣā* (syntactic expectation) of the implied meaning; as *sannidhi,* (phonetic continuity), which makes the utterance coherent; and as *yogyatā* (logical consistency), which permits one to draw conclusions. Owing to this threefold unity of the energy of formation, the instructions apply not only to the ritual, but also to attaining "heaven" through ritual actions.

According to Mīmāṁsā, *śabdabhāvanā* is invisibly present in any instruction as a force that brings about something new. The fulfilment of a ritual duty causes the generation of *arthabhāvanā* energy, which unfailingly ensures good results. In other words, exposing oneself to the inner energy of the instruction one is entitled to partake of Supreme Goodness, or *svarga* (heaven). But this excludes personal effort from striving for *svarga,* since the process becomes automatic and impersonal as soon as man takes in the instruction. Consequently, according to Mīmāṁsā, the

Vedic instruction (*vidhi*) is determined by its own effort and is its own *ratio sufficiens*, and the scriptures have absolute and indisputable relevance.

At the same time, Śabara and Kumārila reduce the notions of the Veda's eternal nature and of that of the word (*śabdanityatā*) to the concept of the eternal nature of syllables as the smallest structural fractions of the Revelation (*varṇanityatā*). This reduction was necessitated by their dissociation from the grammarians' Sphoṭavāda theory and in the first place from Bhartṛhari. Kumārila came closest to the notion of the eternal nature of Śruti, but he failed to accept the grammarians' doctrine of a certain absolute phonetic entity (*sphoṭa*) that existed *beyond* and *above* any uttered syllables and manifested itself *in* them. To understand his reasoning it is enough to recall that Pūrva-Mīmāṁsā is strongly opposed, in a positivist fashion, to the concept of reality as underlying and determining all phenomena.

In philosophical systems that acknowledge the transcendental nature of supreme values (e.g. Advaita), thinking by *analogy*[8] and use of metaphor, myth and symbols play a very important part. The burden of Mīmāṁsā, by contrast, was the variety of spatial-temporal relations; the meanings of words were reduced to the bare ritual context. Mīmāṁsā's terminology was used to formulate instructions, and therefore word meanings had to be unequivocal. A

8. See H. Bruckner's study of the role of illustrative examples (*dṛṣṭānta*) in Śaṅkara's philosophy. To our mind, however, H. Bruckner underestimates the use of analogy and through this arrives at the fallacious conclusion that Śaṅkara's reasoning is purely logical and serves to prove the truthfulness of the Vedic dicta. (H. Bruckner, *Zum Bewelsverfahren Śaṁkaras, Eine Untersuchung der Form und Function von dṛṣṭānta im Bṛhadāraṇyakopaniṣadbhāṣya und Chāndogyopaniṣadbhāṣya des Śaṁkara Bhagavatpāda*, Berlin, 1979.)

pragmatic orientation necessitated the supplanting of the notion of the intrinsic, eternal nature of the word by the concept of the initialness (*ādinityatā*) of uttered syllables as held in "the continual tradition of *gurus*" (*guru-śiṣya paramparā*). This also matches well with the image of an "immature" disciple who should be instructed and should blindly obey the impersonal instructions of the Revelation, which are like a cog in the mechanism of the universe.

Obviously, the situation would have been different if Pūrva-Mīmāṁsā had chosen the Arthavāda type of dictum as a model. It is difficult to tell in what direction the teaching on the truthfulness of the scriptures (*śabda-prāmāṇyam*) would have developed. Probably, it would have become similar either to Ānandavardhana's *Dhvani* or to Śaṅkara's Advaita.

Śaṅkara never regards the Vedas as an auxiliary "instrument," be it a means of "awakening" to required actions or a method of instructing the neophyte, with his poor knowledge, shyness and indolence. The Revelation's dicta are knowledge sufficient for salvation. All the words in Śruti are harmoniously correlated.[9] Figuratively speaking, one has only to pull any of the multitude of threads, and the whole illusory knitwork of the universe comes unravelled, baring the true axis of existence — *ātman*. Moreover, according to Advaita, the lower level of hierarchy of the sacred dicta is instructions and interdictions, which are subsidiary conditions for emancipation, while at the top are the so-called higher dicta (*mahā-vākyāni*) of the Upaniṣads: "Thou art That" (*Chāndogya Upaniṣad*, XI. 8. 7); "This *ātman*

9. To cite Śaṅkara's own words, "no proposition of the scripture can be rejected; but once it is heard, it should be joined with the propositions assimilated previously, even if they are not contradictory and form a whole." (Commentary on *Br. S.*, III.II.18).

is *Brahman*" (*Bṛhadāraṇyaka Upaniṣad*, II.5.19), etc. The higher dicta are of no pragmatic value, they do not lead anywhere or educate anyone; they only help shift one's gaze from the pleasant things of earth and heaven and take a look at one's inner self in order to perceive the unity of *ātman*.

The change of perspective yielded a new concept of the function of language. Instead of its descriptive role, which ensured unequivocal denotation, the evocative function of language came to the fore. The grammarians believed that although the word did not give birth to a new universe, it alone could give an insight into the world's real nature. Incantations and *mantras*, epithets and metaphors, irony and pathos served to produce a colourful vision of the world, a double reflection of the reality concealed behind it. It is for this reason (and not because of fear that rationalism was detrimental to understanding the Revelation[10]) that Śaṅkara argued so vigorously against the "dry reasoning" (*śuṣka-tarka*) of logicians and Mīmāṁsakas.

We have already touched upon the reasons of Śaṅkara's persistent interest in language, but we have so far discussed only his views on poetic expression as a means to cognise qualityless (*nirguṇa*) *Brahman* in terms of apophatic theology. This is more succinctly expressed in Śruti: "The gods seem

---

10. Amongst the latest works discussing the contradiction between faith and reason, which in Advaita took shape in the discrepancy between Śruti and logical argumentation (*yukti*), are: H. Bruckner, op. cit.; T. Vetter, *Studien zur Lehre und Entwicklung Śaṅkaras*, Wien, 1979. These authors deplore the "preponderance" of religious traditions in that historical period and condescendingly "approve" of Śaṅkara's independent thinking and of his bold logical arguments in polemicising with the opponents. In fact, judgements and arguments have a subordinate part in Śaṅkara's philosophy and are strictly dependent on Śruti.

to like indirect (*parokṣa*) allusion and dislike direct naming" (*Bṛhadāraṇyaka Upaniṣad,* IV.2.2). But Śaṅkara assigns the word a cataphatic role as well — it is connected with approaching *Īśvara,* the Creator God (*Saguṇa-Brahman*).

To better comprehend this role it is worth recalling the great European scholiast Thomas Aquinas, who lived about 400 years later than Śaṅkara. Thomas Aquinas believed that the concept of analogy of being (*analogia antis*) was essential for the cognition of God. God becomes known gradually through the study of His creation. Although God's nature is quite different from that of the world, many objects and phenomena can be related to divinity in many different ways. God himself is the primary image. The whole universe is a staircase of being, built by God's grace to make man's path to the divine easier.

Śaṅkara's doctrine is different for obvious reasons. To his mind the creations of *Īśvara* and of an individual *jīva* (human life) are commensurable and in the final analysis identical. Yet it is difficult to communicate knowledge of them to man, whose *ātman* is bound by *avidyā.* This means that initially there must be an intermediate connection between the creator and a soul. This connection is analogy. Continuing the parallel between divine creation and human creative activity, it is pertinent to point out that the modern conception of art suggests a more suitable comparison: the creative efforts of the artist and the viewer are equivalent, but an intermediate analogy, a work of art, is essential to their communication.[11] According to Advaita, *Īśvara* creates

11. See Jean-Paul Sartre: "The act of imagination, viewed in its universality, is an act of consciousness, which implies an absent or as yet non-existent object through the instrumentality of a certain reality. In another work of mine I have termed this reality as *analogon.* It is not just a sign, but a →

the world and the Vedas; man's greatest possible merit is to create something in response. Śaṅkara believes that it is the creative capacity of language that can become, if used to the full, a worthy analogy of the game (*līlā*) of *Īśvara,* who, like an artist or conjurer, puts on the magic performance of *māyā.*

This interpretation may seem to depart from the real meaning of Śaṅkara's writings, but there is some indirect evidence that suggests its correctness. Firstly, as is known, Pūrva-Mīmāṁsā, with its predilection for impersonal instructions, rejected the notion of a creator god, negating the possible existence of an omnipotent and omniscient personality. Secondly, the pattern of reasoning in the first four *sūtras* of Bādarāyaṇa[12] appears to be woven around these problems.

One of the (two) *sūtras* that has been omitted in the cited translation describes *Brahman* as the creator of the world ("Of whom is the birth of this universe and other things. . .", I.1.2[13]), while another *sūtra* speaks of the relationship of *Brahman* and the Revelation. Characteristically, the second *sūtra* (I.1.3) can be interpreted in two

---

→ symbol." ("L'Acteur" in J.P. Sartre, *Un theatre de situations,* Paris, 1973, p. 199.) Sartre's *analogon* is described in his book *L'imaginaire,* which reads in particular: "Once a word turns into an image, it no longer functions as a simple sign."(J.P. Sartre, *L'imaginaire,* Paris, 1940, p. 112).

12. It is these four *sūtras* of the text and commentary that are beyond doubt the most important. They give a clue to understanding the whole work of Śaṅkara. *Pañca-pādikā,* the sub-commentary of Padmapāda, Śaṅkara's direct disciple, deals with these four *sūtras* only. Madhva's compendium *Sarva-darśana-saṁgraha* also refers to these *sūtras* alone in presenting the Śaṅkara system.

13. *janamādyasya yataḥ.*

different ways: "*Brahman* is omniscient, since it is the source ("the birth-giving womb") of the Śāstras", or "*Brahman* is inscrutable without the Vedas, since the Śastras are the source of its cognition."[14] Śaṅkara wrote two independent commentaries on this *sūtra,* being not in the least puzzled by its ambiguity, as it met his own intentions perfectly.

14. *śāstrayonitvāt.*

Chapter Six

Rāmānuja's Interpretation of the Bhagavad-Gītā

VSEVOLOD SEMENTSOV

IN view of the very special character of the Indian tradition of scholastic commenting, according to which a commentary serves as a means to express the commentator's own ideas, it would seem expedient to outline the main conceptions of Viśiṣṭādvaita as presented by Rāmānuja, its most influential exponent, and to delineate, at least sketchily, his exegetic method.

This system is expounded in hundreds of relevant texts. On the one hand, its elements can be traced back to the philosophical mysticism of the Upaniṣads, which is codified in Bādarāyaṇa's *Brahmasūtras* and also related in a more accessible fashion in the *Bhagavad-Gītā*. On the other hand, it is rooted in the religious (predominantly Bhakti) movement of the Āḻvārs and Aṟagiyas, inspired poets and their followers, which flourished in southern India between the sixth and ninth centuries CE.

The earliest Viśiṣṭādvaitist prophet whose teaching has reached us is Āḻvār Āḷavandār (918-1038). He is more widely known by the Sanskrit name of Yāmuna (Yāmunācārya). The system's dual origin — from the Vedic tradition and the Āḻvār religion — is manifest in the other name of this school, Ubhaya-Vedānta (Both Vedāntas). Evidently, Yāmuna had a relationship of some kind with Kāśmīrī

Śaivism, to which one of his treatises owes its title of *Kāśmīrāgama*. He is the compiler of a concise commentary on the *Gītā*, the first one in this school, which became the basis for all subsequent Vaiṣṇavite commentaries.

Yāmuna had many disciples. One of them was Mahāpūrṇa, whose nephew and disciple was Rāmānuja, who, like Yāmuna, bore the title of an Aṛagiya, "an interpreter of the Ālvārs."

Out of Yāmuna's "intuitions" Rāmānuja made a consistent system, which was a very early, yet final codification of Viśiṣṭādvaita.

After Rāmānuja, the school of Viśiṣṭādvaita produced a number of outstanding thinkers. The most prominent of them was undoubtedly Vedānta-Deśika (Veṅkaṭanātha, 1268-1369), a person of versatile genius, an illustrious philosopher, *guru* and poet.

The post-Vedānta-Deśika tradition also lists some commentators, but they were of less importance. In the fourteenth and fifteenth centuries Yāmuna's and Rāmānuja's ideas influenced a number of renowned *bhaktas*, among them Swāmi Rāmānanda and his followers Kabīr, Dādū, Tulsīdās and others.

Viśiṣṭādvaita excelled in solving the problem of correlation between the Divine Absolute and the imperfect, "bestial" world (*saṁsāra*), which, to the mind of a medieval Indian, was a painfully vain and endless cycle of reincarnations. Śaṅkara and his school of Advaita solve this problem simply by "annihilation" of the material world, regarding it as an unreal and meaningless entity. What exists in reality is only the Absolute (*Brahman*), while whatever is perceived in the form of space-time existence (i.e. the whole universe) is *māyā*, the cosmic illusion, a mirage which is to be identified and unhesitatingly discarded.

The Advaitic compendiums usually offer examples meant to demonstrate the agency of *māyā*. For instance, depending on the quality of light, a person may take mother-of-pearl for silver, or be scared in the dusk by a rope lying across the path, mistaking it for a snake. But a more attentive look dispels the illusion. Likewise, adopting a correct viewpoint, a person realises that this world is nothing but *Brahman*, which manifests itself in a variety of forms. *Brahman*, being the substratum of these forms, is real, while the forms themselves are not. There is nothing in the universe but the singular; all plurality is imaginary. For that reason this system was named Advaita-vāda, i.e. the doctrine of the non-duality of existence.

Let us examine how Viśiṣṭādvaita answers the same question. It holds that there are three real entities with the following attributes:

A. The absolute, which is totally independent and possesses consciousness and properties. The Absolute is cognisable.
B. Individual *ātman*, which is naturally dependent on the Absolute. It possesses plurality, consciousness and properties. *Ātman*, like the absolute, is cognisable.
C. Matter, which also is dependent on the Absolute. It is cognisable, possesses plurality and properties, but is devoid of consciousness.

From this classification of attributes it is obvious that the Absolute in Viśiṣṭādvaita is paradoxical in a number of ways: (i) it is simultaneously subject and object of cognition; (ii) it is non-dual but possesses properties, it coexists with two other entities; and (iii) being totally independent, it is however injured when nobody perceives it, because at such a time its supreme qualities seem to become meaningless.

All these discrepancies, however, result from our endeavour to conceptualise the interrelation between God, the world and individual souls. This, as a rule, is not done in Viśiṣṭādvaita. But when it is done in heated polemics, this school proves vulnerable to opponents' criticism. The school's principal "intuitions" have to do not with a scheme, but with an image or a whole set of images. Very often the Absolute, *ātman* and matter are likened to the human being, whose aspects are the soul, the senses and the body. Human life symbolises the manifest natural interaction of the three aspects, while death corresponds to the end of the world, when only the *Paramātman* remains, absorbing individual souls and matter, which turn non-manifest.

There are diverse presentations of this model. Here are a few examples. God is the owner of parts (*aṁśin*), the parts (*aṁśa*) are soul and nature. Or, God is a predominant, independent and self-sufficient entity (*śeṣin*), while everything else (*śeṣa*) is subordinate to and dependent on Him. Or, God is an artist and all else is His paintings and statues. Or, God is a boundless ocean, in which nature and souls are drops, or waves, or flakes of foam. Or, He is the sun and they are His rays. Or, He is fire and soul and nature are His sparks.

Most of these images were used by Yāmuna. Various combinations of them are found in any post-Yāmuna text of Viśiṣṭādvaita.

The "philosophical technique" of Yāmuna and Rāmānuja to some extent resembles Plato's style of philosophising. Plato usually begins by introducing "his Socrates," only to grind various conceptual schemes in the mill of his dialectics, and then finishes by relating a myth (to conjure up an image) — of the island of Atlantis, or of the wise woman Diotima, or of the spherical people, and so on. Fruitless are any attempts to summarise Plato's constructive generalisations by merely rearranging his dialogues into a scheme which is supposed to show his philosophical evolution, or by trying to weave them around some central idea, and so are any attempts to present Viśiṣṭādvaita as a configuration of ideas. These devices do not work in our case, because we have not a conceptual complex, but an image-building methodology.

In this respect Viśiṣṭādvaita deserves special attention, for, like an *aśvattha* (an Indian fig tree), it lays bare its own roots. In the conception of "both Vedāntas" are discerned the main constituent elements of the future system. We shall try to see how the Upaniṣads and Āḻvār poetry contributed to this synthesis.

First, let us examine the Āḻvār influence. Both Yāmuna and Rāmānuja participated in the Bhakti movement in southern India and interpreted the ecstatic Āḻvār hymns. What was this poetry about?

From the brief, yet informative chapter, "Nammāḻvār (Śaṭhakopa)" in the third volume of *A History of Indian Philosophy* by Surendranath Dasgupta we learn the following interesting facts:

(1) Every *bhakta* (devotee) feels absolutely dependent on *Bhagavān*.

(2) He compares his longing for Kṛṣṇa to the longing of a young girl for her beloved, or of a mother for her child, or of a wife for her husband, or of a servant for his master, or of a retinue man for his eminent companion.

(3) He divines the whole world in *Bhagavān*'s body.

(4) He describes in an elaborate and imaginative fashion the amazing qualities of *Bhagavān*.

(5) He cannot bear separation from Kṛṣṇa and goes out of his mind because of deep sorrow, and then Kṛṣṇa gives him consolation.

(6) Separated from the Beloved, he calls for Him and appeals to Him by many different names.
(7) At times he feels that he is God, the Creator of the world.
(8) At times he even feels that the Divine Grace overwhelms him and pours out in verse, and then he is willing and able to console all those who suffer.
(9) He sees forms (reflections) of divinity everywhere.

This list could be continued, but there is no need to do so, since it allows us to see in it the source of the images of God, nature and individual souls in Viśiṣṭādvaita. Indeed, Nammāḻvār's (i.e. the soul's) "attitudes" to *Bhagavān* as described in (2) can be summarised in the *śeṣa-śeṣin* principle (i.e. the relation of the dependent to the depended-upon); (1) "reaffirms" it, the world is rediscovered in the body of *Bhagavān:* (3) is also one of the basic images in Viśiṣṭādvaita.

All these coincidences and analogies are so obvious that there is no doubt as to the origin of the image-building technique which constitutes a specific feature of this system, especially in view of the fact that both Yāmuna and Rāmānuja belonged to the Āḻvār tradition.

The second component part of this school is the philosophical mysticism of the Upaniṣads. We shall try to estimate its role in the crystallisation of the system. Naturally, this task is much more difficult. Unlike the comparatively homogeneous Bhakti movement and Āḻvār poetry, the Upaniṣads are a mixed conglomeration of ideas, largely used by all traditional Indian philosophies. That is why in its theoretical (abstract-logical) sense, the term "teaching" cannot be applied to the Upaniṣads, not even to the 10 to 15 principal texts. It would be wise to attempt a functional approach to the Upaniṣads, regarding them as a certain complex of ascetic training methods, which include continuous recitation of the sacred texts in order to obtain a state of knowledge that transcends subject-object relations.

We feel free to surmise, albeit as a very cautious hypothesis (since this problem is very complicated and requires a meticulous textual analysis), that the concept of the knowledge process plays just as big a part in the ideology of Viśiṣṭādvaita as it does in the opening two chapters of the *Gītā*. Knowledge, acquired with the help of the described phenomena of the "inner exhaustion" of images, restricts and ennobles the quenchless image, thirst, which, if handled without discipline, threatens to derange man's psyche and result in "mystical unruliness." Apparently due to this knowledge the temptingly non-transcendental, grey-coloured, idol-like deity turns into the transcendental Absolute of philosophers. In Viśiṣṭādvaitist parlance, only this knowledge makes the diverse pertinent to non-duality. The variegation and crush of the lower world dies down before the silence of the higher world, and some portion of this silence may even linger in the lower world forever.

This approach is quite handy, for it allows us to bring out, although in a very general outline, the relationship between Śaṅkara's and Rāmānuja's versions of Vedānta. The two schools, in their mutual opposition, countervail each other. Śaṅkara's Advaita is a purely ascetic and transcendental doctrine. It discards the material world altogether and seeks absolute knowledge as a process. But any real human being who has not yet fully renounced his humanity can hardly stand the temperature of absolute perfection — he feels cold and looks for something warmer. His soul warms itself with images, above all the image of a kind and merciful God, who helps and saves. That is why in his commentary on the *Gītā,* Śaṅkara assumes the existence of *Bhagavān, Īśvara* and others. Viśiṣṭādvaita, which is far better adapted to secular life, transgresses the sensual images with the help of the image of God, and then the image of God is overcome with the help of the process of knowledge. This interpretation shows the single essence of the two doctrines.

Turning to the exegetic method of Rāmānuja, we immediately realise that the images of Viśiṣṭādvaita are directly related to it. *Gītā-bhāṣya* opens with an imposing image of *Bhagavān*, Nārāyaṇa, the Supreme *Puruṣa*. It is a hymn in the style of a prosaic *kāvya*. It begins:

> Now, the Consort of Śrī, whose proper form, antagonistic to all that is evil and solely comprising all that is good, is nothing but knowledge and bliss; the ocean of innumerable beautiful qualities, such as boundless and supreme knowledge, power, force, sovereignty, fortitude, mastery, etc., qualities proper to his nature.[1]

Then *Gītā-bhāṣya* describes the numerous good qualities of *Bhagavān*, which do not prevent Him from remaining immutable. This is followed by a description of His wife, the goddess Śrī Lakṣmī, who praises the pious *bhaktas*. Then the hymn relates stories about *Bhagavān*'s incarnations for the sake of saving human beings, and so forth.

Why does this solemn and elaborate hymn open the commentary? Presumably to give a clue to *Gītā-bhāṣya*'s general meaning. This image runs through the whole text: every *śataka* opens and ends with it, sometimes a brief extract from the opening hymn is placed after an important verse or term. Does it mean that we as readers of *Gītā-bhāṣya* are also supposed to keep this image in mind? If so, we have before us an image-bearing commentary on the whole of *Gītā-bhāṣya*, the very kind of knowledge that should accompany the process of reading, i.e. a continuous recitation of the sacred poem.

---

1. J.A.B. van Buitenen, *Rāmānuja on the Bhagavad-Gītā*, Delhi: Motilal Banarsidass, 1974, p. 45.

It is an amazing Indian habit — to interpret ancient culture through images. As is well known, the Brāhmaṇas are nothing but commentaries on the earlier Saṁhitā texts. These commentaries, however, are rich in sacred images, which is testified to by the formula "who so knows" and the relevant technique of mental ritual. At the same time, there are reasons to suppose that the *Ṛgveda*, the most ancient piece of Indian writing known to us, was also intended as a similar commentary on the so-called *nivida*s, still more ancient invocations of gods, regarded as "ancient" even in the *Ṛgveda*. From the time of the Brāhmaṇas onwards, we find similar imagery, meant to "dramatise" the teaching that is commented upon. The *Gītā*, for instance, is such a commentary on the teaching on the indestructibility of *ātman* as expounded in the *Kaṭha Upaniṣad*, while Rāmānuja compiled a commentary of this type on the *Gītā*. Clearly, Rāmānuja does not close this tradition. Of the same type are a number of Buddhist commentaries (*Jātaka*, the commentary on *Dhammapada*, etc.), the *Pañcatantra*, and the like.

Let us examine the exegetic method of Rāmānuja in detail. All the instructions of *Gītā-bhāṣya* form a permanent background for the image of *Bhagavān*, which is introduced in the opening hymn and fragmentarily comes up throughout the text. This compels us to regard this image as the resultant content (meaning, object and aim in one, i.e. *artha*) of the whole treatise. It is nonetheless obvious that the numerous special instructions contained in the commentary (interpretations of terms and certain lines, references to various chapters of the *Gītā* and to the Upaniṣads as well as to other philosophical treatises, often to polemicise with them) have no symbolic meaning and resemble ordinary philosophical or rationalist theological generalisations, like those of Anselm of Canterbury. The question therefore arises, how does this "common-sense logic" connected with the sacral imagery of the opening hymn?

On mature examination, any Indian commentary, including that of Rāmānuja, displays certain "peculiarities." The Dutch Indologist J.A.B. van Buitenen, who has specially dealt with Viśiṣṭādvaita's exegetics, has compiled a list of Rāmānuja's "fantastic" interpretations, paying particular attention to how, in *Gītā-bhāṣya,* Rāmānuja selects quotations from sacred texts, primarily the Upaniṣads and the *Gītā.* Much about it is quite obscure. It is not clear why the commentator holds that the *Chāndogya Upaniṣad* (8.7-12) includes the teaching on individual *ātman* and that the same *śloka* (8.1-3) discusses the Absolute, or why he relates the *Bhagavad-Gītā* (8.3) to the teaching of five fires (*Chāndogya Upaniṣad,* 5.4-10, *Bṛhadāraṇyaka Upaniṣad,* 6.2), or why he interprets *karma* (action) as reproductive. Why does he choose only one out of all the meanings of a polysemantic word, and as a rule not the most important one at that? For instance, *yoga* (in *Bhagavad-Gītā,* 4.28) is interpreted as a pilgrimage to sacred places. The logic of these interrelations seems rather elusive.

To overcome such difficulties encountered by the reader of Indian commentaries at every step, van Buitenen sets forth two basic principles of Rāmānuja's exegetics:

1. All the sacred texts teach the same doctrine, supplementing each other, and in this respect they are equally authoritative.
2. The concepts of the historically determined nature and traditionality of the sacred texts are alien to this approach from positions of eternity, that is why early texts may be interpreted with the help of later ones.

These considerations seem convincing and helpful in explaining Rāmānuja's "inconsistency" (for instance, his arbitrary manner of quotation). This seeming inconsistency is a result of the disagreement between two different approaches — modern (historical) and traditional (exegetic).

Nevertheless, all this fails to fill the gap between Rāmānuja's logic and the methods of modern science.

> The two principles which determine the interpretation, viz. basic assumptions of the consistency and of the eternity of the sacred texts, run counter to the fundamental principles of modern scholarship, and we have to reject them.[2]

In spite of all our efforts to grasp the psychology of the transmitters of this tradition, it still remains largely incomprehensible to us. Furthermore, we could be content with the principles formulated by van Buitenen if they elucidated, at least partially, Rāmānuja's thinking, but in fact they do not. Reverting to the aforementioned exegesis of *śloka* 8.3 of the *Bhagavad-Gītā* (which is explained by reference to the *Chāndogya Upaniṣad*, 5.4-10), the notion that the sacred texts are basically in accord helps us to understand (although only formally) that Rāmānuja alludes to the doctrine of five fires contained in the *Chāndogya Upaniṣad* by turning to *śloka*s 8.23-26 of the *Bhagavad-Gītā,* which contain a similar teaching on the two ways. The latter is also present in the *Chāndogya Upaniṣad* (5.10). But why does he turn (implicitly) from *śloka* 8.3 to *śloka*s 8.23-26 of the *Bhagavad-Gītā,* although they bear no resemblance to each other? Van Buitenen's approach fails to answer this question. Rāmānuja's exegetics remain unintelligible to him.

Let us take a closer look at the above example. Why does Rāmānuja, being totally indifferent to the evolution of the texts and teachings, still interpret one sacred text with the help of another? Our example is characteristic in this regard. A careful reading of the beginning of the eighth chapter of the *Bhagavad-Gītā* suggests that the lucid *śloka*

2. J.A.B. van Buitenen, op. cit., p. 58.

8.3 is explained by the vague doctrine of the two ways (8.23-26), which is then expanded into the doctrine of five fires (*Chāndogya Upaniṣad,* 5.4-9).

Why does the commentator quote the sacred texts? At first it may seem that he simply wishes to corroborate his ideas by their authority, just as modern scholars do. But this assumption is not convincing. Why should one try to prove the doctrines of the *Gītā* by referring (explicitly or implicitly) to the *Gītā* itself? And why should the same text be quoted 10 to 15 times to justify one statement (e.g. *Bṛhadāraṇyaka Upaniṣad,* 3.7.3 ff.), which is rather typical of *Gītā-bhāṣya?* All this creates an impression of the commentator's inexperience, which certainly cannot apply to such a master as Rāmānuja. It means that our interpretation of the function of quotations in the exegetic framework is not acceptable.

Let us now attempt to overcome these difficulties by examining the function of the text as such, which consisted in its continuous recitation. This is the case with the Upaniṣads and with the *Gītā*. What would this practice mean to the commentator?

Here I would like to point out a curious habit of one of the most eminent contemporary interpreters of the *Gītā* — Mahatma Gandhi. During difficult moments of his life, Gandhi turned to the *Gītā* for advice. He opened the book at random and read the first line that met his eye, taking it as God's will. Does this bear in one way or another upon the recitation technique?

Let us imagine an Indian who has for long learnt the *Gītā* and recites it everyday, as well as some parts of the Upaniṣads. Obviously, many years of such practice will tell on his mentality. Apart from its spiritual effect, this practice will result in a habit of recalling the Upaniṣads and the *Gītā* on every occasion — in connection with old and new doctrines and poems, situations of everyday life, all manner of emotions and actions. Clearly, it is this "omnipresence" of the sacred text that Gandhi compensated for by his random reading. For one who knows the text by heart there is no need for such a mechanical exercise, as the appropriate *śloka* springs to mind automatically even before he can think of consulting the *Gītā.*

This view seems to provide satisfactory answers to the questions raised above. Van Buitenen's two principles tie in with it quite well. All the texts liable to recitation would be, to those who practise it, equally indisputable, mutually complementary and unhistorical. Naturally, these exegetic principles are irrelevant to modern culture, which is unfamiliar with the recitation technique. Like any other traditional commentator, Rāmānuja quotes the sacred texts because they come to his mind by association. There is nothing surprising in the fact that sometimes commentators interpret the same text using different references and read different meanings into it. The Indian commentator teaches his disciple not abstract (objective), but concrete (personal) truths. Along with these truths he instils in the disciple part of his personality.

Our brief outline of Viśiṣṭādvaita would be incomplete without an answer to the question that is fundamental to any philosophical school: what is its concept of knowledge? What kind of knowledge can eradicate *avidyā* from the soul of the disciple and set him on the path to inner emancipation? Turning to such authoritative texts of the ancient Vedāntic tradition as the *Brahmasūtras* and the *Gītā,* Rāmānuja substantiates the transcendental mysticism of the Upaniṣads. The Upaniṣads (referred to as *jñāna-kāṇḍa* in Vedānta) deal above all with the problem of knowledge. But knowledge, being indescribable by nature, is not explained but only prescribed. Translating this into modern parlance, we may say that knowledge is instilled not descriptively, but with the aid of an algorithm. Mere understanding is not enough, it requires realisation. Knowledge should be "in-built." Then a digression brings us to the *Gītā*. The first step to realisation is learning of the knowledge (the text) by heart. The second step is its regular worship. Perpetual worship (which is compared to a stream of oil) takes the shape of incessant recalling. Finally, warmed by overwhelming love, knowledge is lit by a ray of reciprocal Divine Love and becomes *bhakti*. The teaching (or, to be more precise, the prescribing) of this knowledge is the burden of the philosophy of the Upaniṣads and (we believe) of the *Gītā*.

CHAPTER SEVEN

Polemic of Viśiṣṭādvaita and Advaita Vedānta

RUZANA PSKHU

THE first systematisation of the Upaniṣads, presented in the *Brahmasūtras,* had put forward the question of the relation of *Brahman* and the soul. Position of the author of the *Brahmasūtras* is that *Brahman* is a source of the origination, subsistence and destruction of the world and that He is the highest object of knowledge. This position was not disputed by any system of Vedānta. But the ambiguity of the text, generated by its aphoristic style, was the reason for the varying understanding of the status of the world in its relation to *Brahman* in the different systems of Vedānta. Śaṅkara, having absolutised the idea of the reality of *Brahman,* had argued that the world is a product of *māyā.* The founders of the different systems of Vedānta were critical of Śaṅkara's *māyā,* which is considered neither real nor unreal. We can see the example of such criticism in the first major work of the founder of Viśiṣṭādvaita, the *Vedārthasaṁgraha.*[1] Rāmānuja, explaining in detail the method of understanding the Upaniṣads, firstly puts arguments against Śaṅkara's total identification of the world and the individual self with *Brahman*. The weakness of the arguments of Advaita is shown and denied by Rāmānuja with maximum pedantry. A detailed and "meticulous"

1. Rāmānuja, *Vedārthasaṁgraha,* ed. and tr. J. Van Buitenen Poona, 1956.

conversation of Rāmānuja with the representative of Śaṅkara occupies most of the first part of the *Vedārthasaṁgraha*. This testifies to the exclusive value of the ideas of Advaita Vedānta for formation of the Viśiṣṭādvaita system.

The essence of the Advaitic philosophy can be expressed in the thesis: "*Brahman* is real, the world is illusory, the soul is identical with *Brahman*." The criticism of the concept of *māyā*, presented in the *Vedārthasaṁgraha*, is realised by Rāmānuja on two bases: on the basis of sacred texts (§10-39) and on the basis of a rational discourse (§40-53). In the third part of the work, devoted to working out the main ideas of Viśiṣṭādvaita, Rāmānuja exposes also the arguments in protection of his own system against the attacks of Advaita (*Vedārthasaṁgraha*, §67-71, §85-90, §95-96, §113).

It is necessary to notice that the criticism of Advaita, put on the basis of sacred texts, occupies actually two thirds of all the criticism of Advaita, exposed in the *Vedārthasaṁgraha*. That is connected both with the exegetic "specialisation" of the *Vedārthasaṁgraha* and with the necessity of the debutant (i.e. Rāmānuja) to demonstrate clear and correct understanding of the Upaniṣads. The pivotal schools of Vedānta, Advaita and Viśiṣṭādvaita, are solid for the ideas, that (1) all is *Brahman*, and (2) the source of the knowledge of *Brahman* is Śruti. Although both Śaṅkara and Rāmānuja agree on the significance of Śruti for the knowledge of *Brahman*, Rāmānuja in contrast with Śaṅkara accepted all Śruti passages as being of equal value. Rāmānuja refused to make any distinction among Śruti passages: for him there is only one meaning for any Śruti text. The main method of Rāmānuja's interpretation of the sacred texts, which can deduce the primary meaning of Śruti, is *sāmānādhikaraṇya*, which is explained in detail in the *Vedārthasaṁgraha*. For Rāmānuja *sāmānādhikaraṇya* is "the application to one object of several words in different functions."[2]

In general the discussion between Rāmānuja and the representative of Advaita, presented in the *Vedārthasaṁgraha*, can be divided into three parts.

The first part contains Rāmānuja's arguments against Advaita, which are based on the interpretation of the sacred texts. Our investigation of this passage of the *Vedārthasaṁgraha* demonstrates that the most quoted text, used in the polemic between Rāmānuja and the representative of Advaita, is the *Chāndogya Upaniṣad* and an axial passage — the passage about clay and its modifications:

> Just as by knowing a lump of clay, my son, all that is clay can be known, since any differences are only words and the reality is clay. — *Chāndogya*, 6.1.4

The reference to the *Chāndogya*, one of the longest and perhaps the oldest Upaniṣads, is not casual. The *Chāndogya* contains an idea of identity of *Ātman-Brahman*: *Brahman* is the Self of all, He is *Ātman*. In the polemic Rāmānuja often uses the well-known refrain "Thou art that" (*Chāndogya*, 6.8.7).

Firstly Rāmānuja contends the Advaitic idea of freedom of *Brahman* from all attributes and characteristics. Rāmānuja quotes many scriptural passages expounding all perfections, which belong to *Brahman*. The result of this quotation is Rāmānuja's affirmation that "the origination, subsistence and reabsorption, etc. of the world are due to the will of *Brahman*"[3] and consequently it means that the world is real. To refute this consequence Advaitin uses the passage from the *Chāndogya* (6.1.4), which demonstrates, in his opinion,

2. Rāmānuja, op. cit., p. 200.
3. Ibid., p. 189.

that "the One, being the cause, is real whereas all transformations have no reality,"[4] in other words that *Brahman* is non-differentiated. Only having learnt the cause-*Brahman* (=clay), Rāmānuja replies, it is possible to learn an effect-world (=clay-modifications).

> The assertion that we can know all by knowing the One is only tenable in case that all has reality of its own by having the One for its soul.[5]

The soul and the world are real and distinct from *Brahman*, but they exist, based on *Brahman* alone. *Brahman* has created this world out of spontaneity and in play (*līlā*). He is the material and the operative cause, the substratum of the entire phenomenal world of spiritual and non-spiritual entities. All texts of Śruti affirm the real existence of the world. *Brahman* animates the world as the inner Ruler (*antaryāmin*) and consequently all words functioning in the world, are His predicates. ". . . Since all spiritual and non-spiritual entities constitute *Brahman*'s body, *Brahman* being thus embodied and modified by all, is denoted by all words."[6] Words are names of objects, which are created and animated by *Brahman*. To explain this idea Rāmānuja uses the analogy of body-soul relationship. Just as the body modifies the soul and has no separate existence from it, yet is different from it, just so the world constitutes *Brahman*'s body, modifying it, yet having no separate existence from it. Rāmānuja states that only in this case we can have the right understanding of the meaning of the sacred texts. Rāmānuja's interpretation of the ordinary language is disputed by the representative of Śaṅkara, for it is nonsense to deduce the

---

4. Rāmānuja, op. cit., p. 189.
5. Ibid., p. 190.
6. Ibid., p. 195.

original meaning of the concrete word (e.g. cow) from *Brahman*. Rāmānuja answers that all words denote the Supreme Spirit only in so far as He is differentiated by the non-spiritual matter and the individual soul.[7] We should understand the passage "Thou art that" (*tattvamasi*) in the sense that "thou" (*tvam*) denotes only the inner Ruler of "thou" as differentiated by the mode "thou." Since *Brahman* is the soul of the embodied individual self, He has the same name as this individual self. It follows that both words "that" (*tat*) and "thou" denote *Brahman*.[8] Advaitin says that "it is impossible to refer to one and the same person as if he were simultaneously connected with incompatible places or durations. So we contend that the two words are only meant to establish a mere proper form and that this proper form is one in itself."[9] Rāmānuja replies that there is no contradiction, when a person, who in the past was connected with one place, is at present connected with another place. There is nothing contradictory in the Supreme *Brahman*, who is the cause of the world, is also the soul of the individual soul inasmuch as He is its inner Ruler.[10]

Advaitin affirms that *Brahman* is pure and non-differentiated knowledge. But according to Rāmānuja, the knowledge cannot be an entity and it is only one of the attributes of *Brahman*. The word "knowledge" has distinctive characteristics in the form of a root and an inflexion and besides it demands an object: knowledge of what? If *Brahman* can be learnt, it means that He possesses

7. Rāmānuja, op. cit., p. 196.
8. Ibid., pp. 195-96.
9. Ibid., p. 199.
10. Ibid., pp. 199-200.

properties, on which He is learnt. If the reality has no distinctive properties, as Advaitin confirms, it cannot be comprehended. Any perception means the presence of any distinctive properties. *Brahman*'s proper form is designated by knowledge as His attribute.[11] The term "pure knowledge" points to a differentiated reality, because this word refers to a differentiated substance. The word "knowledge" tells us that it has an object and a subject and that it is a specific action with a specific nature, which distinguishes it from other actions. Rāmānuja concluded the first polemical part by the affirmation that, if one admits the differentiating attribute characterising pure knowledge and that this attribute is connected with the word standing for *Brahman*, the logical consequence would be that *Brahman*, being characterised by all attributes, affirmed by all the sacred texts, must be admitted.

In the second part of the polemical discussion with Advaitin Rāmānuja puts forward logical arguments against the Advaitic position. First of all, these arguments concern definitions of *Brahman* as pure knowledge and a definition of the world as a product of *māyā*. The Advaitic definition of *Brahman* as pure knowledge and of the world as a product of *māyā* has two logical consequences, which are destructive for the Advaitic position: (1) *Brahman* is not so eternal, not so pure and not so self-sufficient, if *māyā*, illusion, can hide it; and (2) the attainment of salvation is impossible, because anything in this world, including the sacred texts and the idea of salvation, is unreal, being only a projection of *māyā*. We should admit that *māyā* is devoid of foundation of its reality: it can be neither the individual self, which is a projection of *māyā*, nor *Brahman*, which has the nature of self-luminosity. And we should admit that the knowledge,

11. Rāmānuja, op. cit., pp. 199-200.

which destroys *māyā*, cannot be illusive and superimposed individual self. According to Rāmānuja, the Advaitic understanding of the relation between *māyā*, the destructive knowledge and *Brahman* is false, because it is contradictory to the idea of the absolute reality of *Brahman*. It would seem, the opponent (i.e. Advaitin) is crushed. But in the third part of the *Vedārthasaṁgraha* he rises and puts reasonable enough arguments to his own advantage: in the third part Rāmānuja defends the Viśiṣṭādvaita position from the Advaitic criticism. First of all Rāmānuja says that "the sum-total of spiritual and non-spiritual entities is ensouled by the Supreme *Brahman* inasmuch as it modifies Him."[12] Advaitin tries to refute it by the argument that it means that *Brahman* is the material cause of the world, "but being the material cause means being the substratum of evolution."[13] It means, in the opinion of Advaitin, that *Brahman* is cruel and partial. Rāmānuja says, that *karman* of all the various embodied souls, which causes cruelty and partiality of the world, is not *Brahman*. Individual souls are essentially unlimited and perfect knowledge. But they are enveloped by ignorance in the form of *karman*. *Brahman*, on the one hand, has the mode of being of cause and, on the other hand, that of effect. That's why there is no difference between cause and effect, and consequently no Śruti is contradicted. It is the central meaning of Śruti, according Rāmānuja.

But, if *Brahman* is the inner Ruler of all creations of the world and all is caused by His will, it means, Advaitin says, that there is no subject of His prescriptions and prohibitions. Rāmānuja replies that *Brahman* gives everything necessary for activity or inactivity. The person operates voluntarily,

12. Rāmānuja, op. cit., p. 231.

13. Ibid., p. 232.

and God only observes it. When an action of a person is directed for the blessing, God grants a corresponding intellectual spirit, which allows further to make good acts and, on the contrary, if a person makes evil acts, the intellectual spirit from God will be suitable, and a person will be vicious further. God himself is not "contra" and is not "pro" — He only helps prompting good or harm, and the person himself decides what to do. "The Supreme Spirit has bestowed equally upon all spiritual beings all that is required for activity or inactivity. The spiritual being, whose capacities are so dependent on Him, performs of his own accord certain acts or refrains of his own accord from certain acts. But while observing the soul in its doings the Supreme Spirit Himself takes no side. . . . Besides, it depends on every individual case whether He will cause good or evil acts to be performed."[14] It is noteworthy that Rāmānuja uses in the *Vedārthasaṁgraha* for denoting *Brahman*, as the Supreme Cause of the world, the words "Nārāyaṇa," "*Īśvara*" and many other epithets of Viṣṇu, while in the *Śrībhāṣya*, the most important philosophical commentary on the *Brahmasūtras*, Rāmānuja uses the word *Īśvara* only once. He does so "in order to dispel any doubts that the focus of his attention was the *Brahman* of the Upaniṣads and none other."[15]

The last reply of Rāmānuja to any argument of Advaitin is that *Brahman* is omnipotent and His omnipotence resolves any contradiction. "I remind you that the Supreme *Brahman* is Nārāyaṇa, as has been declared before. Then how could there be contradiction?"[16]

---

14. Rāmānuja, op. cit., p. 247.
15. Ciryl Veliath S.J., *The Mysticism of Rāmānuja*, Delhi, 1993, p. 39.
16. Rāmānuja, op. cit., p. 253.

As we see from the above-stated, discussion Rāmānuja does not only criticise the philosophical ideas of Advaita, but also rejects the probable Advaitic critical arguments. The results of the discussion between Rāmānuja and the representative of Advaita presented in the *Vedārthasaṁgraha* are:

1. there is one *Brahman*, the sole cause of all existence, and He is differentiated by all perfect attributes;
2. all sentient and non-sentient matter constitutes the body of *Brahman*, and stands to him in the relationship of attributes; and
3. salvation of the individual soul is not identification with *Brahman* but devotion to *Brahman* through the intellectual love for Him (*bhakti*).

CHAPTER EIGHT

Ancient Indian Culture and Materialism

GRIGORI BONGARD-LEVIN

DESPITE the fact that Indian materialism is discussed in many specialised works, its role in ancient Indian culture is still far from clear, and controversy about it persists.

The subject indeed is a very complex one, particularly because there are no texts of the ancient materialist school (the Lokāyatikas, or the Cārvākas) that can be trusted as indisputably authentic. For an insight into the teaching and evolution of Lokāyata one has to turn to the writings of its opponents, although their presentation of Lokāyata is often quite tendentious.

The sources on Lokāyata studied traditionally are religious and philosophical texts. Scientific and political treatises are usually disregarded, although the influence of materialism was strongest on science and political theory, as becomes obvious, for instance, from an analysis of the essentially political *Arthaśāstra* (Treatise on Material Gain).

Indological works offer various hypotheses as to when the *Arthaśāstra* was written; the existing materials, however, allow us to presume that the final version was compiled not less than 2,000 years ago.[1] The *Arthaśāstra* contains some

---

1. H. Soharfe, *Untersuchungen zur Staatsarechtslehre des Kautilya*, Wiesbaden, 1968; T. Trautmann, *Kauṭilya and the Arthaśāstra* (A Statistical Investigation of the Authorship and Evolution

→

of the earliest information on Lokāyata as a philosophical trend. Chapter 2, "The Place of Philosophy" (*ānvīkṣikī-sthāpanā*), of Part 1, entitled "The Definition of Sciences" (*vidyā-samuddeśaḥ*), deserves special attention. It relates the opinions on the correct classification of the sciences held by various religio-jurisprudential schools (based on the Śāstras) and by political schools.

First comes Mānava's school,[2] which regards the teachings on the three Vedas (*trayī*), on economy (*vārttā*) and on government (*daṇḍanīti*) as sciences, but does not include philosophy, because it is only "a special section of the teaching on the three Vedas" (*trayīviśeṣo ānvīkṣikī*). The school of Bṛhaspati[3] distinguishes between only two sciences — the teachings on economy and those on government. The exponents of this school believe that to the worldly person the teachings on the three Vedas is nothing but a mist before the eyes (*saṁvaraṇamātram hi trayī lokayātrāvida iti; "lokayātrā"* literally means "the worldly path"). The followers of Uśanas cling to an extreme point of view that the teachings on government are the only science.

→ of the Text), Leiden, 1971; A.A. Vigasin, *Problems of Studying the Sources Relating to the Arthaśāstra* (Russian edn.), V.D.I., no. 1, pp. 218-33; G.M. Bongard-Levin, *India of the Mauryan Epoch* (Russian edn.), Moscow, 1973, pp. 23-26.

2. R.P. Kangle maintains that the text refers not to the school connected with *Manu-Smṛti*, but to the arthaśāstra school. (See R.P. Kangle, *The Kauṭilīya Arthaśāstra*, Pt. II, Bombay, 1962.) This point of view is criticised by Debiprasad Chattopadhyaya. (See Debiprasad Chattopadhyaya, *Indian Materialism*, "Neue Indienkunde", *Festschrift Walter Ruben zum 70, Geburtstag*, B. 1970, S. 521.) The problem requires further study.

3. Traditionally, the origins of Indian materialism and of the Lokāyata school have been connected with Bṛhaspati.

Criticising these opinions, Kauṭilya presents another view, which possibly is more ancient, going back to the early treatises on *artha*. There are four sciences — philosophy (*ānvīkṣikī*) and the teachings on the three Vedas, economy and government — that help to cognise *dharma* (religious duty, morality, norms of social conduct, social structure) and *artha* (gain, benefit, material prosperity).

Then Kauṭilya defines philosophy and shows its importance to other sciences. This excerpt needs to be thoroughly analysed. Kauṭilya writes:

> Philosophy (*ānvīkṣikī*) is Sāṁkhya, Yoga and Lokāyata. Philosophy, by studying with the aid of logical reasoning: the lawful (*dharma*) and unlawful (*adharma*)[4] in the teaching on the three Vedas; benefit (*artha*) and damage (*anartha*)[5] in the teaching on economy; correct and incorrect politics in the teaching on statecraft; and by studying also the strong and weak points of these teachings — does good to people, strengthens their spirit in hardship and happiness and teaches them to think, speak and act. Philosophy is always viewed as the guiding star for all sciences, a means to do any job, the logical grounds of any normative principles.[6]

Significantly, praising philosophy as a strong instrument of state policy and a clue to distinguishing between the right and wrong in the orthodox ideology based on the Vedas, Kauṭilya names Lokāyata as one of the three branches of philosophy and assigns it an equal position with other philosophical systems.

---

4. In Kangle's translation: "(What is) spiritual good and evil?" (Kangle, op. cit., p. 6).
5. Material gain and loss (cf. ibid.).
6. *Arthaśāstra* of Kauṭilya with the Commentary *Śrimūlā* of Mahāmahopādhyāya T. Gaṇapati Śāstri, ed. Commentator, Trivandrum, 1924, pp. 16-18.

Another interesting fact is that, along with the consistently materialistic Lokāyata, the *Arthaśāstra* also names Sāṁkhya, a largely rationalistic doctrine close to materialism in a number of conceptual principles, as a philosophical school, while no mention is made of the orthodox systems like Mīmāṁsā and Vedānta. It seems hardly sensible to suppose that Kauṭilya was ignorant of these two orthodoxies, since Bādarāyaṇa's *Brahmasūtras* was written in the second century BCE and the *Mīmāṁsā-sūtras,* ascribed to Jaimini, not later than the first to second centuries CE. The system of Nyāya-Vaiśeṣika had definitely been fully shaped by the time the *Arthaśāstra* was written, but Kauṭilya does not mention it either.[7]

Evidently, the fact that defines Lokāyata and Sāṁkhya as philosophical schools is explained by their considerable influence on ancient Indian culture and ideology, and by Kauṭilya's personal outlook. There is no need to discuss here their place in India's spiritual life at that time, since there are many other works dealing with this subject. We shall examine the relationship between Lokāyata and the views of Kauṭilya — a problem that has been studied very little as yet.

As mentioned above, Kauṭilya regards *ānvīkṣikī* and the teachings on the three Vedas, economy and statecraft as sciences. This distinguishes the *Arthaśāstra* from other schools (legislative and political). Obviously, the *Arthaśāstra* was connected with more ancient teachings on *artha.*

According to Kauṭilya, philosophy is not only a scientific discipline independent of religion, but is also the guiding star of all sciences. This position could be shared only by rationalistic schools and primarily by the Lokāyatikas, since other philosophical and religious systems

7. Chattopadhyaya's hypothesis that by *yoga* the *Arthaśāstra* implies Nyāya-Vaiśeṣika does not appear well grounded or convincing. (See Debiprasad Chattopadhyaya, op. cit.)

looked upon philosophy as exclusively a science of inner spiritual emancipation.

Kauṭilya's philosophical schools do not coincide with the traditionally accepted *darśanas*. Haribhadra cites the philosophies of Buddhism, Nyāya, Sāṁkhya, Jainism, Vaiśeṣika, Mīmāṁsā and Lokāyata. He writes that some people do not recognise any distinction between Nyāya and Vaiśeṣika and include Lokāyata in the six *darśanas*. Mādhavācārya in his *Compendium of All Philosophies* (*Sarvadarśana-saṁgraha*) discusses the following doctrines: Cārvāka (Lokāyata), Buddhism, the systems of Rāmānuja and Madhva, four schools of Śaivism, Vaiśeṣika, Nyāya, Mīmāṁsā, the school of Pāṇini, Sāṁkhya, Yoga, and Advaita. The compendium, *Sarvadarśana-siddhānta-saṁgraha,* relates the doctrines of Lokāyata, Jainism, four Buddhist schools, Vaiśeṣika, Nyāya, the schools of Prabhākara and Kumārila, Mīmāṁsā, Sāṁkhya, Yoga, Vedānta, Vedavyāsa Bhaṭṭa's system, and the teachings of the *Mahābhārata*. The *Sarvamata-saṁgraha* speaks about Buddhism, Jainism, Vaiśeṣika, Nyāya, Yoga, Sāṁkhya, Mīmāṁsā and Vedānta.

As can be seen, Lokāyata was regarded as an autonomous system opposite to the schools of *āstika,* while Sāṁkhya and Yoga were reckoned among the orthodox *darśanas* and were usually followed in compendiums by Vedānta, admittedly the finest expression of orthodox ideology.

Mānava and his followers did not rank philosophy among the sciences. According to Kauṭilya, they regarded *ānvīkṣikī* as part of *trayī* and reduced the entire philosophical tradition to notions about the sacred nature and absolute authority of the three Vedas (hence the term *trayī*). In *The Laws of Manu, ānvīkṣikī* is identified with *ātmavidyā* (of the orthodox system), which corresponds with the evidence of the *Arthaśāstra* in the views of Mānava's school (as interpreted by Chattopadhyaya). It is significant that Bṛhaspati, the originator of Lokāyata, acknowledges the teachings on economy and statecraft as sciences, but does not rank *trayī* as such. Lokāyata does not consider *trayī* as science either, while recognising the importance of material welfare in worldly life and the primacy of secular power.

Kauṭilya not only numbers philosophy among the sciences, but also gives it priority over other disciplines; this was quite daring for his times, considering Kauṭilya's understanding of the term *ānvīkṣikī* as well as the general tendency of the treatise. For him a philosophy (i.e. Sāṁkhya, Yoga and Lokāyata) means the supreme form of knowledge which allows assessment of the results achieved by other sciences (and thus also by state policy) from positions of practical use. According to Kauṭilya, the aim of philosophy was to justify by means of logical argument (*hetu*) the lawful and unlawful (*dharma* and *adharma*) statements contained in the three Vedas, which were the foundation of Brāhmanical ideology.

Apparently, the exponents of the theories enunciated in the *Arthaśāstra* (in fact, statesmen and politicians) were allowed and required to determine, using their own authority, the validity or invalidity of the sacred orthodox commandments. This partly explains why Kauṭilya classified the teachings on the three Vedas with other principal sciences.[8] As is obvious from the text, an essentially materialistic philosophy was necessary to bring out, with the help of logical categories, the applicability of certain

8. The general tendency of the *Arthaśāstra* makes clear the reasons for including *trayī* as a science: an advocate of strong monarchy, Kauṭilya supported the idea of a close alliance between the kṣatriyas and the brāhmaṇas.

Vedic principles to the practical interests of the state, that is, to make them "do good to people and strengthen their spirit in hardship and happiness," as well as to facilitate practical activity.

This shows that despite his close contact with brāhmaṇa circles, Kauṭilya, unlike the exponents of the orthodox doctrines, did not accept Vedic theology as the main factor of his ideological programme. Judging by the treatise, Sāṁkhya, Yoga and Lokāyata served to analyse *trayī* in terms of practical applicability (although Kauṭilya certainly was no supporter of heretical doctrines, let alone the consistently materialistic teaching of Lokāyata). However peculiar Kauṭilya's general conception of philosophy, his position in this respect draws an unmistakable distinction between the Dharmaśāstras and the treatises on *artha*.

What aspects of Lokāyata attracted Kauṭilya's attention, and what points of contact did he as a politician have with the materialist theory?

Kauṭilya attaches primary importance to logical methods of finding solutions to practical problems of the state and providing them with theoretical justification (*hetubhir-ānvīkṣamāṇa*). In a number of ancient texts the terms *tarkavidyā* and *hetuvidyā* (sciences of logical reasoning) are used as synonyms of *ānvīkṣikī*. According to the *Amarakośa*, for instance, *ānvīkṣikī* means *tarkavidyā* (logic).[9] For Kauṭilya philosophy is, above all, a logical discipline, which deprives it of any mystical or irrational meaning. Pāṇini explains *ānvīkṣikī* as a derivative of *ānvīkṣā* (that which is based on true knowledge). Hence Kauṭilya's interest in Lokāyata, logic being one of the key elements of its doctrine. Some ancient texts describe the Lokāyatikas as faithful adherents of the teaching on logic, while Medhātithi, the

9. See Debiprasad Chattopadhyaya, op. cit., p. 511; P.V. Kane, *History of Dharmaśāstra*, vol. III, Poona, 1946, p. 48.

commentator on *Manu-Smṛti,* speaks of the Cārvākas' *tarkavidya.*[10]

The tendency of orthodox brāhmaṇa circles to interpret *ānvīkṣikī* as *ātmavidyā* and even to include Vedānta in it[11] prevailed in the Middle Ages over other interpretations, and this was reflected in many medieval texts. Kauṭilya's rationalistic position was tendentiously revised.

An analysis of the *Arthaśāstra* shows that Kauṭilya, proceeding from certain practical considerations, sometimes expressed ideas that were at variance with the orthodox religious norms and notions. Kauṭilya gave royal decrees and orders priority over any other legislation.

The interests of the state override considerations of religion and priestly privileges. Thus it is stated that of the four legs of law, *carita* (custom), *vyavahāra* (agreement), *dharma* (the provisions of the law-books) and *rājaśāsana* (royal edicts), the succeeding item overrides the preceding one. This clearly implies that royal edict supersedes all other sources of law. Moreover, it is explicitly stated that whenever Śāstra (the Brāhmanical law-book) comes into conflict with a royal decree based on the customs of the people (*dharmanyāya*), the latter shall prevail.[12]

This principle of priority of state interest over the traditional Brāhmanical Śāstra can be compared to the attitude of the Lokāyatikas to the sacred texts and divine revelation. While the brāhmaṇas claimed these sources of knowledge to possess supreme authority, the Lokāyatikas refused to admit their omniscience, believing that neither revelation nor the

---

10. K.K. Mittal, *Materialism in Indian Thought,* p. 43.
11. P.V. Kane, op. cit., p. 48.
12. R.S. Sharma, *Aspects of Political Ideas and Institutions in Ancient India,* Delhi, 1968, p. 189.

scriptures could add anything to knowledge obtained from experience.

As to the relationship between the state and official religion, "there seems to be some indication of state control of even Brāhmanical institutions. Kauṭilya provides for an officer known as the superintendent of temples (*devatādhyakṣa*), who is charged with the function of collecting at one place various kinds of property of the gods of the capital and countryside and depositing them in the royal treasury."[13] Kauṭilya "apparently wants to convince his ruler that religious practices have so many superstitions, of which the latter should take advantage in serving his interests."[14] Kauṭilya places profit above *dharma* and *kāma*. *Artha* is the basis of law and the guarantee of pleasure. His interpretation of the correlation of human actions and fate (i.e. divine acts) is quite rationalistic. Man's actions are visible; they are "correct politics" if they result in welfare and "bad politics" if they cause unhappiness. Human actions can be explained, while divine acts cannot. Thus, being a realist and rationalist, Kauṭilya discards many religious dogmas and traditional norms, giving priority instead to the interests of the state. He reckons *artha* to be the main principle of any sensible action and *dharma* as dependent on *artha*. To cite the words of R.S. Sharma, Kauṭilya "made the first serious attempt to reconstruct the science of polity and emancipate it from the influence of religion and theology."[15]

Obviously, Kauṭilya's ideas were in tune with his times. The image of a statesman who is critical of religious dogma and traditional norms contradictory to state interests and is guided in his activity by common sense, is to be found in

---

13. R.S. Sharma, op. cit., p. 190.
14. Ibid., p. 194.
15. Ibid., p. 192.

many Indian literary writings of antiquity and the early Middle Ages. One example is Rāma's minister Jābāli, graphically portrayed in the *Rāmāyaṇa*. Jābāli's views have much in common with some notions of the Lokāyatikas. This fact sheds some light on the relationship between materialism and political theory in ancient India.[16]

The view that the ideas of the *Arthaśāstra* were borrowed from the Dharmaśāstra tradition seems to be erroneous. Recent investigations have proved the ancient schools of political thought in India to be quite independent of the Brāhmanical codes of law. Moreover, it is probable that the Dharmaśāstras borrowed quite a few propositions and judgements on politics and the state from the *Arthaśāstra*. This approach to the sources of the *Arthaśāstra* and other similar treatises is instrumental in studying the relationship of the political theories of ancient India with rationalism and materialism.

Some valuable information can also be obtained by comparing the opinions on the political treatises of the *Arthaśāstra* type contained in the early Dharmaśāstras (whose antiquity, however, remains doubtful) with those in the later codes of law and medieval commentaries.[17]

The early Smṛti considered the *Arthaśāstra* and the Dharmaśāstra to be two independent authorities on political issues, albeit stressing the latter's priority over the former in case of contradiction between them. Later, the *Arthaśāstra*'s authority was intentionally diminished and even denied, and its propositions came to be regarded as part of the Smṛti. Early Buddhist writings describe the

16. See W. Ruben, *Studies in Ancient Indian Thought*, Calcutta, 1966, pp. 3-24; M. Winternitz, *Geschischte der indischen Literatur*, Leipzig, Bd. 3, 1922, S. 507.
17. See J.S. Negi, *Some Indological Studies*, vol. 1, Allahabad, 1966, pp. 1-11.

autonomous political science known as the *artha-śāstra* (or *kṣatravidyā*), whose central principle, unlike the Dharmaśāstra, was *artha* and not *dharma;* the *Arthaśāstra* was not based on religious dogma and morality.

The distinct practical aspect of this political science, its concern for benefit (including Kauṭilya's *Arthaśāstra*) were subjected by the religious authorities to sharp criticism and often described as an immoral and disastrous logic. Clearly, the religious authorities attacked their deviation from doctrinal norms and prescriptions.

It is indicative that a number of ancient sources mention the followers of the *Arthaśāstra* along with the Lokāyatikas. *Jātaka* 528 in Pāli expounds the ideologies of Lokāyata and *kṣatravidyā,* among other teachings. The exponents of the latter considered *artha* to be their chief purpose, which has analogies in ancient Indian materialism.

The followers of the *Arthaśāstra* felt free, for *artha,* to transgress the conventional moral norms and even resort to killing their close relatives, which the orthodox tradition deemed a very grave sin. Vātsyāyana's *Kāmasūtra* compares the materialists (*laukāyatikaḥ*) and the followers of the *Arthaśāstra* (*arthacintakaḥ*).

The *Jayamaṅgalā,* a commentary on the *Arthaśāstra,* emphasises Lokāyata's relevance to affairs of the state and identifies it with Bṛhaspati's philosophical system. According to the *Jayamaṅgalā,* Lokāyata is important because it provides knowledge about worldly affairs.[18] Somadeva's *Nītīvākyāmṛta* says that "with the help of Lokāyata the king gets rid of thorns in his kingdom."[19] The *Bṛhaspati-sūtra,* a

18. *lokāyataṁ bārhaspatyam: lokāya buddhim tanoti iti nairuktam.* See R.P. Kangle, op. cit., p. 6.

19. *lokayatao hi rājā rāṣṭra-kaṇṭakān ucchedayati.* See R.P. Kangle, op. cit., p. 6; M. Winternitz, "Anvīkṣikī und Ātmavidyā", *Indologica Pragnesia,* 1929, no. 1, p. 7.

relatively late political treatise, contains a most interesting remark concerning Lokāyata: "At a time of acquisition of profit it is necessary to follow only Lokāyata" (*sarvathā laukāyatikāmeva śāstram arthasādhanakāle*). And further: "If someone rejects *dharma* as useless and aspires for profit, he is a lokāyatika" (*vṛthā dharmam vadatyarthasādhanaṁ laukāyatikaḥ*).[20]

All this shows that it was the position of the priority of *artha* over *dharma* that impelled the ancient Indians to draw a parallel between political science and Lokāyata's materialism. The comparison is corroborated by two compendiums — Haribhadra's *Ṣaḍdarśana-samuccaya* and Mādhava's *Sarvadarśana-saṁgraha* — each containing an epitome of the doctrine of Lokāyata. It should be observed that both consider the Lokāyatikas to be followers of Bṛhaspati, to whom the *Arthaśāstra* and a number of other treatises attribute the creation of one of the political schools of the time.[21]

Significantly, Śrutadeva Sūri, the author of a commentary on Somadeva Sūri's political treatise entitled *Yaśastilaka* (tenth century), associated Bṛhaspati's teaching with the teachings of the Cārvākas (i.e. the Lokāyatikas).

Numbers of people, in accordance with the science on politics (*nīti*) and pleasure, believe wealth (*artha*) and pleasure to be man's sole object (*puruṣārtha*), discarding the notions of another world and following exceptionally the doctrine of the Cārvākas. This is why this teaching is also known as the Lokāyata, which corresponds with its essence.[22]

20. *Bṛhaspati-sutra*, ed. and tr. by F.W. Thomas, Lahore, 1931.

21. The *Pañcatantra* and the *Mahābhārata* mention a science (*nīti*) compiled by Bṛhaspati.

22. To quote Mādhava's presentation of Lokāyata, "For the good of the majority of people it is needful to follow the teaching of the Cārvākas" (*bahūnāṁ prāṇināmanugrahārtaṁ cārvākamatamāśrayaṇiyam*).

Although Kauṭilya himself was not a Lokāyatika, Mādhava's explanation of the widespread acknowledgement of Lokāyata accounts also for the special attention that Kauṭilya paid to this teaching. Kauṭilya was an ardent adherent of the science of political administration (*daṇḍanīti*), regarding *artha* as the central principle of his doctrine. Mādhava's epitome of Lokāyata is identical to that contained in the treatise *Bṛhaspati-sūtra:* both consider man's striving for *artha* (*puruṣārtha*) to be the cause of Lokāyata's great popularity. Kauṭilya believes *artha* to be of greater importance than law (*dharma*) and love (*kāma*), which are dependent on *artha*. Hence the title of his treatise: *Arthaśāstra* (On Material Gain).

The Lokāyatikas' ideas of a state leader, as cited by Mādhava, reflect their concept of a powerful centralised state: "There is no supreme deity except the *rājā,* whose existence is obvious to all";[23] "the *rājā,* whose existence is obvious to the world, is the only omnipotent being, and not something from the other world."[24] Thus denying the orthodox view on the divine, the Lokāyatikas uphold secular power as natural and expedient and reject the attitude that looks upon the monarch as an incarnation of a deity in this world. Although Kauṭilya never challenges the theory of the divine origin of state power, his outlook is in full harmony with the Lokāyatikas' view of the science of government as a means to preserve what has been attained and to expand what has been preserved. Their science is purely secular and down-to-earth. The monarch rules and protects his people with a rod of iron; the people are faithful to their duties and enjoy prosperity in their secure abodes.

---

23. *lokasiddho rājā parameśvaraḥ; lokasiddha* can be translated as "successful in this world".

24. *lokasiddho bhavedrājā pareśo nāparaḥ smṛtaḥ.*

Śaṅkara, one of Lokāyata's chief opponents and an ardent Vedāntist, cites the Lokāyatikas' statement that all the joy of a wise man in this world results from his work in agriculture, trade, the civil service, etc. Kauṭilya attaches special importance to the teachings on economy (*vārttā*) and government (*daṇḍanīti*). According to the *Arthaśāstra,* the teachings on the economy which comprise the teachings on plant and animal husbandry and also on trade, relate to economic gains such as grain, cattle, gold, timber, woodwork, and compulsory labour. Relying on these teachings on the economy, the king rules his supporters and enemies with the help of his treasury and his army. This shows that Kauṭilya, like the Lokāyatikas, set great store by practical activity and above all such activity that brings about material gain.

But Kauṭilya and the Lokāyatikas held entirely different views on Vedic religion and priesthood because of their ideological differences. While Kauṭilya advocated the caste system as hallowed by the Vedas and upheld a close alliance between the kṣatriyas and brāhmaṇas, the Lokāyatikas strongly argued against the authority of the Vedas, denying their role as revelation; they criticised Brāhmanical rituals and priestly privileges and accused priests of fraud and cupidity. (There is evidence suggesting that Kauṭilya himself was a brāhmaṇa.) Nevertheless, the *Arthaśāstra* does contain some analogies with certain ideas of Lokāyata. It is noteworthy that although Kauṭilya never defied the doctrinal tradition, as did the Lokāyatikas, his pragmatism often challenged the orthodox norms and attitudes.

Haribhadra writes that according to Lokāyata there is neither *dharma* nor *adharma,* its opposite. Mādhava cites the statement of Lokāyata that the defects of the three Vedas are mendacity, contradictoriness and excessive verbosity. Kauṭilya believes that philosophy (wherein he includes

Lokāyata) reveals the *dharma* and *adharma* in the three Vedas. He considers *artha* to be the prime goal of politics and adheres, therefore, to pragmatic principles, denouncing prejudice and superstition. He warns that a silly man who asks the stars what he should do will miss his *artha*. *Artha* is its own star, and the stars of heaven are of no help, he insists.

Discussing the issue of destroying a hostile ruler, Kauṭilya recommends that one should stop at nothing, not even desecrating sanctuaries. Poison should be mixed in the food of the ruler to be served at the religious feast during the ceremony of sacrifice. Spies disguised as ascetics should wait in ambush, hiding in a hole made in the effigy of a deity, or they should come to the ruler clothed as magicians and induce him to hold a sacrifice for a local deity in order to destroy him. These "recommendations" characterise Kauṭilya as a relentless politician shunning no means to achieve his aims and playing on other people's superstitions and religious prejudices.

Had it been possible to present it as a piece of good advice to a ruler, and to cite it in a political treatise, Kauṭilya, perhaps, would have repeated the sarcastic and scathing remark of the Lokāyatikas that *agnihotram*, the three Vedas, *tridaṇḍa*, and besmearing oneself with ashes only serve those deprived of wisdom and industry. Those who praise oblations maintain that the Lokāyatikas are liars, and that they are the same tramps who have established the practice of eating sacrificial meat. If *śrāddham* (oblations) pleases the dead, then oil should sustain fire even in a broken lamp. If those who live in heaven are pleased with our *śrāddham*, why not offer it to one standing on the roof of a house?[25]

Although no texts of Lokāyata have remained, this school is frequently mentioned in various ancient Indian

25. See *An Anthology of World Philosophy*, vol. I, pp. 170 ff.

writings, which shows their popularity. Scholars believe that Pāṇini (fourth century BCE) was already familiar with it.[26] Lokāyata is mentioned in the Jātakas and other early canonical Buddhist texts.[27]

Beyond doubt, Lokāyata greatly influenced the spiritual climate of ancient India. However, in those times any materialistic doctrine was inevitably attacked by the idealistic orthodox schools. The orthodoxies did their best to misinterpret and defame the Lokāyatikas' teachings and to destroy their writings. This seems to explain why the orthodox philosopher Bāṇa, strongly criticised Kauṭilya and described his "recommendations" as contemptible for their ruthlessness.[28]

Apparently, many brāhmaṇas looked upon Kauṭilya as an extreme rationalist undermining the traditional norms of social and religious life, and his ideology was regarded as too bold and hence heretical. His conception of the priority of *artha* over *dharma* and *mokṣa* was in contradiction with the Brāhmanical religious norms and met with a storm of criticism. While the orthodox brāhmaṇas censured Kauṭilya for his fidelity to the "cruel" principle of *artha,* the Vedāntists and other opponents of Lokāyata reproached him for immorality and alleged advocacy of carnal pleasures.

Although the Lokāyatikas were quite outspoken in their opposition to asceticism and any form of mortification of the flesh, they never preached brutish hedonism. Their alleged immorality manifested itself, in fact, in their rationalistic treatment of the code of social behaviour and

26. See V.S. Aggarwal, *India as Known to Pāṇini,* Lucknow, 1953, p. 394.

27. See G.P. Malalasekera, *Dictionary of Pali Proper Names,* vol. II, London, 1960, p. 787.

28. See Debiprasad Chattopadhyaya, op. cit., p. 513.

in their endeavours to overcome dogmatism. In assigning a special role to *artha* and *kāma*, the Lokāyatikas did not mean to advocate moral licentiousness, but a denial of the religious ethical ideal and connected with it a nihilistic attitude to the joys of earthly life. However different their view of the purpose of human life from that of Kauṭilya, ethical rationalism was their common ground. It seems plausible that Kauṭilya would have supported the Lokāyatikas' claim that it was foolish to renounce sensual pleasures as leading to suffering. No one wishing to gain real *artha*, they maintained, would throw away grains of rice only because they are covered with dust and husk;[29] a copper coin (*kārṣāpaṇa*) that one possesses is better than a golden coin (*niṣka*), the future possession of which is uncertain.

As a politician, Kauṭilya took interest in Lokāyata because it provided rationalistic explanations and empirical interpretations of natural and social phenomena and challenged the standing Brāhmanical norms and dogmas, holding out new moral ideals instead of preaching pious submissiveness, asceticism and suffering. Practical activity and full-blooded life in complete harmony with nature were more dear to him than the concepts of heavenly emancipation and spiritual immortality.

Obviously, in discussing *ānvīkṣikī*, which he regarded above all as a teaching on logic, Kauṭilya laid special emphasis on the principle of logical generalisation, which was close to the rational, scientific approach to the nature of things. Hence his interest in Lokāyata and Sāṁkhya, the latter being closely connected with the development of ancient science. His mention of Sāṁkhya and Yoga together was perhaps a tribute to tradition, since it was customary to consider these two doctrines as complementary. The very word *sāṁkhya*

---

29. See *An Anthology of World Philosophy*, vol. I, p. 166.

("number," "quantity," "analysis," "thinking") is probably indicative of this school's essential rationalism and scientism, i.e. a logical approach to the principal philosophical problems rather than reliance on the authority of the scriptures. To illustrate this, it would seem appropriate to cite Kauṭilya's statement on the importance of science: heeding leads to understanding, understanding to practical experience, and practice experience to complete self-realisation. The realism of the *Arthaśāstra* is clearly crystallised in this thesis, which also explains why Kauṭilya turns to Lokāyata and Sāṁkhya.

In conclusion, we feel impelled to subscribe to the judgement of Guiseppe Tucci about the close relationship between Lokāyata and the early Indian schools of political theory (the *Arthaśāstra* and other similar doctrines). Later, the two teachings increasingly diverged, as the *Arthaśāstra* was influenced by religious ideology, to which Lokāyata remained determinedly opposed.[30]

30. See Guiseppe Tucci, "A Sketch of Indian Materialism", in *Proceedings of the First Indian Philosophical Congress,* Delhi, 1925, pp. 36, 40-41.

CHAPTER NINE

Logical and Methodological Schemes of Indian Religious Philosophy and their Interpretation

ANDREY TERENTYEV

WHEN selecting non-orthodox Indian religions as a subject for study, one should remember that the spread of free thinking in the middle of the first millennium BCE, which challenged the dogmas of Brāhmanism, was not an entirely new phenomenon in India. Notes of scepticism have been heard in Indian religious philosophy ever since the time of the *Ṛgveda:*

> The source from which this universe has risen,
> And neither it was made, or uncreated,
> He only knows, who from the highest heaven
> Rules, the all-seeing lord — or does not He know?[1]

The same type of doubt is found scattered in the Upaniṣads. There is doubt about a dead person: "He exists," says one. "He does not exist," says another.[2]

It is not, however, the declaration of doubt itself that interests us here, but its philosophical "consequences" manifested in the fact that some Indian philosophers

---

1. *The Ṛgveda*, by Kaegi, p. 90, *RV*, X. 129, cited in Surendranath Dasgupta, *A History of Indian Philosophy*, vol. I, Delhi, 1975, p. 24.
2. *Sechzig, Upanishads des Veda aus dem Sanskrit ubersetzt von P. Deussen*, Leipzig, 1879, S. 270.

accepted the idea of the existence of certain "epistemological situations" with immanent doubt and this gave them the grounds for rejecting the conventional law of the excluded middle, and for acknowledging the "existential reality" (however paradoxical) of the simultaneous being and non-being of certain objects.

The Ājīvikas were the first (or among the first) to use the formula: "exists and does not exist." They assumed that certain objects required ambivalent definitions, such as "soul and no soul," "world and no world," and the like.[3] They found it possible to say about anything that it "is and is not," while as early as in the *R̥gveda* we come across an utterance exactly opposite to this in form: "There were at that time neither existent nor non-existent things." Thus, by the sixth to fourth centuries BCE Indian thought had at least four different ways of describing reality, and the scheme comprising these four ways came to be known as *catuṣkoṭika* (possessing four peaks). The adherents of *catuṣkoṭika* maintained that about any object one of the following is true: (1) it exists; (2) it does not exist; (3) it both exists and does not exist; (4) it is neither existent nor non-existent.

Catuṣkoṭika and the congeneric doctrines of Ajñānavāda and Syādvāda, elaborated in India long before the birth of Christ, have of late increasingly attracted scholars' attention for their great likeness to some twentieth-century logical conceptions. Now that the view that Aristotle's logic is but one out of a multitude of possible logics is shared by many, and a dialectical way of thinking embraces science ever more strongly, the "paradoxical" ideas of some Indian philosophers meet with increasing understanding. Relevant publications have grown in number, especially abroad. However, some of the views, above all the neo-positivists', are difficult to agree with. For that reason we shall try in

3. A.L. Basham, *The History and Doctrines of Ājīvikas*, L., 1950, p. 275.

this article to offer a more adequate interpretation of the neo-Brahmanist conceptions that were current in classical Indian philosophy.

The three aforementioned theories developed, each in its individual way, the method that interests us — studying an object through contrary definitions of it. We shall begin our analysis with the simpler doctrine — *catuṣkoṭika* — which obviously served as a basis for further modifications.

Let us first try to clarify its origins. Many publications wrongly classify *catuṣkoṭika* as a Buddhist doctrine.[4] This opinion is based on the fact that most of the information about *catuṣkoṭika* is contained in Buddhist texts. The question arises, however, why did Buddhists address this doctrine?

It would be expedient to consider several well-known examples. The neo-positivist philosopher K. Jayatilleke has thoroughly studied *catuṣkoṭika.* He proceeds in his analysis from the following excerpt ". . . this world is finite . . . this world is infinite . . . this world is both finite and infinite . . . this world is neither finite nor infinite . . ."[5] taken from the *Brahmajāla-sūtta,* a well-known text of the Pāli canon. But Jayatilleke overlooks the fact that this formula is mentioned amongst the heretic doctrines criticised by Buddha. Summing up the description of the formula, the text reads:

> And so, monks, Tathāgata understands: "These notions are reached in such and such a way, lead to such and such things, and bring such and such things in the future

4. See: L. de la V. Poussin, *The Way to Nirvāṇa,* Cambridge, 1917, p. iii; S. Miyamoto, "The Logic of Relativity as Common Ground for the Development of the Middle Way", in *Buddhism and Culture,* Kyoto, 1960, p. 80; K. Jayatilleke, *The Early Buddhist Theory of Knowledge,* L., 1964, p. 339 (quoted in Pāli).
5. K. Jayatilleke, ibid., p. 340.

> existence." And Tathāgata understands them, and he understands that which is above them, and he does not attach himself to this understanding. . . .[6]

Here is another excerpt from the *Poṭṭhapādasūtra,* where Buddha explains to the brāhmaṇa Poṭṭhapāda, Tathāgata's existence after death:

> "I did not say, Poṭṭhapāda, that Tathāgata exists after death, that this is the truth and all the rest a delusion. . . . I did not say, Poṭṭhapāda, that Tathāgata does not exist after death, that this is the truth and all the rest a delusion. . . . I did not say, Poṭṭhapāda, that Tathāgata both exists and does not exist after death, that this is the truth and all the rest a delusion. . . . I did not say, Poṭṭhapāda, that Tathāgata neither exists nor does not exist after death, that this is the truth and all the rest a delusion."
>
> "Why did Bhagavat not say this?"
>
> "Because this, Poṭṭhapāda, does not do good, is not connected with the *dhamma,* pertains not to chastity, leads neither to [the] renunciation [of the world], nor of impassivity, nor to destruction, nor to consolation, nor to revelation, nor to awakening, nor to *nibbāna*. That is why I did not say this."
>
> "What then did Bhagavat speak about?"
>
> "This is suffering — this, Poṭṭhapāda, I spoke about. This is the beginning of suffering — this, Poṭṭhapāda, I spoke about. This is the end of suffering — this, Poṭṭhapāda, I spoke about. This is the way that leads to the end of suffering — this, Poṭṭhapāda, I spoke about."
>
> "Why did Bhagavat speak about this?"

---

6. *"Tayidam, bhikkhave, tathāgato pajānāti: 'Ime ditthitthānā evam gahita evamparamaṭṭhā evam-garikā bhavissanti evaṁ-abhisamparāya ti.' Tan ca tathāgato pajānāti, tato ca uttaritaram pajānāti tan ca pajānaṁ na paramasati. . . ". The Dīgha Nikāya,* vol. I, ed. Rhys Davids and J.E. Carpenter, L., 1890, p. 24.

> "Because this, Poṭṭhapāda, does good, is connected with the *dhamma*, pertains to chastity, leads to renunciation, to impassivity, to destruction, to consolation, to revelation, to awakening, to nibbana. That is why I spoke about it."[7]

The above excerpt is of interest to us not only because it contains a refusal to expose *catuṣkoṭika,* but also because it explains the reasons for this refusal. This shows that *catuṣkoṭika* is essentially alien to Buddhism. Being above all a religion of mysticism, Buddhism never had anything to do with attempting to formulate in words, by mere reasoning, the true nature of reality.

This statement may at first strike one as strange, for the logical treatises of prominent Buddhist philosophers (such as Dharmakīrti, Diṅnāga and others) are known to

---

7. *"Avyākatam kho etam poṭṭhapāda mayā: 'Hoti tathāgato param maraṇā. Idam eva saccam mogham aññan ti'. . . Etam pi kho poṭṭhapāda mayā avyākatam: 'Na hoti tathāgato param maraṇā. Idam eva saccam mogham aññan ti'. . . Avyākatam kho etaṁ poṭṭhapāda mayā: 'Hoti ca na ca hoti tathāgato param maraṇā. idam eva saccam aññan ti'. . . Etam pi kho poṭṭhapāda mayā avyākatam: 'N'eva hoti na na hoti tathāgato param maraṇā. Idam eva saccam mogham aññan ti . . . 'Kasma bhante Bhagavata avyākatam ti?' 'Na hetaṁ poṭṭhapāda attha-saṁhitaṁ na dhammasaṁhitaṁ nādibrahmacariyakaṁ na nibbidāya na viragāya na nirodhāya na upasamāya na abhiññāya na sambodhāya na nibbānāya saṁvattati. Tasmā tam mayā abyākataṁ 'ti. 'Kiṁ panaṁ bhante bhagavatā byākataṁ 'ti?'Idaṁ dukkhaṁ 'ti kho poṭṭhapāda mayā byākataṁ. 'Ayaṁ dukkhasamudayo 'ti kho poṭṭhapāda mayā byākataṁ.'Ayaṁ dukkha-nirodho 'ti kho poṭṭhapāda mayā byākataṁ.'Ayaṁ dukkha-nirodha-gāminī patipāda 'ti kho poṭṭhapāda mayā byākataṁ 'ti. 'Kasmā panetaṁ bhante bhagavata byākataṁ 'ti? 'Etaṁ hi kho poṭṭhapāda attha-saṁhitaṁ etam dhamma-saṁhitaṁ etaṁ ādibrahmacariyakaṁ, etaṁ nibbidāya virāgāya nirodhāya upasamāya abhiññāya sambodhāya nibbanāya saṁvattati. Tasmā etaṁ mayā byākataṁ 'ti.* (*Dīgha Nikāya*, I. IX, 27-30).

every scholar. These treatises were logical indeed in the strict sense of the word, they dealt with the rules and forms of verbal expression, errors of reasoning and other problems in the sphere of the linguistic apparatus of science. They were valuable for propaedeutics, polemics with representations from other philosophical and religious schools, and for other auxiliary purposes. But no Buddhist philosopher ever held that the essence of reality, or of the Buddha, can be expressed in any combination of words.

Catuṣkoṭika and other similar doctrines are subject to Buddhist criticism exactly because they attempt to offer an adequate description of the real order of things. Representatives of linguistic philosophy fail to understand this because of their methodological principles. They identify philosophical analysis with the analysis of language, and therefore they tend to find in centuries-old doctrines their own modern problems. Neopositivists consider it pointless to deal with things that lie outside any verbal framework, and this obscures the essential nature of the doctrines in question.

It should be noted that a negative attitude to *catuṣkoṭika* as an adequate descriptive method is expressed not only in the Pāli canon, referred to by K. Jayatilleke as the principal source of information, but also in some later Mahāyāna-oriented texts. Nāgārjuna criticises all four propositions on the existence of things. The problem of *catuṣkoṭika* comes up several times in the *Laṅkāvatāra-sūtra*, one of the most venerated texts in northern Buddhism:

> Those who see the world as evolving out of reasons and conditions cling to *catuṣkoṭika* and cannot grasp My Teaching. The world is born not out of being, not out of not-being, nor of being-and-not-being, nor out of anything different, nor out of reasons and conditions as the foolish think: a complete revolution in psyche and baselessness

> can be reached only when the world is seen neither existing, nor non-existing, nor both, nor other. . . .
>
> . . . the ignorant and simple-minded being fascinated from the beginningless time with their primitive self-imaginations and reasonings, keep on dancing and leaping about. They are unable to understand the discourse on self-realisation and, denying to the external world, they cling to the study of theories which are a means only, and do not know properly how to ascertain the truth of self-realisation, which is Truth unspoiled by four propositions of *catuṣkoṭika*. . . .[8]

The quoted extracts compellingly bear out the suggestion that *catuṣkoṭika* is by no means a Buddhist doctrine.

But what philosophical schools did the opponents of Buddhism, who were wedded to *catuṣkoṭika* belong to? To the best of our knowledge, neither Jain nor Hindu texts, traditionally regarded as contemporaneous to the ancient core of the Buddhist canon, approved of the *catuṣkoṭika* doctrine, whereas, judging by Buddhist texts, *śramaṇa*s and wandering brāhmaṇas were acquainted with it.

Evidently, within the period under review, the doctrine had become a matter of common knowledge amongst Indian philosophers. But one cannot discard altogether the supposition, based on some indirect evidence, that it was the Lokāyata[9] adherents who clung to *catuṣkoṭika* more than

8. D. Goddard, *A Buddhist Bible*, 1938, p. 277.

9. The research work done by K. Jayatilleke (*The Early Buddhist Theory of Knowledge*, pp. 46-57) leaves little doubt as to the fact that the identification of the philosophical school of Lokāyata with Indian materialism is not totally correct. In antiquity and the Middle Ages the term "Lokāyatikas" referred not only to materialists, but to all philosophers who were inimical or indifferent to the universal Indian religious ideal of salvation (*mokṣa*), discussions and cosmological theories.

others. This hypothesis is corroborated by the use of the epithets "foolish" and "simple-minded" in the above passage from the *Laṅkāvatāra-sūtra.* These epithets were usually bestowed upon Lokāyatikas. We also come across direct mention of Lokāyata in the same text: ". . . 'eternal and temporary', 'created and uncreated', 'this and the other world' — all these and other similar misconceptions have to do with Lokāyata."[10]

If our opinion about the non-Buddhist nature of *catuṣkoṭika* is right, we are bound to call into question interpretations that are based on the wrong premise that *catuṣkoṭika* is a purely Buddhist doctrine and pay attention exclusively to Buddhist doctrines in trying to explain it.[11]

As to the four-proposition scheme used by Buddhists for propaedeutic purposes, it is explained, among other texts, in *Gung-Lun,* a commentary on Nāgārjuna's *Mādhyamaka-śāstra:*

> In order to save the living beings, they (the Buddhas — *A.T.)* teach some: "Everything is true." They teach some: "Everything is untrue." They teach some: "Everything is true and untrue." They teach some: "Everything is neither true nor untrue."
>
> Everything is true. (If) one seeks after the true property of the *dharmas,* then everything in the supreme sense presents itself as burdened with this property, which is propertylessness. Just as waters that look different (*nāmarūpa*) and taste different flow into the great sea and then acquire one look and one taste.

10. . . .*nityamanityaṁ kṛtakamakṛtakaṁ paramaparām evamāyāni sarvāṇi lokāyatanayaṁ bhavet.* — *Laṅkāvatāra-sūtra*, p. 182.

11. See Rhys Davids, C.A.F. "Logic (Buddhist)", in *Encyclopaedia of Religion and Ethics,* vol. 8, ed. J. Hastings, New York, 1926, p. 133; B. Barua, *A History of Pre-Buddhist Indian Philosophy,* Calcutta, 1921, p. 47.

> Everything is untrue. So are the *dharmas* that have not yet come into the property of truthfulness, each one is studied separately, all without exception are untrue, and stand out owing solely to the conditions (*pratyaya*).
>
> Everything is true-and-untrue. The living beings (*sattva*) fall into three kinds: (standing) high, in the middle and in the depth. Those who are superior regard the property of the *dharmas* as neither true nor untrue. The middling regard the property of the *dharmas* (in this way): everything true, everything not true. The inferior regard with superficial rationalism *nirvāṇa* as an uncreated (*asamskr̥ta*) *dharma,* for it does not vanish, and therefore as true; they regard *saṁsāra* as a created (*saṁskr̥ta*) *dharma,* for it is illusory, and therefore as untrue. (Him) who (says) "not true but not untrue", for he disputes "true (and) untrue," Buddha teaches: "Neither true nor untrue."[12]

Thus, we see, for Buddhist preachers *catuṣkoṭika* was no more than a scheme for working out individual approaches to different kinds of people, and it never laid claim to any autonomous role within the framework of teachings.

Matters stood otherwise with two other doctrines that developed the principles of *catuṣkoṭika* further — Ajñānavāda and Syādvāda. Ajñānavāda was extensively used by Indian sceptics who, as is testified by the *Sūtrakr̥tāṅga,* one of the most ancient texts of the Jaina canon, had founded by the sixth to fifth centuries BCE at least four different schools.[13]

Sceptics have questioned the possibility of expressing the truth through the use of any of the four propositions of *catuṣkoṭika:.*

---

12. M. Walleser, *Die Mittlere Lehre des Nagarjuna. Nach der chinesischen Version ubertragen,* Heidelberg, 1921.
13. *The Jaina Sūtras,* tr. H. Jacobi, in The Sacred Books of the East, vol. 45, Oxford, 1895, pp. 138-39.

> If you questioned me: "Does the other world exist?" and if I believed that the other world exists, I should reply that the other world exists. (But) I do not say so. I do not speak so. I do not speak otherwise. I do not say no. I do not say not-no.
>
> If you questioned me: "Does the other world not exist?" and if I believed that the other world does not exist, I should reply that the other world does not exist. (But) (1) I do not say so. (2) I do not speak so. (3) I do not speak otherwise. (4) I do not say no. (5) I do not say not-no. If you questioned me: "Does the other world both exist and not exist?" and if I believed that the other world neither exists nor does not exist, I should reply that the other world neither exists nor does not exist. (But) I do not say so. I do not speak so. I do not speak otherwise. I do not say no. I do not say not-no.[14]

The canonical Buddhist text *Sāmaññaphala-sutta* ascribes these words to the wondering ascetic Sañjaya Bellathiputta. On these grounds Arthur Keith[15] and Hermann Jacobi[16] believed that it was Sañjaya who first formulated the above five propositions. However, the already mentioned *Brahmajāla-sūtta* talks about a number of ascetics and brāhmaṇas who shared the same positions and answered questions evasively, "like a slippery fish": "I do not say so. I do not speak so. I do not speak otherwise. I do not say no. I do not say not-no."[17]

---

14. *"Atthi paro loko 'ti iti ce maṁ pucchasi", "atthi paro loko 'ti iti ce me assa", "atthi para loko 'ti iti te naṁ byākareyyaṁ". Evaṁ pi me no. Tatha ti pi me no. Aññatha ti pi me no. No ti pi me no. No no ti pi me no 'ti . . . "Natthi paro loko?" . . . "Dīgha Nikāya,* vol. I, ed. T.W. Rhys Davids and J.E. Carpenter, p. 58.
15. A. Keith, *Buddhist Philosophy in India and Ceylon*, Oxford, 1923, p. 309.
16. H. Jacobi, *The Jaina Sūtras: Introduction*, in The Sacred Books of the East, vol. 45, Oxford, 1895, p. XXVII.
17. *Dīgha Nikāya*, vol. I, p. 25.

This permits us to assume that the five-proposition scheme of negative predication was current in the diverse sceptical schools of the time. The Buddhist commentator Buddhaghoṣa offers two explications of this scheme. The first explication is based on the supposition that the statement "I do not say so" is concrete. That means that the first statement is a general reply to the question, while the subsequent statements "unfold" the answer, as it were, in keeping with *catuṣkoṭika*.

The other explication, according to K. Jayatilleke,[18] may be presented as follows. Designating the object of the proposition as *A*, we present ajñānavāda as follows: (1) it is wrong that *A* exists; (2) it is wrong that *A* does not exist; (3) it is wrong that *A* both exists and does not exist; (4) it is wrong that *A* neither exists nor does not exist; (5) it is wrong that 1 to 4 are true.

Indeed, 1 and 2 negate each other; 3 negates 1 and 2; 4 negates 1, 2 and 3; 5 negates the negation contained in the judgements 1 to 4.

It must be observed that the word "wrong" here is not synonymous with the negation "not," as it does not connote contrariety. The five propositions, therefore, are not incompatible, even though they negate each other.

Both explications proceed from the structure of the question: "Does the other world exist, or not, or both, or neither?" and seem equally convincing.

The immediate translation of the word *ajñānavāda* is "agnosticism." It is, however, a consistently sceptical doctrine, since its adherents deny at once the possibility of any description of any object and this denial itself. The Ajñānavādin does not know whether he knows or not,

---

18. See K. Jayatilleke, *The Early Buddhist Theory of Knowledge*, p. 136.

whereas the strict agnostic is absolutely certain of his ignorance.

The views of sceptics are thoroughly analysed in the works of Russian philosophers, and there is no need to dwell on them in this article.

More complex is the Jaina doctrine of Syādvāda. Any object, according to it, can be described in seven ways. It (1) exists in some way (*syād-asti*); (2) it does not exist in some way (*syādnāsti*); (3) it both exists and does not exist in some way (*syādāstināsti*); (4) it is non-predicative in some way (*syād-avaktavyam*); (5) it exists in some way and is not predicative (*syādasticāvaktavyam*); (6) it does not exist in some way and is non-predicative (*syād-nāsticāvaktavyam*); and (7) it exists and does not exist in some way, and is non-predicative (*syād-astinacāsticāvaktavyam*).[19]

As in Ajñānavāda, Syādvāda's seven propositions are not incompatible. However, by contrast, they can all be true at the same time, each on its own premises, of which there are four: colour-form (*rūpa*), substance (*dravya*), place (*kṣetra*), and time (*kāla*).

The term *syād* (somehow) was important not only theoretically, as specifying the limited and concrete nature of a stated truth, but also practically, for it was helpful in conducting disputes. It limited the scope of a statement and prevented the opponent from deliberately extending its subject, thus rendering the statement vulnerable to objection.

Let us illustrate this. Saying of some object, for example, a pitcher, that it exists, the Jaina philosopher points out that he means a concrete pitcher, let us say, (1) a big red earthen pitcher that is now in this room. Without the term *syād* it is not clear what pitcher is being referred to, and one

19. See *Śrī Hemacandrācārya viracita Anyayogavyavacchedikā ca Śri Malliṣeṇa Sūri praṇītā Syādvādamañjarī*, Poona, 1926, p. 190.

may suppose that the opponent has in mind (2) a silver pitcher. But then, from his standpoint, proposition 1 is wrong and proposition 2 is right, whereas 2 is wrong for one who is referring to the earthen pitcher.

Any Syādvāda adherent, therefore, begins a discussion by giving every term an accurate definition, for otherwise the discussion may turn into empty talk about confused objects.

Proposition 2, in the words of the twelfth-century Jaina logician Malliṣeṇa, who alludes to the ancient authority of *Tattvārthaśloka-vārttika,* is introduced "because of the establishment of the non-given by the given (when what is not stated is obvious from what is stated)."[20] It is implied that the absence of a definite pitcher means the presence of a new situation, for the existence of a thing is also a non-existence — the negation of all the other things in the given determinacy. Vice versa, the non-being of one thing is the existence of another. If a pitcher is defined as in some way non-existent, the negation may have the following grounds: the pitcher is in some way not a pitcher but a piece of baked clay, a commodity, or just another pitcher, not the one referred to.

> Significantly, the understanding of non-existence as absence of the existence of a certain thing is found in Hegel's work: Such a Nothing opposed to Something, therefore, such a negation of Something, is a determinate Nothing.[21]

Although the propositions of Syādvāda can be considered true only with regard to their own premises, Jaina philosophers do not absolutise the relative nature of this truthfulness. Describing each of the propositions as

---

20. Malliṣeṇa Sūri, *Syādvādamañjarī,* tr. F.W. Thomas, Berlin, 1960, p. 135.
21. Hegel's *Science of Logic,* vol. I, London, 1929, p. 95.

incomplete, Malliṣeṇa writes that they possess "the own-nature of complete expression (*sakalādeśa*), and the own-nature of incomplete expression (*vikalādeśa*)." Of these, complete expression is

> a statement making out, with simultaneity, an entity composed of endless attributes adopted for demonstration, with primacy of occurrence with non-distinction. . . . Incomplete expression through implication of distinction or through primacy of distinction states the same with succession. . . .[22]

By "complete expression" here is meant not just a verbal utterance, but a mystical synthesis of all the "incomplete expressions" on a non-discursive plane. According to the Jaina conception, "complete expression" is attained through the subject's spiritual evolution as he advances along the way to salvation mastering clairvoyance, telepathy, and finally, *kevala* (absolute omniscience). It is a transformation of logic into mysticism; philosophical methodology becomes a phase of religious theory — a specific trait of the Indian mentality.

Let us now dwell on proposition 3 that attributes to an object contrary predicates, thus asserting the unity of existence and non-existence in any material thing. The sixth-century Jaina writer Sāmantabhadra, commenting on proposition 3 of Syādvāda in his treatise *Gandhahasti-mahābhāṣya*, convincingly demonstrated the universal character of this unity for objective reality, justly believing that with complete exclusion of non-existence "things become all-pervading, beginningless, endless, indistinguishable and inconceivable,"[23] whereas complete exclusion of existence asserts its own non-existence.

---

22. Malliṣeṇa Sūri, *Syādvādamañjarī*, p. 139.
23. S.C. Vidyabhusana, *A History of Indian Logic (Ancient, Medieval and Modern Schools)*, Calcutta, 1978, p. 184.

Many scholars,[24] however, believe that proposition 3 is a mechanistic combination of the two previous propositions: an object simultaneously exists and does not exist when viewed from two different standpoints at a time.

A simplified (as compared to Sāmantabhadra's) interpretation of a similar sort is also to be found in the canon of the Śvetāmbara sect.[25] One example is the *Bhagava* text that explains Syādvāda against the general background of the Jainist atomistic theory of the structure of matter. It maintains that proposition 3 is applicable only to objects which occupy two or more units of space (*pradeśa*). Such complex objects simultaneously "(1) possess (dialectical) reality if they are considered from the point of view of their own (properties) . . . and (2) do not possess that reality if they are considered from the point of view of (the properties of) another object. . . ."[26]

Proposition 4, postulating that an object is in some way non-predicative, indescribable and inexpressible, is illustrated in *Bhagava* as follows: "One cannot say if they (hells and heavens — *A.T.*) possess or do not possess reality if they are considered simultaneously from both these points of view,"[27] i.e. of their own properties and of the properties of another object.

A number of nuances make proposition 4 substantially different from 3. First, the whole object is considered from the standpoint both of its own properties and the properties

24. See Debiprasad Chattopadhyaya, *A History of Indian Philosophy* (Russian edn.), Moscow, 1966, p. 188; S. Chatterjee, and D.M. Datta, *Ancient Indian Philosophy* (Russian edn.), Moscow, 1954, p. 82.

25. Śvetāmbaras and Digambaras are the two major Jainist sects.

26. J. Deleu, *Viyāhapannatti (Bhagavat)*, Brugge, 1970, p. 191.

27. Ibid.

of another object. That signifies that proposition 3 is also applicable to simple objects occupying one unit of space. Second, it is postulated that to some questions there are no answers. Thus, for instance, the question about a pitcher's colour may to a first approximation be answered by stating that in some way (e.g. in the sunlight) it is yellow, and in some way not yellow (e.g. by candlelight, when it is red). But what would the answer be if it is asked what the pitcher's colour is in reality — while reality is always definite?

Hence, proposition 4 affirms the existence of questions that are to remain unanswered because of their very nature and accentuates that any verbal description is incomplete, conditioned and limited by the subject's standpoint, i.e. in some way false and impossible. Here again a parallel suggests itself between this judgement and Hegel's idea: "*Unter dem wirklichen Versuche es (Stück Papier) zu sagen, würde es daher vermodern . . .*" (If ever a genuine attempt were made to express it (a sheet of paper) in words, it would be turned to ashes).[28]

It is remarkable that the Jainas do not absolutise this point of view either. Malliṣeṇa points out that a thing is indescribable only in some way, since the very word "non-predicative" is in itself a predicate.[29]

Propositions 5, 6 and 7 reproduce the same pattern of reasoning as in 1, 2 and 3, taking into account the criticism expressed in 4 of the possibility of predication in general.

Proposition 5 in the atomistic interpretation expounded in *Bhagava* is viewed as formulated while considering one part of an object from the standpoint of its own properties and the other part from the standpoint both of its own properties and of the properties of another object simultaneously.

28. G.W.P. Hegel, *Phenomenologie des Geistes,* Berlin, 1970, S. 88.

29. Malliṣeṇa Sūri, *Syādvādamañjarī,* p. 132.

Proposition 6, likewise, is formulated while considering one part of the object from the standpoint of the properties of another object and its other part from the standpoint both of its own properties and the properties of another object. Proposition 7 can only be framed through considering material bodies that occupy not less than three units of space. In this case three parts of an object may be visualised, one from the standpoint of its own properties, another from the standpoint of the properties of another object, and the third part from both standpoints simultaneously.

On the logical plane proposition 7 may be presented as the conjunction either of 3 and 4 or of all the four initial propositions. 5 and 6 are conjunctions correspondingly of 1 and 4 and of 2 and 4.

The ever-present term *syād* (somehow) indicates a certain inadequacy and deficiency of each proposition. Quite a few authors writing on Syādvāda have been misled by this term. *Syād* is the singular form of the Sanskrit verb *as* (to be) in the third person of the optative mood. A literal translation of it as "may be" or "possibly" would irreparably distort the whole meaning of the doctrine. For example, W. Ruben's presentation of Syādvāda is as follows: "It is impossible to say definitely that the thing (1) exists, or (2) does not exist, or (3) exists and does not exist simultaneously. . .".[30]

This interpretation cannot be accepted, for, as is obvious from all the quoted Jaina texts, Syādvāda states exactly the opposite: it is possible to say about any object definitely that it exists, does not exist, etc., as long as this definiteness is not absolutised. According to Malliṣeṇa, the particle *syād* signifies "not unequivocally" (*anekanta*).[31]

---

30. W. Ruben, *Geschichte der indische Philosophie*, Berlin, 1956.

31. Malliṣeṇa Sūri, *Syādvādamañjarī*, p. 22.

Made through misunderstanding a term, this mistake is yet another reminder that the translation of Indian philosophical texts should not be based on a purely etymological meaning of a word. Each term is a clue to a certain context, and it very often does not correlate with its immediate meaning. In order to translate such terms correctly it is vital to know the text they refer to, in which the pertinent context is contained in full.

An even more frequent mistake is the reduction of Syādvāda to a purely logical level. Many authors tend to lose sight of the fact that ancient teachings are generally of a syncretic nature, that "logic originates in the womb of the one indivisible and all-embracing science of philosophy and is above all ontological, i.e. it is basically concerned with the order of things and not with the order of ideas."[32] The same is emphasised by S. Chatterjee and D.M. Datta, who point out that Syādvāda's propositions are not just subjective ideas, but that 'they reveal the different real aspects of the object."[33] Jainists believe that the relative character of judgements about things is "dependent upon not simply the mood of the judging mind, but upon the relational character of the many-sided reality itself."[34]

Founded on a study of the quoted texts, these considerations leave no room for the neo-positivist interpretation of Syādvāda as a purely linguistic doctrine.[35] For the same reasons, the comparison of Syādvāda with the intuitionist (constructivist) trends in mathematical logic,

---

32. A.O. Makovelsky, *A History of Logic*, Moscow, 1967, p. 4.
33. S. Chatterjee and D.M. Datta, *An Introduction to Indian Philosophy*, Calcutta, 1968, p. 86.
34. Ibid.
35. K. Jayatilleke, *The Early Buddhist Theory of Knowledge*, pp. 347-67.

which refuse to adopt the law of excluded middle, does not seem fully convincing.

The "ontological wealth" of Syādvāda prompts one to draw a parallel between this doctrine and some modern methodological concepts rather than compare it to logical-mathematical theories. One example is the principle of complementarity which, in the words of Niels Bohr, physics was forced to resort to after the principle of indeterminacy was defined by Werner Heisenberg and the quantum of action discovered by Max Planck.[36]

The complementary method of description states, in much the same way as Syādvāda does, that the result of an investigation is conditioned by the investigator's approach to the problem. We can demonstrate this using the following well-known example: (1) the electron is in some way a particle; and (2) the electron is in some way not a particle, but a wave. The expression "in some way" refers here to a certain empirical context. Although this example is borrowed from physics, the concept of complementarity is important not so much scientifically as methodologically. Niels Bohr wrote that this principle retains its heuristic use not only for microcosmic physics, but also for psychology, linguistics, biology, culturology, etc. Bohr also saw some similarity between his own ideas and some religious conceptions of the East.

Much attention has been given to the principle of complementarity in Soviet philosophical publications. It has been argued that its weak point is that this concept fails to acknowledge the dialectical contradictions inherent in any reality. "Materialist dialectics . . . has never been satisfied

36. Bohr, *Kausalität und Komplamantarität, Erkenntniss,* 1937, S. 293-303.

with 'gliding from one side to the other' or 'musing over their contiguity in space and time'."[37]

In assessing the principle of complementarity we are inclined to agree with those concluding that "complementarity is a necessary cognitive phase of scientific progress and at the same time a temporary state of any science in its advancement."[38]

It should be observed that even Jaina philosophers did not think of Syādvāda as the final method of cognition. They did realise the need for a synthesis of diverse approaches and definitions. Yet they expected to attain such a synthesis not by means of scientific research but through the mystical revelations of a saint.

---

37. G.S. Batishchev. "The Conflict and Development of Opposites", in *Lenin on the Components of Dialectics* (Russian edn.), Moscow, 1965, p. 240.
38. I.P. Gavrilova, "The Principle of Complementarity as a General Law of Scientific Cognition", in *The Principle of Complementarity and Materialist Dialectics* (Russian edn.), Materials of a Scientific Conference, Obninsk, 1972, p. 47.

CHAPTER TEN

Correlation Between Philosophy and Religion
The *Īśvara-parīkṣā* in Śāntarakṣita's *Tattvasaṁgraha*

VALERI ANDROSOV

THE creative method of the noted eighth-century Buddhist philosopher Śāntarakṣita was based on the conceptual principles of the Yogācāra-Mādhyamika-Svatantrika school. Following Nāgārjuna in subjecting the views of his opponents to slashing criticism, Śāntarakṣita took an independent stand in viewing consciousness (*svatantra*). On the whole, this stand is quite similar to the Yogācāra view of the self-validity (irrelativeness) of consciousness. However, in contrast to the *vijñānavādins*, his Consciousness was not an absolute reality; further, it was multiple.

According to Śāntarakṣita, the flow of consciousness is registered in self-produced conceptions whose verity is rooted inside rather than outside ourselves. Śāntarakṣita makes use of Diṅnāga's and Dharmakīrti's epistemology in refuting the principles propounded by his opponents. Being an adherent of the negative dialectics of Nāgārjunism, the philosopher aims to completely destroy the opponent's line of arguments by carrying it to a logical absurdity (*prasaṅga*).

Tattvasaṁgraha[1] is considered a brilliant piece of

1. *Tattvasaṁgraha of Śāntarakṣita with the Commentary of Kamalaśīla*, in two volumes, GOS, Baroda, 1926.

logicophilosophic thought precisely because of the faultless system of inferential knowledge developed in it. The commentary (*pañjikā*) by Kamalaśīla, Śāntarakṣita's follower, is in no way inferior to the *kārikās* of his teacher.

Śāntarakṣita examines the creative principle propounded by the Nyāya-Vaiśeṣika philosophy in the context of contraposing the Buddhist doctrine of dependent co-arising (*pratītyasamutpāda*) to the concepts of causality (*āstika*) advocated by the orthodox schools and other systems of thought. *Tattvasaṁgraha* opens with the following statement:

> Being independent from an influence of the *Prakṛti,* the Creator, both of them, the *Ātman* and others, the revolving system (*calam*) of Life depends on acts, their results, a relation, an arrangement and so on. Because of the tricks of a quality, a substance, an action, a universal, an inherence and the like, the vacuity (*śūnyam*) became a field of terms and conceptions attributing only one word to other.

Two valid means of cognition joined with an obvious mark (*lakṣaṇa*) provide the basis for such criticism and for the statement by Śāntarakṣita of his own standpoint. He views the soteriological role of a theory as the criterion of its verity and expediency. Because of the tricks of conceptions, the illusory (*pratibimba*) systems developed out of nothing by yet unnamed opponents proved to be useless, stagnant (*agatam*) and not contributing to salvation. It was the Buddha, unprejudiced towards an independent revelation (*svatantraśruti*), who, being filled with great compassion, announced for the sake of the welfare of the world the teaching about dependent co-arising. Worshipping his omniscience, the *Tattvasaṁgraha* was created as an offering to him.

In the second chapter of this treatise, Śāntarakṣita

investigates the Nyāya-Vaiśeṣika doctrine of the intelligent creative cause of the universe (*Īśvara*). He begins by introducing the arguments of a number of representatives of this school such as Aviddhakarṇa, Praśastamati (an acquaintance with whose works, incidentally, can only be derived from the commentary by Kamalaśīla) and Uddyotakara, the noted Naiyāyika, and also the arguments which were generally accepted within the system of their philosophy. Then, Śāntarakṣita analyses this conception and finds at least two and, not infrequently, more logical faults in each of their inferences.

According to Śāntarakṣita, the Nyāya-Vaiśeṣika position basically states that the one eternal intelligent Creator is the efficient cause of the universe along with other causes — which, unlike him, are unconscious — such as atoms, *ākāśa, dharma-adharma,* time (*kāla*), etc. The latter are potentially consequential (passive) and insentient and in producing their effects they need *Īśvara* and His intelligence as the active principle. Every integral creation or complete form of an object is preceded by certain knowledge of its arrangement, which cannot be in any place other than *Īśvara*'s intelligence (*buddhi*). In this sense, he resembles Plato's Demiurge contemplating a sphere of archetypal ideas and transforming them into worldly forms.

Śāntarakṣita disagrees with the Nyāya-Vaiśeṣikas when they say that the precedence of the conscious cause to worldly diversity is beyond doubt, but various effects are created not by the one and eternal *Īśvara,* but by *karma* — an interminable stream of meritorious and demeritorious actions. The Naiyāyika opinion that during the destruction of the world (*pralaya*) all conscious manifestations disappear and *Īśvara*'s intelligence alone remains, is also wrong. On the contrary, people retain their memory and consciousness at the time of *pralaya,* since they are reborn in other worlds until this world is restored. The plurality of consciousness that has thus been preserved is at the source of the plurality of creative acts of the present universe. Śāntarakṣita also consistently refutes Aviddhakarṇa's conception of the whole, which Kamalaśīla called "bare babbling" (*pralāpamātra*). At first glance, the contents of *Tattvasaṁgraha* seem to be far from the quests and feelings of believers. It may seem that the author is only concerned with exposing the logical inconsistency of the doctrines propounded by his opponents. Yet this is far from being the case. Here is an example to illustrate our point. In giving an account of the Naiyāyikas' arguments in defence of *Īśvara*, Śāntarakṣita points out that they infer the omniscience of the Creator of the universe from His omnipotence as its Lord and Manager. The existence of an omniscient (*sarvajña*) person was assumed in early Indian philosophic literature as well — both orthodox and Buddhist. Subsequently, this idea was developed further.

Śāntarakṣita had already declared the thesis of Buddha's omniscience, to the proof of which he devoted the last chapter of his treatise. What, then, did he find unacceptable in the Naiyāyikas' line of argument? Replying to his opponents, he writes: "It is clear that by the refutation of *Īśvara*'s creatorship His omniscience is also turned down in the same way as the argument for 'omniscience' has been based just on the strength of 'creatorship'."[2] Moreover, Śāntarakṣita goes on to say, the analysis has revealed fresh difficulties: "If the Creator is not one, the attributing of omniscience only to Him is erroneous." The ending is quite significant: "If the proof is such, then the [Naiyāyikas'] argument is directed against those who are with Jaimini."[3]

2. *Tattvasaṁgraha*, p. 91.

3. Ibid., pp. 92-93.

One may ask, why should Śāntarakṣita bring up this issue when it relates to Mīmāṁsā, which repudiates an "Omniscient Being," and not to Buddhism?

The essence of Śāntarakṣita's refutation is hard to discern in his laconic *kārikās* consisting mostly of technical logicophilosophic terminology, whereas the literary form of *pañjikā* enabled Kamalaśīla to demonstrate not only the logical, but also the soteriological ineptitude of the conception of *Īśvara*'s omniscience. Since the Naiyāyikas derive the concept of omniscience from the idea of creatorship (for the Creator must surely know the results of His activity), and the latter was refuted as a result of the analysis which revealed faultiness (*doṣa*) in inferences, the refutation of creatorship applies to omniscience as well, for the truth cannot be inferred from a lie. Even if one were to agree with the Naiyāyikas' assertion of the omniscience of the intelligent Creator, their arguments in favour of His being the one and only one are erroneous and superfluous, since every effect can have its own cause, and the concept of wholeness of creation is devoid of any foundation: its only purpose is to make the understanding of the theory simpler.

These concepts of Kamalaśīla are based on the strict apparatus of Buddhist logic. But along with the polemic between the two logical systems and the two philosophies, the author of *pañjikā* also dwells upon the religious contradistinction of the two systems. In his commentary to *śloka* 54 he poses the following question: "In what way is the omniscience of *Īśvara,* who may become the object of worship (love, devotion — *bhakti)* for those who aspire for well-being and salvation, i.e. believers, demonstrated?" Here, in our opinion, Śāntarakṣita's disciple reveals the essence of the opponents' views (*pūrvapakṣa*) on the role of God in human life ascribed to Him by a particular religious cult.

Most Naiyāyikas were Śaivas, which was pointed out by Winternitz in his days.[4] Their philosophical terminology was easily comprehended by the devout members of that sect. *Īśvara* is not only a speculative principle, but also one of the epithets for Śiva, the Supreme Deity of Śaivism. Bringing him closer to everyday reality, the Naiyāyikas ascribe to Him the role of the first Teacher of mankind, the Progenitor of consciousness and the Manager of people's "pleasure and pain" (*sukha-duḥkha*) over and above His cosmological functions. Thus, the Creator of the universe becomes the supervisor of people's souls and deeds. It is this amount of work "done" by Him which gives the Naiyāyikas grounds to consider Him omniscient. For, says Praśastamati, everything in this world has its creator who knows its material and other causes. For example, a potter is the creator of a jar and other such things, its material cause is a lump of clay, its instrumental cause is a potter's wheel and so on, its purpose is to be a container for fetching water, etc., and a householder is known to be its consumer. Similarly, *Īśvara* is the Creator of all worlds. He knows that their material causes are atoms, etc., that their instrumental causes are merit, demerit, space, time, etc., that the assistant causes are characterised as generality, particularity and inherence, that the purpose is the experiencing, and that people are the consumers. Consequently, His omniscience is proved.

Apparently, the last argument in the Nyāya-Vaiśeṣika conception, reconstructed by Śāntarakṣita, was specifically directed against the Buddhists, since the latter, while recognising *pratyakṣa* as a *pramāṇa*, repudiated the possibility of perceiving any real object (*vastu*). It is obvious that at

---

4. M. Winternitz, *Geschischte der indischen Literatur*, B. III, Leipzig, 1922, S. 477.

least *someone* should be capable of perceiving matter (*vastu*), which has become a point of disagreement, since matter, living beings (*sattva*), etc. are distinguished in the same way as pleasure, pain, and so on.

It is significant that the Naiyāyikas chose an epistemological problem — though viewed in its soteriological aspect — as a point of disagreement. Later Buddhist syncretic philosophy adhered to Nāgārjuna's doctrine of two truths, according to which, from the point of view of the absolute truth, the phenomenal world is invalid since the contraposition between a subject and an object is invalid. Apparently, the aim of the method of negative dialectics was to bridge the gap between the subject and object of cognition through the absorption of both by knowledge, understood as a pure relation, i.e. knowledge abstracted from gnoseological duality. In other words, in this situation there is neither a designator, a gnoseological subject, nor a designatum, a gnoseological object: there is only the *designated*, or the *recognised*, as a moment of valid knowledge or knowledge of facts. Thus, cognition becomes a polystructural and multilevelled flow of factual information that has neither a source nor a receiver. Apparently, the correlates of consciousness (both objective and subjective) are rejected from the dominant standpoint in Buddhism — that of withdrawal from the infinity of births and deaths, from the continuous round of events.

However, the Naiyāyikas were also well informed about another Buddhist conception, namely the conception of three types of omniscience. Maitreyanātha in *Abhisamayālaṁkāra*, as well as his commentators, among them Śāntarakṣita's disciple Haribhadra, regarded the following types of cognition as supreme.

1. Buddha's special omniscience consisting of his ultimate direct knowledge of all the aspects of

absolute and empirical existence simultaneously (*sarva-ākāra-jñātatā*).

2. Omniscience with respect to the Hīnayāna and Mahāyāna paths to salvation (*mārga-jñātatā*), possessed by the Buddha and *bodhisattvas* who have embarked on the path of saintliness (*ārya*).
3. Omniscience with respect to objects (*vastu*) of the empirical world, possessed by the Buddha, *bodhisattvas*, and Hīnayāna saints (*śrāvakas* and *pratyekabuddhas*) — *sarva-jñātatā* or *vastujñātatā*. This type of cognition, corresponding to the Hīnayāna capacity for comprehension, represents the cognition of all empirical objects from the standpoint of their non-relation to a real and independent individual ego.

This doctrine played an outstanding part in Mahāyāna soteriology, in which the methods (*prayoga*) of realisation of the three types of omniscience were investigated in detail. One should not forget that at the level of soteriology this doctrine did not contradict the negation by the Mahāyānas (such as Candrakīrti) of a subject of cognition at the level of epistemology. In the opinion of the Buddhist methodologists of the Pramāṇa school, perception as a method of valid cognition of reality is not a relation between the agent (the receiver of information) and the object (the source of information). They describe it as cognition, which includes the moment of perception and carries information only about the presence or absence of a single object, in contrast to inference (*anumāna*), which is wholly devoid of perceptive aspects.

There exists, however, still another type of cognition which Diṅnāga refers to as *svasaṁvitti*, and others (for example, Dharmakīrti and Dharmottara) call *yogīpratyakṣa*, which is a soteriological rather than epistemological means. This intuitive "self-cognition, is attained through progress along the path of perfection (*sambhara-mārga*), comprehension (*dṛṣṭi-mārga*), and special training (*prayoga-mārga*)."

From this it clearly follows that the Naiyāyikas' "attack" was definitely directed against the Buddhist soteriological doctrine of omniscience for the purpose of defending an equally soteriological thesis of *Īśvara*'s omniscience. The strict and logical character of the opponents' conception as presented by Śāntarakṣita is quite admirable. Perhaps, in its orderliness and completeness, it surpasses the Naiyāyikas' constructions of Īśvaravāda scattered over numerous treatises by several authors.

Kamalaśīla clarified the reasoning of his ideological opponents by citing some passages from their works. Perception, which has become a matter of argument for some people, possesses the property of arising-non-arising, it is similar to reality (*sat*), and so on, for the reason that there is a subject. Colour is an example of this. In turn, the real, the commentator proceeds, possesses six inherent properties, namely it exists, it is non-eternal, it is a substance, it has its effects, it has its cause, and it possesses the general and the particular, which are all inherent in substance, quality and action. These three categories (substance, quality and action) determine the emergence of perception. A similar idea was advanced by Kaṇāda, who said that the term "object" applies to substance, quality and action. However, according to the Nyāya-Vaiśeṣikas, this triad of categories is not sufficient for gaining a perception of the universal and the like; therefore, the rest is determined by other *pramāṇa*s. Philosophical categories describe the real state of things. Thus, various manifestations are characterised by the category of quality and the arising-non-arising (*praspanda*) of things by the category of action. The substratum of both is substance as an indispensable cause.

Hence, according to Kamalaśīla, the Naiyāyikas

conclude that the object of perception is established, for otherwise we would see hair growing on a tortoise's shell. Here an example of proof by dissimilarity (*vaidharmya*) plays the part of the law of sufficient reason. If one accepts the Buddhists' hypothesis that the receiving cognition is not similar to the external world, why then has nobody ever seen horns on a hare or known a son of a barren woman? As can be seen, the Naiyāyikas' argument and their "attack" on Buddhist positions were quite sound.

In answer to this, Kamalaśīla, like Śāntarakṣita, points out that, if it is being proved in general that there is *someone* who is omniscient, this is refuted not by us but by the Mīmāṁsakas, whereas we object to calling this omniscient being *Īśvara,* a god of blind faith, whose existence and omniscience cannot be demonstrated by any method of cognition. "You," says Kamalaśīla, "have declared this doctrine for the sole purpose of confusing others." The Mādhyamika-Svātantrikas oppose this omniscient *Īśvara* with the Buddha, who acquired great compassion and omniscience in innumerable births of many *kalpa*s, which means that only a human being, a substratum of *saṁsāra,* may hope to attain omniscience by living through his own kārmic experience. And only such a being can become a knower (*adhiṣṭhātṛ*) of human thoughts and actions. Thereby Śāntarakṣita substitutes a "valid" object of the Buddhist cult for the object of the Śaivas' religious devotion.

The Naiyāyikas' proof is not valid, stresses the author of the commentary, precisely for the reason that *Īśvara* (Creator, Śiva, God) is regarded as the knower of all, which cannot be confirmed by any positive example taken from reality, i.e. an essential condition of Buddhist and Nyāya logic is not fulfilled here. "That is why it is recognised that the whole world is directed (or known) through the mercy of our *Bhāgavat,* the Enlightened One, the greatest of all that has ever been (*loka*), and owing to this the righteous (the noble) ones can even now attain success in salvation and well-being." Indeed, the religious aspect is at its greatest height in this phrase, because here soteriological essence, liberation, constituting the contents, takes the place of the outward, cult form.

It should be stressed once again that the Buddhist conception of omniscience finds its full expression only in the last chapter of *Tattvasaṁgraha*. What is important to us here is the existence of an indissoluble connection of philosophical and religious problems in Buddhism. It is significant that in this part, which is traditional for Buddhist treatises refuting *Īśvara*,[5] Śāntarakṣita and Kamalaśīla deliberately bring up the question of the soteriological meaning of philosophy, which essentially is the existential problem of choosing the way. For the masses of believers, the latter meant the choice of religion.

---

5. Suffice it to name Nāgārjuna, Vasubandhu and Śāntideva, who gave attention to this problem both in their general and special treatises.

CHAPTER ELEVEN

The Vaibhāṣika Teaching on Determinants of Psychic Activity

VALERI RUDOY

THE philosophico-religious system of Vaibhāṣika is known to belong to the Abhidharmist (Hīnayāna) trend in Buddhism. *Abhidharmakośa* (*The Treasury of Higher Law*), written in the fifth century CE by Vasubandhu, is one of the main sources for the study of the Vaibhāṣikas' philosophical views. Though the Sanskrit original remained unknown until 1937, its Tibetan translation and two Chinese versions have always attracted scholarly attention.

We have studied the *Abhidharmakośa* in the original to reconstruct as far as possible traditional Buddhist views on the human psyche. To this end we have developed a *synthetic approach*, which involves distinguishing between three different levels of Buddhism, none of which can be inferred from the others. Two of these levels are religious doctrine and philosophical discourse, according to O.O. Rosenberg, a Russian scholar who studied the Chinese versions. Apart from these, we single out a third (psychotechnical) level, which was not studied by Rosenberg, namely the level of religious psychic exercise — Buddhist *yoga*. These three levels are clearly discerned in the diachronic perspective of Buddhism, and they unfold independently upon a synchronic "cross-section" of the functioning of any Buddhist school. Structural polymorphism is characteristic of any Buddhist trend.

Rosenberg adopted an analytical approach to Buddhism, trying to divide its complex ideology diachronically into Buddhist religion and Buddhist philosophy. In our study of *Abhidharmakośa* and other ancient texts we have concentrated on the synchronic aspect, trying to analyse how a traditional philosophical treatise is "mediated" by religious doctrine and by Buddhist *yoga*. In other words, we approach each of the texts as an ideological synthesis of religion, *yoga* (spiritual exercises) and philosophy.

The aim of this article is to reconstruct the Vaibhāṣika conception of the determinants of psychic activity proceeding from Part I of the *Abhidharmakośa*. We shall examine these determinants in the light of the Abhidharmist classificational method and discuss the units of classification from the perspective of Buddhist structural polymorphism.

The Abhidharmists studied the subjective nature of the human psyche in its dynamism, as an ontological reality. The temporal irreversibility of existence is inseparable from the continuous process of perception, which makes time a general determinant of everything causal, both in the world of objects and in the psyche, as the law of causality functions irreversibly in time.

This standpoint presupposes that being as a whole is divided into two spheres: that which falls under the law of causality (i.e. that which is concrete and transient), and that which is absolute and eternal. This division was accepted by all subsequent Buddhist trends.

Transformation of consciousness, according to Vaibhāṣika, consists in a shift from the causal-resultive and temporal to the absolute and timeless. This problem required, for its logical justification, a systematic analysis both of the unchanged states of consciousness and of the stages of psychic exercise intended to control individual subjectivity. It should be observed, however, that the basic categories involved in such an analysis are predetermined by the doctrine. The doctrinal texts contained the basic classificational concepts, though their correlation remained quite obscure.

In expounding the traditional Abhidharmist concept of the psyche, Vasubandhu sought to clarify this correlation, proceeding from canonical Abhidharma and the *Sūtta Piṭaka*. *Kārikās* 21-28 of Part I of the *Abhidharmakośa*[1] enable us to reconstruct the views of Vaibhāṣika on the problem of the dependence of consciousness upon the sensual level of reflection of objective reality.

Vasubandhu also touches upon certain questions connected with the logico-argumentative approach to the practical psychological aspect of this problem.

Kārikā 21 and Vasubandhu's commentary on it contain a doctrinal substantiation of the classification of mental phenomena (*caitta* or *caitasika*), all of which fall into four classes — *sensitivity, notions, formative factors* and *consciousness.* The class of consciousness includes types of consciousness superior to all other mental phenomena, which are simply *modi* or dependent derivatives. Formative factors are mental phenomena united into one class on the basis of dispositionality, their common characteristic. The division of the rest of the *caitasika* into two other classes — sensitivity and notions — is, according to Vasubandhu, not psychological but purely doctrinal.

The *caitasika* belonging to the class of sensitivity condition the individual's potential attachment to sensual pleasure and are, in fact, the cause of this attachment, which Vasubandhu defines in his commentary as attachment to the sensual world. The term "sensual world" (*kāmadhātu*) is not only synonymous with *saṁsāra,* but it also denotes the

1. *Abhidharmakośabhāṣya of Vasubandhu*, ed. P. Pradhan, Patna, 1967, VIII, pp. 14-22.

opposition of the transformed and untransformed states of consciousness, the former being achieved through mental exercise. That is why the view that the class of sensitivity embraces only sensations, expressed in many modern studies on Buddhism, cannot be regarded as historically correct. This interpretation adjusts this five-class taxonomy to the modern scientific outlook, which has nothing to do with the Buddhist tradition, and disregards the classification's doctrinal origin.

The *caitasika* of the class of notions characterise man's adherence to certain beliefs, which are regarded by Vaibhāṣika as incomplete and therefore false (*dṛṣṭi*). Emotional perception is the source of false views.

As has been shown, apart from sensations the class of sensitivity includes emotional perception, which results in sense formation. The class of notions comprises *caitasika* that can be interpreted, depending on their individual character, either as acts of perception or as actual notions, from which universals are formed. In other words, both classes comprise specific *modi* of consciousness which we refer to as mental phenomena. This is indicated by the fact that the term *mānendriya,* describing the instrumental aspect (*mānas*) of consciousness, is found in the analysis of both classes in Vasubandhu's commentary.

Traditional Buddhist psychology, as presented by Vasubandhu, regards the mental processes — sensation, perception and imagination — not independently, but in relation to consciousness, as its mediating manifestations (*caitasika*). Herein lies the distinction of the Buddhist approach to the psyche as against that of European philosophy. This distinction is due to the doctrinal character of traditional theories of the psyche in Buddhism, which shows that Buddhism is a close-knit system of religious and philosophical concepts.

In *kārikā* 22 Vasubandhu explains the relationship of the Absolute with the five categories of mental phenomena and comments on their doctrinal hierarchy. As mentioned above, the Absolute comprises three unconditioned *dharmas*, namely *ākāśa*, and two types of cessation of the flow of *dharmas* — *pratisaṁkhyā-nirodha* and *apratisaṁkhyā-nirodha*. Division into classes can be valid only for cause-determined *dharmas*. For that reason Vasubandhu points out in his commentary that the term *asaṁskṛta* does not imply any classificational distinction.

Absolute *dharmas* cannot form a sixth class, for they do not correspond to the doctrinal definition of a category as presented in the *sūtra*. They do not conform to the "technical" meaning of the term "class," since the Absolute has no formal distinctions as generalised in this definition.

The classification of cause-determined *dharmas* is in fact a traditional method of psychoanalysis; it is connected with the school's religious pragmatism.

This can clearly be seen in the correlation of two terms: "the attachments class" (*upādāna-skandha*) to "class" (*skandha*). While the first indicates the cause of impurity (*saṁkleśa*), the second points to the sources both of impurity and purification (*saṁkleśavyavadāna*). Absolute (uncaused) *dharmas* are not subject to affective influence (*anāsrava*), which makes it impossible to tie in the term *asaṁskṛta* with the notions *saṁkleśavastu* and *vyavadānavastu*. This would be a purely logical justification of the absence of any semantic correlation between the Absolute and the classes of cause-determined *dharmas*.

The sequence in which the classes of *dharmas* are enumerated is explained by Vasubandhu in a logical vein and in conformity with the Abhidharmists' rationalist maxims. He introduces such qualitative and quantitative criteria as "degree of grossness" (*audārikatva*) and "affective impurity" (*saṁkleśa*). Vasubandhu also relates this sequence to the mental exercises which result in a changed individual consciousness.

Vasubandhu states that the classes are arranged in order of dimunition of their "grossness," by which he implies the simplicity of qualities of manifestation. Matter is characterised by the quality of impenetrability (*sapratighatva*), the class of sensitivity, by the dependence of sensations on the individual's physical constitution, etc. The subtlest mental phenomena are those least connected with material existence.

The succession of the five classes can also be explained by the affective quality of psychics as a fundamental characteristic of an individual's saṁsāric existence. Vasubandhu explains this asymmetric, yet not unsystematic, arrangement with the help of a metaphor, illustrating the inner logic of the sequence. This is in accordance with the traditional principle of metaphorical explanation of doctrinal propositions. Interpretation of doctrinal concepts is always preceded by their syncretic metaphorical realisation in common parlance.

Thus, the sequence *"matter — sensitivity — notions — formative factors — consciousness"* may be metaphorically equivalent to the sequence *"vessel — food — spice — cook — one-who-enjoys-food."*

This sequence also has correlatives on the psychotechnical level. It corresponds to the three spheres in the Buddhist psychocosmos, or the three spheres of empirical existence and meditative concentration — the *perceptible world,* the *world of forms* and the *world of non-forms.*

The immutable states of consciousness are determined by the primacy of psychic reflection of the sensual qualities of matter (*kāmaguṇa-rūpa*). That is why psychoanalytically these states correlate with the class "matter" as dominating the first sphere of empirical existence, the perceptible world. The mutable states of consciousness, denoted by the term "world of forms" (*rūpa-dhātu*), represent the four stages of meditative concentration (*dhyāna*) in which the class of sensitivity is determinative.

The next three states of yogic concentration (*samāpatti*) are termed "world of non-forms" (*arūpya-dhātu*); they are determined by the notion of class (*saṁjñā-skandha*).

According to the classical Buddhist tradition of psychic exercise, there are eight stages in *yoga*. The final stage, the acme of experience (*bhavāgra*), is described as the state of being in a sphere devoid of sensual or mental distinctions. However, since it is a matter of concentration, the psychic disposition which leads to concentration pertains to this stage too. In this case the class of formative factors is determinative.

The organic unity of these psychocosmoses, or spheres of existence, is determined by consciousness, and for this reason consciousness as a class complements the five-class classification. The semantic metaphor used to justify the doctrinal sequence of the classes on the "psychotechnical" level is the image of a seed in a field. With this Vasubandhu ends his analysis of the classification of cause-determined *dharmas*. The two following types of ternary classification are the sources of consciousness (*āyatana*) and the elemental classes (*dhātu*). As defined in *kārikā* 23, they correspond to the six senses, which is typical of all the Indian philosophical traditions.

Kārikā 23 logically justifies the accepted order of enumerating the six organs of sense. The five senses of sight, hearing, smell, taste and touch come first, as they are directed at a given object, explains Vasubandhu. The temporal characteristic of the intentional use of sense organs is of particular importance. The original text uses the formula *vārttamānārthya,* which denotes both an existing (perceptible) object and attraction to it.

The logico-semantic variable *arthya* indicates the direct relationship between the senses and their objects as well as the relation of the senses to the types of consciousness that are based (*āśrita*) on the senses and sensory information (*viṣaya*). Reason (*mānas,* or *mānendriya*), the sixth sense, is opposed to the previous five, for its object is not temporally unambiguous (*aniyata*).

The vector of reason can be determined by an object actually existing or by objects in any other time *modi* (*trayadhvā*), or it can be temporally indeterminate (*anadhvan*).

Another important argument for the enumeration of the senses in the above order is the interpretation of the material characteristics of their objects. The first four senses perceive derivative (*bhautika*) forms of matter. By contrast, the fifth sense — touch — can perceive the great elements (*mahābhūtāni*), derivative matter, or both simultaneously, i.e. objects that are materially not unambiguous.

To explain the order of enumeration, Vasubandhu adopts the principle of necessity and sufficiency conditions for introducing its determining characteristics. Contraposing reason to the other five senses, on the basis of the temporal modality of objects, Vasubandhu justifies its concluding position in the sequence. He also introduces the characteristic of materiality to define the fifth position in the sequence, that of touch, as opposed to the previous four.

To further specify the sequence, Vasubandhu introduces additional characteristics of the sense organs, namely the remoteness and rapidity of perception (*dūrāsūtaravr̥tti*), whereupon the positions are counted in direct order, beginning with sight.

The organ of sight is capable of perceiving objects at a greater distance and in less time than the organ of hearing. The smell and taste organs have a short reach of perception, while taste can only be felt through direct contact with the object.

In addition, Vasubandhu justifies the sequence by the location of the sense organs. The sight organ is located higher than the other four. The organ of touch is all over the body. However, treating reason as one of the senses (*mānendriya*), Vasubandhu points out in his commentary that it has no location (*adeśastha*). Consequently, the interpretation of reason as a sense should be regarded as formalisation of the functional aspect of the human psyche in the framework of the Abhidharmist analysis, and not as a naïve mechanistic interpretation of psycho-physiological processes.

In *kārikā* 24 and in the commentary to it Vasubandhu discusses two very special sources of consciousness — colour-form (*rūpāyatana,* the visible) and the dhārmic (*dharmāyatana*).

The eye as an instrument of consciousness perceives the visible (a content-source). This function includes the reflection of existing material objects, which are derivatives of the great elements. The visible is characterised by visual information (*viṣaya*). This information comprises colour and form, which means that the visible as a source of consciousness pertains to the objective world.

Explaining in his commentary the difference between the common and "technical" meanings of various terms, Vasubandhu notes that colour and form commonly imply matter. Impenetrable (*sapratighatva*) matter can also be detected by touch, but it is only due to its visibility (*sannidarśana*) that it can be referred to in existential propositions like "This is blue," etc. That is why colour-form as a source of consciousness is given a predominant position (*prādhānya*). These explanations are particularly valuable for the study of the history of traditional psychology and its specific descriptive terminology. One of the major achievements of Buddhist psychology is the discovery of the paradox in the description of mental processes: visual information describes the process of seeing, yet it cannot be translated into any terms other than those of the objective world. Oversight of this important detail has frequently led to terminological errors in works on Buddhism: for example, a scholar would mistakenly refer to allusions to visual information (*viṣaya*) for judgements about the objective world and conclude that the subject of discourse has been ontological knowledge, and not traditional psychoanalysis.

Along with colour-form, which pertains to gross material objects, Vasubandhu assigns a special role to the dhārmic source of consciousness and explains in great detail the meaning of the term *dharmāyatana*. All sources of consciousness are *dharmas*, but *dharmāyatana* is not homogeneous, for it comprises a multitude of *dharmas*, and being *dharmas* is the only thing they have in common. Hence the term *dharmāyatana*.

The dhārmic source of consciousness consists of cause-determined *dharmas* and the Absolute, the latter being referred to in Vasubandhu's commentary as "the supreme *dharma*," i.e. *nirvāṇa*. Its being included only in the dhārmic source of consciousness determines the special position of "the supreme *dharma*" among the twelve sources of consciousness.

Kārikā 25 elucidates the correlation between doctrinal terminology (as used in the classification of *dharma*) and the technical usage of terms. In the section of his commentary dealing with the previous *kārikā*, Vasubandhu argues that other connotations of the terms "class," "source of consciousness," and "class of elements" also occur in the *sūtras*. He points out that these connotations do not exist independently but are logico-semantic correlatives of the classificational categories "class," "source of consciousness" and "class of elements."

The whole doctrine can be regarded as 80,000 classes of *dharmas* as enunciated by Śākya Muni; yet, depending on whether the commentator (Abhidharmist) chooses to term the notion "dhārmic class" as "word" (*vāk*) or "name" (*nāma*), these classes can be included either in the class "matter" or in the class "formative factors." The term "word" implies articulated speech, i.e. sounds. Thus, *vāk* denotes the ontological quality of speech and therefore of the 80,000 dhārmic classes as well. This interpretation includes the dhārmic classes in the class of matter.

Abhidharmists who regard the essence of the teaching as a "name" (*nāma*), i.e. an idea that can be expressed in writing, include the dhārmic classes in the class of formative factors. This inclusion is explained by the fact that a "name" (idea) is the object of the formation of a certain individual psychic disposition, since to a Vaibhāṣika the formation of a semantic concept is closely connected with the underlying idea. The relationship between a semantic concept and the relevant idea (the referent object), is deemed indissoluble.

It is essential to point out that linguistic philosophy as a part of Buddhism is in no way an autonomous discipline. It evolved at the heart of Buddhist hermeneutics and dealt with the verbal-argumentative interpretation of the general Buddhist doctrine. Linguistic philosophy served the purposes of religious pragmatism, just like any other Abhidharmist philosophical discipline. It also served to specify descriptive terminology which allowed diverse doctrinal propositions and principles to be systematised on a verbal-argumentative plane.

In *kārikā* 26 Vasubandhu expounds the socio-psychological meaning (speaking in modern terms) of the 80,000 doctrinal dhārmic classes as stated by Śākya Muni.

An analysis of empirically observed human behaviour made it possible to define 80,000 typological classes of behavioural reactions (*carita*) conditioned by such formative factors as attraction (*rāga*), hatred (*dveṣa*), delusion (*moha*), arrogance (*māna*), etc. The 80,000 dhārmic classes provide a method of neutralisation (*pratipakṣa*) of the corresponding sāṁsāric behavioural stereotypes. *Kārikā* 26 allows us to conclude that Vasubandhu tended to interpret the doctrine of the 80,000 dhārmic classes as a *nāma*, including them in the class of formative factors. This shows that in analysing empirically observed behaviour he proceeded from the individual's motivation.

Vasubandhu dwells upon the distinctive criteria (*pramāṇa*) for each of the 80,000 dhārmic classes. In addition to his own essentially socio-psychological approach to this problem he cites examples of other approaches. Some Abhidharmists suggested as a criterion the canonical text *Dharma-skandha,* thus reducing the criteria *to canonical dogma;* others regarded the *descriptive* terms which form the vocabulary of logico-analytical discourses as suitable criteria.

The doctrine of the 80,000 dhārmic classes can therefore be justified in three ways: by canonical dogma; by philosophical argumentation (mediated criteria); or directly by a socio-psychological analysis of types of behavioural reactions.

Kārikā 27 explains the correlation between the use of the terms "class," "source of consciousness" and "class of elements" as classificational categories and specific units of descriptive terminology.

As specific descriptive units, these terms denote combinations of *dharmas* — a concept employed for the doctrinal description of the system's "psychotechnical" level — in contexts other than classificational. Nevertheless, dhārmic combinative compounds should be regarded in the context of primary classificational categories — 5 classes, 12 sources of consciousness and 18 classes of elements. In each case they are correlated according to the inner qualities (*svalakṣaṇa*) of compounded *dharmas*, as it is these qualities that form the basis of primary doctrinal classification.

In his commentary Vasubandhu illustrates this principle with descriptive terms of the "psychotechnical" level. The psychophysical structure of the non-egocentric individual is described by five "pure classes": morality (*śīla*), contemplation (*samādhi*), wisdom (*prajñā*), emancipation (*vimukti*) and vision of emancipative knowledge (*vimukti jñānadarśana*). These "pure classes" do not coincide with the five classes as a classificational category, for the class "morality" is included in the class "matter" on account of *dharmas* comprising the former class, whereas the other four "pure classes" are dhārmic compounds which represent certain psychic dispositions. For this reason Vasubandhu attributes them to the class of formative factors.

Then the commentary examines the terms in relation to an analysis of the terminology used to describe specific psychic practices. Ten spheres, designated as ten sources of universality (*kṛtsnāyatanāni*), characterise the stages of meditative concentration. At each stage the transformed states of consciousness are described by the terms "class," "source" and "element." At the same time the specific meanings of these terms can be presented as accepted classificational categories through an analysis of the meanings of the *dharmas*.

The text of the commentary and the logic of argumentation display the essential unity of the descriptive terminology on all three levels — doctrinal, "psychotechnical" and logical.

Regardless of the contexts in which the terms "class,"

"source of consciousness" and "class of elements" come up, their explicit relationship as specific units of descriptive terminology with the basic classificational categories (5 "classes," 12 "sources of consciousness," 18 "classes of elements") is always brought out by an analysis of the meanings of the *dharmas* they describe. It is also significant that these classificational categories always involve numerical indexing, which designates whether the term is used in its narrow "technical" sense or as a classificational category.

Vasubandhu then proceeds to explain the non-classificational meaning of the term "element" *(dhātu)* as used in the *Vahudhātuka-sūtra,* a part of the first section of the Buddhist canon. This *sūtra* enumerates 62 elements, six of which (earth, water, fire, air, *ākāśa,* and mind) are described as fundamental. Vasubandhu inquires whether *ākāśadhātu* (the element of *ākāśa*) is identical to *ākāśa,* one of the three non-conditioned (*asaṁskṛta*) *dharmas*, and whether the element of mind is identical to the mind itself. *Kārikā* 28 answers this question.

The Buddhist doctrine describes 62 types of misconception concerning the objects of the inner and outer worlds. The 62 demerits in the *Vahudhātuka-sūtra* are in fact a list of the doctrinal oppositions for neutralising the corresponding misconceptions. It follows that the term *dhātu* is used in this *sūtra* not as a classificational category, but as a specific descriptive terminological unit.

Ākāśadhātu is not identical to the *ākāśa dharma,* since the former carries the notion of hollow space (*chidra*). It should be stressed that Buddhist philosophy does not accept geometrical space (*diś*) as a separate *dharma.* Spatial characteristics fall under the definition of matter (*rūpa*), since there is no other way to include them in the process of visual perception. The designation of space as "the space element" (*ākāśadhātu*) is meant to dispose of the term "geometrical space." *Ākāśadhātu* is defined as a void related to dense matter (*aghasāmantakarūpa*). Light and darkness, the conditions of visual perception of dense matter, embody the perceptive essence of the void, as it cannot be perceived without either. Dense matter is impenetrable (*sapratighatva*), for it consists of atomic agglomerates (*sañcita*), and not of separate atoms, which the Vaibhāṣikas believed did not have the same property. The void is therefore limited by dense matter, and that is why *ākāśadhātu* is seen as related (*sāmantaka*) to dense matter.

Proceeding from this analysis, Vasubandhu correlates the term *ākāśadhātu* with the classificational category of the eighteen "classes of elements," attributing it to the class of the visible (colour-form), since this element is related to dense matter and perceived as light and darkness.

The element of mind is not identical with the mind proper, for the term *vijñānadhātu* describes a mind liable to affective influence. Consequently, the element of mind as a specific unit corresponds to the seven classes of the elements of consciousness, which in turn goes under the category of the 18 classes of elements.

The use of the term *dhātu* as a specific unit of descriptive terminology is correlated with its use as a classificational category (18 classes of elements) through the identification of the generic characteristics (*jātīyatva*) of the *dharmas*.

In conclusion, we deem it necessary to point out that our analysis of *kārikās* 21-28 of Part I of the Encyclopaedic Compendium of Abhidharma corroborates the correctness of the synthetic approach to the philosophical texts of Indian Buddhism.

The traditional analysis of the problems of consciousness would hardly be intelligible without a study of the Buddhist religious doctrine. It was this doctrine that regarded consciousness as the central factor of psychic activity and placed it in the focus of the Abhidharmists' attention. This meant that the human psyche was to be analysed with regard to this factor. The Abhidharmists regarded mental processes as meaningful cause-determined mental states, or phenomena of consciousness. This traditional approach ruled out functionalism, a philosophical method which wrongly considers psychic processes to be functions external to the subjective integrity of the psyche. Seeking to overcome individual subjectivism with the help of sacral psychic exercises, Abhidharmist theoreticians framed a highly elaborated philosophical theory of the subject.

Vasubandhu further developed the school's notional and terminological apparatus, paying particular attention to the classificational categories: "class," "source of consciousness" and "class of elements" in relation to the doctrinal contexts of usage. This was done in a linguistic-philosophical vein. As underlined by Vasubandhu, the doctrinal concepts are polysemantic and they require specialised philosophical interpretation. In fact, the linguistic-philosophical aspect is typical of all traditional Indian philosophico-religious systems, since their ideologies are determined by their religious doctrines, whose philosophical terms, i.e. monosemantic, are terminological units of logical treatises.

CHAPTER TWELVE

Polemics Between Buddhists and Jainas about the Rules of Inference

As Presented in the Tattvasaṁgraha by Śāntarakṣita, and the Commentary Pañjikā by Kamalaśīla[1]

NATALYA KANAEVA

The *Tattvasaṁgraha* is one of the most well-known compendia of Indian philosophic thought.[2] It was written (presumably about the middle of the eighth century CE) by the famous Buddhist author Śāntarakṣita and commented on by his pupil Kamalaśīla. A chapter of this compendium, titled *Anumānaparīkṣā* (The Examination of Inference) contains an interesting discussion between representatives of the major *darśana*s about the problem of the inferential

1. This paper is based on parts of the author's monograph, *"The Problem of Inferential Knowledge in India"* (published in 2002 in Russian). Cf **Канаева Н.А.** ***Проблема выводного знания в Индии.*** **Заболотных Э.Л.** ***Логико-эпистемологические воззрения Дигнаги и его идейных преемников.*** **Москва, «Восточная литература»,** 2002 (N.A. Kanajeva, *Problema vyvodnogo znanija v Indii*. E.L. Zabolotnykh, *Logiko-epistemologicheskije vozzrenija Dignagi i ego ideijnykh prejemnikov*. Moskva: "Vostochnaja Literatura", 2002).
2. Cf. Śāntarakṣita, *Tattvasaṁgraha,* with the *Pañjikā* Commentary of Kamalaśīla / ed. E. Krishnamacharya. vols. 1-2, Baroda, 1926 (Gaekwad's Oriental Series, no. XXX-XXXI).

knowledge (*anumāna*).The author of this paper has made an attempt to reconstruct and analyse the issues of the polemic as well as the methods of discussion employed here by the theoreticians of the "mature" Buddhism. The reconstruction and analysis have been conditioned, of course, by the viewpoint of the author, that is, by the perspective of Western tradition of logic.

The term *anumāna* stands in Indian philosophy not only for such kind of knowledge as a result but also for the very act of cognition. The literal meaning of the word *anumāna* in Sanskrit is something like "measuring after," "forming an opinion after." This refers to the fact that inferential knowledge is obtained after empirical recognition of a logical sign or a logical mark (*hetu, liṅga, apadeśa*), and by way of establishing in one's mind an unbreakable connection (*vyāpti, avinābhāva*) between that mark and the inferential judgement or inferential quality (*sādhya, anumeya*).[3] The polemics in the *Anumānaparīkṣā* touch several issues and are directed against different schools. Here is the list of the problems discussed and of the opponents in the discussions:

(1) the rules for the reason of inference (*hetu*), against Jainas (*śloka*s 1361-1428);
(2) the structure of the *anumāna,* against Naiyāyikas (1429-40);
(3) the classification of the types of inference, against Mīmāṁsakas and the Sāṁkhyakas (1441-54);

---

3. Cf. the reference of Dharmottara to the literal meaning of the word *anumāna* in his *Nyāya-bindu-ṭīkā* as translated by Th. Stcherbatsky (Th. Stcherbatsky, *Buddhist Logic,* 2 vols., New York: Dover Publications, Inc., 1984, vol. II, p. 13). There was no definition of *sādhya* even in Dharmakīrti's time which would have made it possible to differentiate between a thesis and inferential quality.

(4) the inclusion of inference in the list of the means of valid knowledge (*pramāṇa*), against the Cārvākas (1455-85).

It is not accidental that the discussion of the problem of inferential knowledge begins with defining the rules for *hetu*. The purpose of these rules is to establish the basis for transition from the observation of a *hetu* in any location to an inferential judgement about the unperceived, inferential quality (*sādhya*) of the same location. In Western comparative studies the discourse which contains this transition got the name "Indian syllogism." Now the "Indian Syllogism," even though christened so by European scholars, differs quite substantially from the traditional European syllogism which originated in the works of Aristotle. The main dissimilarities between them have been often pointed out and discussed by a number of distinguished scholars (H.N. Randle, Th. Stcherbatsky, S. Schayer, I.M. Bocheński, B.K. Matilal et al.). The dissimilarities, which we take into account here, while interpreting in this paper the *Anumānaparīkṣā* with the commentary, are related to the three basic issues:

1. the ontological presuppositions,
2. the understanding of the very operation of inferring, and
3. the understanding of logical relations.

The ontological presuppositions of the traditional European logic are conditioned by the fact that this theory emerged from the depths of idealism, which brought about the constituting of the sphere of thought as a kind of special reality "inhabited" by forms of thought — that is, by logical forms. Syllogism was always interpreted exactly as a form of thought, and traditional European logic for the past three hundred years (roughly, since the beginning of the modern period) has been understood as "the science of thought."

As a special science of thought, formal logic did not consider and was not supposed to consider the relations between "things" on the one hand, and the structures of thought, on the other. These relations were considered to be outside the sphere of logical theory.

In the Indian tradition only Yogācāra Buddhists in their Anumāna-vāda were moving the same way, that is, towards the separation of (or at least distinguishing between) the sphere of thought and the world of "things." As Th. Stcherbatsky remarked, Yogācāra Buddhists had *de facto* introduced in the Buddhist ontology what may be called a "third reality." From the time of Buddha only two kinds of reality had been recognised — the higher or (using a European term) the metaphysical one (*paramārtha-sat*) and the lower or empirical one (*vyavahāra*). Yogācāra Buddhists introduced one more reality, the "logical" one (*kalpanā*), "where, — as Th. Stcherbatsky put it, — there is no Matter at all, there are only Ideas."[4] All *āstika* schools of logic, as well as all Jaina schools, were realist and had to include in their investigations the relations between the things and ideas — understood as universals (*sāmānya, viśeṣa*) — and between the latter and their linguistic expressions. This shows that Indian logic, being a part of epistemology, was not formal[5] but only formalised and not extensional but only intentional.

One more dissimilarity in the sphere of the ontological presuppositions is very important. In Western traditional logic Being has a subject-predicate structure. In Indian logic

4. Th. Stcherbatsky, *Buddhist Logic*, 2 vols., vol. I, p. 509.

5. The non-formal character of Indian logic has been pointed out by one of the famous specialists in this field, B.K. Matilal: Matilal B.K. *The Character of Logic in India*, ed. G. Ganeri and H. Tiwari, Albany: State University of New York Press, 1998, p. 17.

the World is described as an aggregate of locations and locatable properties. There are of course subject-predicate sentences, e.g. "The mango is sweet," where "the mango" is the subject and "sweet" is the predicate. But there are also sentences with the locus-locatee relations, e.g. "The mango is sweetness-possessing," where "the mango" is the locus, and "sweetness-possessing" is the locatee.[6] In Sanskrit sentences with locus-locatee relations it is not always easy to differentiate between a concept and a statement, which are the basic logical forms in Western tradition. It seems that in Indian logic this kind of differentiation has not been there.

Within Indian tradition itself, between various *darśana*s, there were considerable differences in understanding the operation of inference, as well as in understanding logical relations as a whole.

By the eighth century, several patterns of inference had been developed in India, the most popular of them being the five-membered[7] (*pañca-avayavāḥ*) model of Naiyāyikas and two other models of Buddhists. The classical five-membered syllogism of the Nyāya was developed in the *Nyāyasūtra* of Gautama (*c.* the second century CE). The *Nyāyasūtra* (I. 1.32-39) gives a list of the members (*avayavāḥ*) of the syllogism and the *Nyāya-bhāṣya* illustrates them in this way:

(1) the Thesis (*pratijñā*): "Sound is not eternal";
(2) the Reason (*hetu*): "Because it is created";
(3) the Example (*udāharaṇa, dṛṣṭānta*) which could be either positive (*sādharmya*) or negative (*vaidharmya*): "Like a jar" or "That which is eternal is not created like the Soul";

---

6. Matilal, ibid., p. 29.
7 B.K. Matilal interprets them as "limbs" or "steps" of the inferential process, ibid., p. 4.

(4) the Application (*upanaya*) that could be positive (with a positive example) or negative (with a negative example): "And here likewise" or "Not so in this case";

(5) the Conclusion (*nigamana*): "Therefore sound is not eternal."[8]

From the viewpoint of the traditional (European) syllogistic we may interpret the *avayavāḥ* of Gautama's syllogism as attributive statement, rather than terms. It must be also noted that the first of these statements is attributive without being categorical, whereas the remaining four are both attributive and categorical ones.

Quite a numbr of attempts have been made to analyse and explain the Indian syllogism by means of various Western theories and devices (the theory of syllogistic inference, Venn diagrams, the theory of induction, the locus-locatee relations[9] and even the economic theory of risks,[10] etc.). In our study of the polemic between Buddhists and Jainas we use, for comparison, the traditional (European) syllogistic as interpreted by J. Lukasiewicz. So a few words about this system of syllogistic should be said here.

---

8 *Nyāyadarśanam with Vātsyāyana's Bhāṣya, Uddyotakara's Vārttika, Vācaspati Miśra's Tātparyaṭīkā, and Viśvanātha's Vṛtti*, Critically ed. with notes by Taranatha Nyaya-Tarkatirtha and Amarendramohan Tarkatirtha, 2nd edn., New Delhi: Munshiram Manoharlal. 1985, pp. 369-419.

9. Cf. D.H.H. Ingalls, *Materials for the Study of Navya-Nyāya Logic*, Harvard: Harvard University Press, 1951; B.K. Matilal, *The Character of Logic in India*, eds. G. Ganeri and H. Tiwari, Albany: State University of New York Press, 1998.

10. C. Oetke, *Indian Logic and Indian Syllogism*, Review article on: Jonardon Ganeri (ed.), *Indian Logic: A Reader*, Richmond, Surrey: Curzon Press, 2001; *Indo-Iranian Journal* 46, 2003, pp. 53-69.

The Aristotelian syllogism is strictly structured, by means of definitions, on two levels. First, on the level of statements, there are two premisses (the statements from which a new one is deduced; the two may well change places) and the conclusion (the statement which is deduced from the premisses). The premisses and the conclusion may be of several types:

universal affirmative (All *s* are *p*) – designated as A,
particular affirmative (Some *s* are *p*) – designated as I,
universal negative (No *s* are *p*) – designated as E,
particular negative (Some *s* are not *p*) – designated as O.

Secondly, there are three terms — the minor (*s* — the subject of deduction; that "thing" which is told about in the conclusion), the middle (*m* — the term which is present in the premisses but is absent in the conclusion), and the major (*p* — the predicate of the conclusion; that quality which is told about the subject) ones; the copula "is/are," "is not/ are not"; quantifier "all," "none," "some." All structural elements are introduced by means of the definitions.

Using the Western definitions of relevant terms, we may now give the list of the "members" of the five-membered syllogism of Naiyāyikas, using as the symbols the initial letters of their Sanskrit names:

p (from *pakṣa*) — the minor term (in our example,"sound");

p_s— the subject of affirmative example (in this case, "jar");
p_v— the subject of negative example (in this case, "Soul");
s (from *sādhya*) — the predicate of the conclusion, the major term (in our example, "non-eternal");
h (from *hetu*) — the middle term (in this case, "created").

In addition, let us employ the symbol "$\vdash$" to designate a logical inference in general, the symbol "$\vDash$" to designate a deductive sequence, the symbol "$\approx$" for the relation of likeness and the symbol "$\Diamond$" for the modality "it is possible" or "it is necessary to prove."

With the help of the symbols introduced above and taking into consideration that there were no quantifiers in the syllogism of Naiyāyikas, we now can write down the structure of the Nyāya syllogism and compare them with that of the Aristotelian one. (Later we will use the same symbolic notation for the analysis of syllogisms in other Indian schools, those of Buddhists and Jainas.)

The formula of the Nyāya syllogism with an affirmative example should look like this: $\lozenge\ ps, ph, p_s h, p_s s, p \approx p_s \vdash ps;$ The formula of the Nyāya syllogism with a negative example should look like this: $\lozenge\ ps, ph, p_v \neg h, p_v \neg s, \neg (p \approx p_v) \vdash \neg ps.$	The Aristotelian Syllogism in the form Barbara (in the usual symbolic notation): $Amp, Asm \models Asp$

The structural differences between the Aristotelian syllogism and that of Naiyāyikas demonstrate the different conceptions of the inferential process and its contents in the two traditions. The Aristotelian syllogism is based on the relation of deduction betwen its constituent statements: the two premisses and the conclusion. The deduction as such (the deductive sequence) is warranted by the logical form of the premisses. The "matter," the specific contents of the premisses is not taken into consideration, because they are conceived as the "thoughts" (or "ideas"), not as "things." A deductive sequence takes place only if one of the premisses is a general one. In such a premiss all elements of one class of thought objects are either included in another class of objects or excluded from it. The second premiss subsumes a third class of elements under the two other ones either as their element, or as some of their elements, or even as a whole class. These relations are the basis for the transition from the premisses to the conclusion.

In the realist logic of Naiyāyikas and Jainas the *anumāna* was understood as a dual process: the cognition in which the sensual (or empirical) and the rational (or intellectual) were intertwined.[11] The first step is the sensual perception, the "seeing" of a logical sign (*liṅga-parāmarśa*) in some locus. At the second step there is established in the mind a logical connection between the sign and quality which is inferred (*sādhya*). As Indian logicians based their reasoning on sensual (empirical) perception, they were compelled, as it were, to prove the logical connection between the terms of a syllogism by means of illustrative examples. It may be noted here that this method of proving the logical connection is probably the most telling demonstration of those limits that were (self-)imposed on Indian logical theories by their subsuming into epistemology and by their dependence on metaphysics. Such a dependent status of Indian logic has prevented it from abstracting the *forms* of reasoning from its *contents*. The latter was defined not so much by the

11. There were substantial divergences in the explanations of inference mechanism into details. So Naiyāyikas hold that the result of this comprehension is "the knowledge of the subsistence of the proban in the subject qualified by the knowledge of universal concomitance." Jainas "did not agree with such subsistence in the subject as the necessary condition for *anumāna*" (Yaśovijaya, *Jaina Tarkabhāṣā*, ed. with Translation and Critical Notes by D. Bhargava, Delhi–Varanasi–Patna: Motilal Banarsidass, 1973, p. 116).

objective reality as by the epistemological "portrait" of reality as "painted" by philosophers. Indian thinkers always have to take into account the "matter" of premisses, whereas the Aristotelian syllogistic ignores the "matter" of deductions. On the other hand, the use of illustrative examples for demonstrating a logical connection means that the established connections were inductive rather than deductive ones. It is normal for Indian logic, becaue, as B.K. Matilal pointed out, ". . . the usual distinction, so well-entrenched in the Western tradition, between deduction and induction was not to be found in the same way in the Indian tradition."[12] The use of illustrative examples also shows that the value (the truth or the falsity) of premisses is not preset in the Indian syllogism; it should be substantiated in each individual case.

In the *anumāna* of Naiyāyikas there is no general proposition, though there is the subsuming of one class of elements (*pakṣa*) into another one by means of *dṛṣṭānta* and *upanaya*. *Pakṣa* is understood as a one-element class, as a perceived object, a possessor (*dharmin*) of some qualities (*dharma*) and also as a "locus" (location) of these qualities. An example is supposed to demonstrate the logical connection between the attributes (*dharmas*) *h* and *s* of this particular *dharmin*, this particular *pakṣa*. This connection is intuitively obvious for Naiyāyikas but not so obvious for the non-realists. For the former this connection exists in syllogism because the relation between *h* and *s* is real and it was perceived in the past. The example brings to memory that experience, that perception.

---

12. See, B.K. Matilal, *The Character of Logic in India*, eds. G. Ganeri and H. Tiwari, Albany: State University of New York Press, 1998, pp. 14-15.

Buddhists could not possibly accept this kind of realist validation of inference. They made a revolution in logic in order to emancipate logical theory from intuitive and realistic (but not from empirical) presuppositions and to make it a more reliable instrument of reasoning. The revolution consisted in introducing the formal rule for the *hetu,* what is known as the *trairūpya*-rule or the three-aspect rule (in B.K. Matilal's translation, the rule of the triple-conditioned inferential mark).[13]

This rule, according to K. Potter,[14] had been there before Buddhists took it up. It is mentioned, e.g. by the Vaiśeṣika author Praśastapāda. But it attained its full significance only in Buddhist logic. It happened when Diṅnāga subdivided inference into two varieties, "for oneself" (*svārtha*) and "for others" (*parārtha*). It is true that neither variety contained explicit formulations of all the premisses involved in the process of inference. But, with the *trairūpya*-rule, a common premiss was introduced, though not manifestly, in the process of inference. That way Buddhists made their *anumāna* more like the Aristotelian deductive inference. Thus the probability of conclusions being true has been increased.

Diṅnāga was the first Buddhist thinker to put forward the three-aspect rule. In his formulation of this rule, the understanding of the relations between the elements of the *anumāna* is quite close to the understanding of the relations between elements in the Western logic of classes. Due to this innovation, Western historians of Indian logic, e.g. Karl

---

13. About *trairūpya*-rule see: *NBT* 51.4 // *BL*, vol. II, p. 143; R. Chi, *Buddhist Formal Logic*. Preface by K. Potter. L., 1969 (Repr. Delhi, 1984); B.K. Matilal, *The Character of Logic in India*, pp. 6, 90 etc.

14. R. Chi, *Buddhist Formal Logic*, p. xliv.

Potter,[15] often credit Diṅnāga with discovering the relation of penetration (*vyāpti*).

According to Diṅnāga, the *trairūpya*-rule includes three points:[16]

(1) *pakṣadharma, pakṣadharmatā* — "the logical mark should be the property of the subject of the conclusion." In terms of modern logic, one might say that this rule is related to the minor premiss, "There is smoke on the mountain" [*Aph*], and requires it to be true;

(2) *sapakṣe sattvaṁ,* or simply *sapakṣa* — "The logical mark should occur in cases similar to the inferred one" (or "the *hetu* should be contained in a class of objects similar to the inferred one; for instance, in the hearth [p_s] which contains at once fire [*s*] and smoke [*h*]");
this rule can be written down thus: $p \approx p_s$, Ap_sh, Ap_ss;

(3) *vipakṣādvyāvṛtti,* or simply *vipakṣa* — "the *hetu* should not be present in cases that are not similar to the inferred case" (or: "The middle term should be absent from a class of objects not similar to the inferred one; for instance, from a lake that contains neither fire [$\neg s$] nor smoke [$\neg h$]");
this rule can be formalised like this: Epp_v, Ep_vh, Ep_vs.

Th. Stcherbatsky and many other scholars after him interpreted the three-aspect rule only as an analogue of positive minor premisses in the European tradition, but the third point (rule), technically called *vyatireka,* may be compared rather to a negative minor premiss.

Yogācāra Buddhists understood *anumāna* only as an intellectual process (*kalpanā*), because for them the

15. R. Chi, *Buddhist Formal Logic*, p. xliii.

16. *BL.*, vol. I, p. 244.

perception of a logical mark (as a result of the process of perceiving) was nothing but a mental construction (*kalpanā*).[17] Their models of *anumāna* (we may say as well, their models of syllogism), as presented in Dharmakīrti's *Nyāya-bindu* and in Dharmottara's *Nyāya-bindu-ṭīkā* were twofold: inference "for oneself" (*svārtha-anumāna*) and inference "for others" (*parārtha-anumāna*).

The inference "for oneself" contains two members (*avayava*) and three terms. The two "members" are:

1. what is to be inferred or proved (*sādhya, anumeya* — *s* or *sp*):
   "There is fire on the mountain";
2. the logical ground or logical attribute (*hetu* — *h*):
   "Because there is smoke."
   Within these "members" three terms may be discerned:
   1. the major term, *sādhya, anumeya* — *s;*
   2. the minor term, *pakṣa* — *p;*
   3. the middle term, *hetu* — *h.*

Thus the structure of the inference "for oneself" is: $Aph \vdash Aps$.

In the *svārtha-anumāna* we do not see anything like the quantifier "all," but in fact it is contained here implicitly within the *hetu*, because the latter conforms to the *trairūpya*-rule. Not all premisses which are actually present in this inference, are explicitly formulated. Its actual structure is

17. As pointed out by Dharmakīrti: "Construction (or lodgment) implies a distinct cognition of a mental reflex which is capable of coalescing with a verbal designation (*abhilāpa-saṁsarga-yogya-pratibhāsa-pratītiḥ kalpanā*" — *NB* I.5 / / *BL*, vol. II, p.19. Dharmottara's commentary: "(Pure) sense-perception thus becomes a (real) source of our knowledge only when it has elicited a judgement" — *NBT* 16.7 / / BL, vol. II. p. 45.

more complex than the apparent one and may be symbolically presented in the following way: *Aph*, ($p \approx p_s$, Ap_sh, Ap_ss), (Epp_v, Ep_vh, Ep_vs) $\vdash$ *Aps*. We may say that the illustrative examples as a whole play the role, as it were, of an extended general premiss, which ensures the unbreakable connection between *hetu* and *sādhya*.

The inference "for others" was formulated in two varieties: as "the syllogism of similarity" and "syllogism of difference (dissimilarity)." The forms of their premisses are somewhat different from the forms of the premisses in the inference "for oneself."

According to Dharmakīrti, "the syllogism of similarity" consists of three "members":

1) The major premiss: "[All] produced things (*h*) are impermanent (*s*)" — *Ahs*;
2) An example by similarity: "Just as a jar (p_s) etc." — ($p \approx p_s$, Ap_sh, Ap_ss);
3) Minor premiss: "The sounds of speech (*p*) are such produced things (*h*)" — *Aph*.

The conclusion of such a syllogism was not supposed to be formulated, since it was, according to Buddhists, self-evident: "Consequently, the sounds of speech are impermanent" — *Aps*.[18]

So the logical form of this kind of inference we may write down symbolically in the following way: *Ahs*, ($p \approx p_s$, Ap_sh, Ap_ss), *Aph* $\vdash$ *Aps*.

Now comes the "syllogism of difference" which also consists of three "members":

1) The major premiss: "Eternal entities (s) are not produced (*h*)" — *Ash*;
2) An example by dissimilarity [with *sādhya*]: "As, e.g. Space (p_v)" — Epp_v, Ap_vh, Ap_vs;

18. Dharmottara, *Nyāya-bindu-ṭīkā* 42.16 / / *BL*, vol. II., p. 113.

3) The minor premiss: "But the sounds of speech (p) are product ($\neg h$)" — *Eph*.

[Conclusion: "Consequently, they (p) are impermanent ($\neg s$)" — *Eps*].[19]

The overall structure of this kind of inference looks like this: $Ash, (Epp_v, Ap_vh, Ap_vs), Eph \vdash Eps$.

Now let us bring all the syllogistic models discussed above in one Table. This will bring into relief the differences between the conceptions of the *anumāna* in the Nyāya and in the Buddhist thought.

The Nyāya syllogism with an affirmative example $\Diamond\, ps, ph, p_sh, p_ss, p \approx p_s \vdash ps$; The Nyāya syllogism with a negative example: $\Diamond\, ps, ph, p_v \neg h, p_v \neg s, \neg (p \approx p_v) \vdash \neg ps$.	The Aristotelian Syllogism in the form Barbara (in the usual symbolic notation): $Amp, Asm \models Asp$
The Buddhist *parārtha-anumāna* (a) *the "syllogism of similarity"*: $Ahs, (p \approx p_s, Ap_sh, Ap_ss), Aph[\vdash Aps]$ (b) *the "syllogism of dissimilarity"*: $Ash, (Epp_v, Ap_vh, Ap_vs), Eph [\vdash Eps]$	The Buddhist *svārtha-anumāna* $Aph \vdash Aps$

19. *NBT* 42.19 //BL, vol. II., p. 114.

The *trairūpya*-rule was a nominalist solution of the central problem in Indian logic, the problem of validating the logical connection (*avinābhāva, vyāpti, anyathānupapatti*) between the *sādhya* (what is inferred) and the *hetu* (its "sign," i.e. the basis of the inference) in Indian syllogistic. But this solution aroused the opposition of all other, non-Buddhist schools of logic. Jainas were one group of the opponents. In the *Tattvasaṁgraha* and in the *Pañjikā* Śāntarakṣita and Kamalaśīla put forward their counterarguments aimed at Pāttrasvāmin, who must have commanded a considerable authority in the seventh century, but today is not known well even to the historians of Indian philosophy, because his works have not been preserved. These polemics between Buddhists and Jainas seem to be an important episode in the history of Indian logic, because we may discern here a movement from intensionalism to extensionalism. This tendency was pointed out by J. Bocheński in his *Formale Logik*.[20]

Against the *trairūpya*-rule Jainas put forward an alternative rule for the middle term — *anyathānupapatti* or *anyathānupapannatvā* (literally "non-appearance otherwise" or "invariable concomitance"). What is the gist of the polemics between Buddhists and Jainas?

The founder of Jaina logic Siddhasena Divākara in his *Nyāyāvatāra* offered a definition of *anumāna* which shows the similarity of Jaina ideas about inference with the ideas of Naiyāyikas:

> That cognition of the inferred, which is produced from the mark which is inseparably connected with it, is known as inference (*anumāna*).
>
> *sādhyāvinābhūto liṅgāt sādhyaniścāyakaṁ smṛtam anumānaṁ*.[21]

---

20. J. Bocheński, *Formale Logik*, Freiburg-München, 1956, p. 505.

21. Siddhasena Divākara, *Nyāyāvatāra: The earliest Jaina Work on Pure Logic*, ed. with Candraprabha Sūri's Vivṛti by S. Ch. →

But the polemics between Buddhists and Jainas reveal to us that in Jaina logic there was some similarity with Buddhist views as well. Thus Jainas, like Buddhists and following their lead, used both affirmative and negative forms of syllogism. But whereas Buddhists didn't define what is the *anvaya* (what should be the object of comparison in the *dṛṣṭānta* – the *pakṣa* or the *sādhya*?) and only allowed the partial presence of the *hetu* in the *anvaya*, Jainas, on the contrary, did define the *anvaya*. According to their definition the *hetu* must always be there in the *anvaya* and always absent in the *vyatireka*.[22] J. Bocheński remarked in this connection that the Jaina theory of the *anyathānupapatti* is rather similar to the extensional theory of the *vyāpti* which became widely spread much later, with the establishment of the Navya-Nyāya.[23]

In the *Tattvasaṁgraha*, Śāntarakṣita begins the polemics with his Jaina opponent, expounding the fundamentals of Buddhist Anumāna-vāda according to Dharmakīrti's *Nyāya-bindu* (which we have discussed above). Śāntarakṣita states that there are two types of the inference — *svārtha-anumāna* (the "inference for oneself") and *parārtha-anumāna* (the "inference for others"). The inference "for oneself" is a

→ Vidyabhushana, Arrah, 1915, vol. II, p. 9. Cf. *Nyāya-Bhāṣya* of Vātsyāyana: *mitena liṅgena liṅgajo rthasya paścānmāna-manumānam* — "An inference is a thought next after knowledge of object's mark together with match making [of this mark and inferred quality]" (*Nyāyadarśanam: Gautama Nyāya-sūtras, with Vātsyāyana's Bhāṣya and Uddyotakara's Vārttika, Vscāspati Miśra's Tātparyaṭīkā & Viśvunātha's Vṛtti*, ed. Taranatha Nyāyatarkatirtha and Amarendramohan Tarkatirtha, Introd. by Narendra Chandra Vedantatirtha, 2nd edn., New Delhi: Munshiram Manoharlal 1985, p. 88).

22. Siddhasena Divākara, ibid., p. 17.

23. I.J.M. Bocheński, *A History of Formal Logic*, tr. and ed. I.Thomas, 2nd edn. New York, 1970, p. 507.

cognition of an inferred object, which cognition is effected by means of a three-aspect "mark" (*śloka* 1361). The inference "for others" makes explicit these three aspects verbally (*śloka* 1362). Kamalaśīla, in his commentary on these *śloka*s demonstrates the efficiency of the *trairūpya*-rule (taken from Diṅnāga's *Pramāṇa-samuccaya*), giving as examples the syllogisms in which only one or two points of the rule are raised; such syllogisms are shown to yield false conclusions. Here are the examples of Kamalaśīla:[24]

The Syllogism	**The number(s) of the point(s) realised**
Sound is eternal because it is created	1
Sound is eternal because it is material	2
Sound is eternal because it is unknowable	3
Sound is non-eternal because it is perceived with the eyes	2, 3
Sound is non-eternal because it is perceived with ears	1, 3
Sound is non-eternal because it is non-material	1, 2

In his turn, the Jaina Pāttrasvāmin refutes the Buddhist *trairūpya*-rule by means of the following arguments. First, he puts forward such examples of inferences (of syllogisms) in which the *hetu* conforms to the *trairūpya*-rule, but the conclusions are false. Next, he puts forward such examples of inferences in which the *hetu* does not conform to the *trairūpya*-rule, but the conclusions are true. So, concludes Pāttrasvāmin, the only attribute of a valid *hetu* is *anyathānupapatti*: "This object is one-featured, but not [three-] or four-featured" (*śloka* 1364); "whether or not two examples are given, [it is insignificant] for it is not they which are the reason [of the inference]" (*śloka* 1367).

24. Here and further in this paper the translations from Sanskrit, if not stated otherwise, are mine – N.K.

Śāntarakṣita and Kamalaśīla, in their turn, conduct the defence (or the counter-attack?) in the form of an indirect disjunctive proof, in which the refutation of the anti-thesis ($\neg T$) is taken to be the validation of the thesis: $T \vee T, \neg\neg T \vdash T$. This form of argumentation was one of the favourite ones with Indian philosophers.

In order to refute the position of the antagonist they use two methods. The first one consists in the explication of the meaning of the term *anyathānupapatti*. Śāntarakṣita invites us to consider three possible interpretations of the concomitance between the *hetu* and the *sādhya*. And all the three cases he illustrates with syllogisms in which he finds fallacies and therefore rejects these syllogisms. Which, for him, means the rejection of the Jaina principle of the *anyathānupapatti* as a whole. The logical fallacies which our Buddhist authors point out in the syllogisms of Pāttrasvāmin have been culled mainly from Dharmakīrti's *Nyāya-bindu* and Dharmottara's *Nyāya-bindu-ṭīkā*.[25]

The three conceivable cases of the concomitance between the *hetu* and the *sādhya* are deduced by Śāntarakṣita from the two Jaina ideas:

1. the idea that there are two kinds of the inseparable connection (=concomitance = *vyāpti*) — the internal one (*antar-vyāpti*) and the external one (*bahir-vyāpti*). This idea was accepted in Buddhist logic as well;[26]
2. the idea that all inferences are of three kinds: "the inference about an effect from a cause" (*pūrvavat*), "the inference about a cause from an effect" (*śeṣavat*) and "the inference on the basis of the perception of universals" (*sāmānyato-dṛṣṭa*).[27]

---

25. The list of logical fallacies are cited in *BL.*, vol. II, pp. 171-253.

26. The origin of the distinction between the "external" and "internal" concomitance "has not been conclusively established" — Matilal, op. cit, p. 124.

27. J. Sinha interpreted it as "inference of an unperceived event from a perceived event, which are uniformly co-existent" or →

These ideas were accepted in the Nyāya as well. So we may conclude that our Buddhist authors aimed their criticism here against all realist schools of epistemology and logic. The intrinsic concomitance (the *antar-vyāpti*), as it was defined by Vidyabhushana, "occurs when the minor term itself as the common abode of the middle term and the major term, shows the inseparable connection between them."[28] In other words, *antar-vyāpti* is a connection which is perceived straight in the subject of *anumāna* (*p*). The extrinsic inseparable connection (the *bahir-vyāpti*) "occurs when an example from outside is introduced as the common abode of the middle term and the major term to assure the inseparable connection between them."[29] In other words, *bahir-vyāpti* is a connection which is perceived straight in the subject of an illustrative example (p_s or p_v). The perceiving of the *anyathānupapatti* in different locations shows that Jainas, quite like Naiyāyikas, understood this relation as a special kind of reality which may or may not be there in different locations.

So Śāntarakṣita has examined three possibilities of invariable concomitance (*anyathānupapatti*):

(a) as a common rule or a universal relation (*sāmānyena gamyate*) which is there independently from any *dharmin*; in this case it is perceived as such in the middle term and so the *hetu* may be understood as being a *dharmin*, locus, and *sādhya* as being a *dharma*, locatee.

(b) as a common rule or a universal relation treated in a particular case, in a concrete syllogism. There the

→ "inference by elimination" — J. Sinha, *Indian Epistemology of Perception*, Calcutta: Sinha Publishing House Private Ltd.,1969, p. 215.

28. S.C.Vidyabhusana, *A History of Indian Logic: Ancient, Mediaeval and Modern Schools*, Delhi, etc. 1978, p. 177.

29. Ibid.

pakṣa is the *dharmin*, whereas the *sādhya* and the *hetu* are the *dharmas*, which are tested by the inference (*jijñāsita-viśeṣe*). In this case the invariable concomitance of the *hetu* and the *sādhya* is perceived in the subject of the syllogism (*p*), which is the locus, whereas the *hetu* together with the *sādhya* are the locatee qualities;

c) as a common rule or a universal relation treated in another particular case, namely in the *dharmin* of an illustrative example (*dharminyathā nidarśane*).[30] In this case the invariable concomitance of the *hetu* and the *sādhya* is perceived in the *pakṣa* of the illustrative example (p_s or p_v), which is the locus for the locatee qualities of the *hetu* and the *sādhya*.

It seems that Buddhists saw the case (a) in the *sāmānyato-dṛṣṭa-anumāna*. Buddhists tried to prove that universal concomitance is impossible, because there are syllogisms in which the predicates and the middle terms are always connected in empirical reality (for example "visibility" and "impermanence"), but it is impossible to prove — by means of an inference — their universal concomitance in such an object as "sound." In order to avoid this kind of fallacy it is necessary to choose such middle term, which would designate a real predicate of a *dharmin*, so that the first point of the *trairūpya*-rule would be effected. This rule being effected, the Jaina conception would be transformed into the Buddhist one. The *hetu* cannot be a locus or a *dharmin*, but only a locatee, which pervades the *dharmin* partially. There must be another perceived *dharmin*. "Even the teachers told such definition of infcrcncc briefly" (*śloka* 1384).

The case (b) may be interpreted in the following way: Śāntarakṣita speaks about the unbreakable relation between

30. Śāntarakṣita. *Tattvasaṁgraha*, with the *Pañjikā* Commentary of Kamalaśīla ed. E. Krishnamacharya, vols. 1-2, Baroda, 1926 (Gaekwad"s Oriental Series, No. XXX-XXXI), *śloka* 1379, p. 499.

the *hetu* and the *sādhya* as intrinsic (the *antar-vyāpti*), if it is perceived in the *dharmin* of the inference. This is what takes place in the *pūrvavat-* and *śeṣavat-anumānas*, because the causes and the effects, which play the role of a *hetu*, are not universal: they are the causes of particular effects and, vice versa, the effects of particular causes. By such an interpretation of the *anyathānupapatti* there appears the fallacy of a circle in argumentation (*anyonyāśrayadoṣaḥ*), because "unbreakable perception of the *hetu* and the *sādhya* in the *dharmin* of inference" means that:

either

(1) there is no problematic situation in the affirmative form of inference and there is the knowledge before the inference

or

(2) there is no reason for inference in the negative forms of syllogism, because the *hetu* is absent together with the *sādhya*. So the second interpretation, which leads to situations where an inference is impossible at all, also demonstrates the fallacy of the Jaina rule of the *anyathānupapatti*.

In the third case (c) the unbreakable relation is extrinsic (the *bahir-vyāpti*) and therefore it is demonstrated in the *dharmin* of the illustrative example in the *pūrvavat-* and *śeṣavat-anumānas*. Śāntarakṣita, while considering this possibility and the syllogisms in which it is represented, also finds in such syllogisms logical fallacies. So he says:

> Even if this [i.e. the unbreakable relation] is demonstrated in the illustrative example, it may be absent in the *dharmin* [p], because its *vyāpti* does not embrace [the entire Universe].[31]

Indeed, two predicates (*dharmas*) may be related between themselves, but may as well have no relation to any *pakṣa*.

The second method of refutation used by our Buddhist

---

31. Śāntarakṣita. *Tattvasaṁgraha, śloka* 1388, p. 501.

authors consists in the critical analysis of Pāttrasvāmin's syllogisms. In the course of this analysis the Buddhists demonstrate the facts, not discerned by their opponent, when the *trairūpya*-rule is effected in valid inferences and is not effected in invalid ones.

The net results of the polemics between the Jainas and the Buddhists may be presented in the following way:

	The Anumānas	**The fallacies according to Pāttrasvāmin**	**The fallacies according to Śāntarakṣita and Kamalaśīla**
1.	He [unborn child will be] swarthy because he is a son of a woman whose other [previously born] children are swarthy.	The Conclusion is ambiguous, though the *hetu* is threefold.	The Conclusion is ambiguous; there is no *vaidharmya*; the *hetu* is neither the *kārya-hetu*, nor the *svabhāva-hetu* nor the *anupalabdhi-hetu*.
2.	As they are comprehended one way or another, both Being and non-Being has a [relatively] real nature.	The *hetu* is not threefold; one of the two examples are missing, but the Conclusion is true.	The Conclusion is ambiguous; a second example may be found; there are the fallacies of reasoning: *anāśraya* =*anaikāntika* (ambiguity) and *vyartha* (senselessness).
3.	Something which has a hare-sign is not non-Moon because it has the denotation of Moon-quality.	The *hetu* is not threefold; the *anvaya*-example is absent, but the Conclusion is true.	The Conclusion is true, because the *hetu* is threefold, an example may be found in the field of conventional word usage.
4.	"This sensation of mine is produced by a flying insect" — this is certified by the [sensation] appearance which has been received from the [sense organs] contact with a flying insect.	The *hetu* is not threefold; the *anvaya*-example is not given, but the Conclusion is true.	The Conclusion is false; the *hetu* is equivalent to the *sādhya*; there is a fallacy of reasoning: *vyabhicāritva* = *anaikāntika* (ambiguity).

5.	When a colour is perceived, the eye is always the main cause, because it activates the deciding potency, [in other words, it is] the eye that sees [a colour].	The *hetu* is not threefold; the *anvaya*-example is not given, but the Conclusion is true.	The Conclusion is false; the *hetu* is not universally admitted, therefore the following fallacies are possible: *asiddha* (unreal), *vyabhicāra* and *viruddha* (contrary) reasons.
6.	I, a jar and other objects, have in a way an unreal nature because they are not perceived in certain ways, like a donkey's horns.	The *hetu* is not threefold; the *vyatireka*-example is not given, but the Conclusion is true.	The Conclusion is false; the *hetu* is fallacious, it is *vaiphalya* (barren), *aprasiddhi* (has no force of a proof); there are two examples – they are of their own nature (*sadātmatva*).
7.	Sometimes in some way these have real nature [even such things as] a hare's horns, for the reason of their relative perceptibility similarly to I, a jar and other objects.	The *hetu* is not threefold; the *vyatireka*-example is not given, but the Conclusion is true.	The Conclusion is true, there are two examples — of their own nature (*sadātmatva*).
8.	"There is your [father] in the house" — such a conclusion is made because of the audibility of the sounds of your father's [voice] in the house.	The *hetu* is not threefold; there is no *vyatireka*-example, but the Conclusion is true.	The Conclusion is true, the *hetu* is threefold, the *vyatireka*-example may be found in the previous experience.
9.	It is due to the invariable concomitance in syllogisms with such things as sound (or word, *śabda*), light and the like, that, even if there is no relation with *pakṣa* there is perceived something which gives some infor-mation.	The *hetu* is not threefold; there is no *pakṣadharmatā* for the *hetu*, but the Conclusion is true.	Syllogism is wrong, it is impossible to use sound (word) and light as reasons for an inference, because they do not have the qualities of the minor term.

Besides typical fallacies from Dharmakīrti's list, we see in the 4th column of this Table two mistakes of a different kind. In the first syllogism the error is associated with the Buddhist threefold classification for the *hetu* and *anumāna*. There are the *kārya-hetu* and the *kārya-anumāna* (the ones "based on a cause-effect relationship"), the *svabhāva-hetu* and the *svabhāva-anumāna* (the ones "based on an identity"), *anupalabdhi-hetu* and *anupalabdhi-anumāna* (the ones "based upon non-perception"). "It [i.e. the middle term in the syllogism] is neither *kārya-*, nor *svabhāva-*, nor even *anupalabdhi.* As it does not enter in [these three kinds of reasons], it does not have the invariable concomitance with the *sādhya.*"[32] As for the inference no. 9 in our Table, Śāntarakṣita understands it in a metaphysical sense: as the proof of possibility to infer on the ground of a sound (a word) and light. Sound (*śabda*), as we know, was included in the list of the means of valid knowledge (*pramāṇa*s) by all realists. When Śāntarakṣita points out errors in such kinds of inference, he criticises not only the purely logical but also the ontological ideas of the opponents of Buddhism. He says "A word informs us, but not about real things. Because there does not exist one-to-one correspondence [between the signifier and the signified], a word conveys only an imagined meaning."[33] A light as well as a lamp, which is a light source, cannot possibly be a reason (*hetu*) for an inference, "because there is absent a logical mark [in them] like "blue colour" and so on."[34] A lamp and its light only help us to see things.

By way of conclusion it may be noted that all the arguments of Pāttrasvāmin in favour of the invariable concomitance as the *anyathānupapatti* have been effectively refuted by Śāntarakṣita with the help of Kamalaśīla. In spite

32. Śāntarakṣita. *Tattvasaṁgraha, śloka*1417, p. 508.

33. Ibid., *śloka* 1408, p. 507.

34. Ibid., *śloka* 1410, p. 507.

of this victory Buddhists, in the end, lost the battle against realist logic, but their ideas have remained in the logical theories of their opponents. The fragment (of the *Tattvasaṁgraha* along with the *Pañjikā*) discussed in this paper demonstrates the great role which the method of explanation by means of syllogisms as examples played in polemics between Indian *paṇḍit*s. The study of Indian syllogisms, of their logical structures in the first place, should help us to adequately understand the nature of the problems discussed by the Indian logicians and to reconstruct the factual history of Indian logic, till now little known in the West.

CHAPTER THIRTEEN

The Modernisation of Vedānta

VLADISLAV KOSTYUCHENKO

OF the numerous messianic religious organisations that emerged in India and spread their activities to other regions of the world, the two most influential in the history of neo-Vedāntism are the Ramakrishna Mission, founded by Vivekananda in 1897, and the Ashram founded by Aurobindo Ghose in 1926. Both organisations have been active in spreading the idea of a synthesis of the spiritual values accumulated by the Oriental and Western civilisations. With this prospect in mind, they seek to combine the revised (purified) version of Hinduism with elements of other religions, and compare Vedānta, which is held to be the heart of Hinduism, to some conceptions current in modern European science and philosophy. As a result, Vedāntic ideas deviate increasingly from tradition both in form and essence. While the philosophical views of the leading nineteenth-century theoreticians of Vedānta can be traced back, although with considerable reservations, to the classical Vedāntic trends of the past, Aurobindo Ghose's Integral Vedānta, the most influential trend in the twentieth century, has no such prototype if viewed in its complexity.

As a matter of fact, the above-mentioned comparison of Vedānta is regarded by its initiators as a means of demonstrating its advantages rather than as a modification. This attitude was shared by Vivekananda, who tried to identify the conclusions and methods of Advaita with those of modern science. But even the very approach to the problem reveals the essentially non-traditionalistic character of neo-Vedāntism as compared with the outlook of Śaṅkara. The latter propounded the idea of the limited power of reason and its submission to authority and argued with the proponents of the independent role of reasoning which is not founded on Śruti in the interpretation of the world (recall his polemics with Sāṁkhya philosophers over this issue). Actually, Śaṅkara rejected authority-free methods and any kind of scientific approach in philosophy. Therefore, Vivekananda's description of Vedānta as "a scientific religion," despite its very eulogistic tone, was not traditional and closely connected with the ideology of enlightenment.

In corroborating this definition, Vivekananda advanced a number of arguments which in the twentieth century have become classical and travelled from one neo-Vedāntic treatise to another. Vivekananda's arguments in favour of correlating Vedānta with science include:

(i) the underlining of the priority of any kind of pantheism over creationism;
(ii) an underestimation of the religious aspects in Vedānta;
(iii) an emphasis on the naturalistic concepts assimilated by Vedānta;
(iv) modernisation of the natural-philosophical schemes contained in Vedānta; and
(v) an attempt to discover a methodological similarity between Vedānta and science.

Let us now examine the said arguments in detail. Vivekananda persistently points to the antithesis between pantheism and creationism. He believes that it is the unsoundness of creationism that makes it difficult for science to accept religion. First, creationism contradicts the laws of conservation of matter and energy. Second, it is connected with the doctrine of a temporally and spatially finite universe, and is, therefore, contrary to the scientific conception of the universe, which was adopted in the late nineteenth century. Third, it does not conform to the theory of evolution that has prevailed, thanks to Darwin.

Vivekananda's objections to creationism are sometimes reminiscent of the well-known antitheses of Kantian mathematical antinomies. The Indian scholar wrote:

> If you can give a beginning to time, the whole concept of time will be destroyed. Try to think of a limit where time began, you have to think of time beyond that limit. Try to think where space begins, you will have to think of space beyond that. Time and space are infinite, and therefore have neither beginning nor end.[1]

This part of Vivekananda's argumentation is very convincing. He propounds a number of dialectical ideas concerning the relationship between part and whole (and the reflection of an integral structure in its parts), the unity and interpenetration of the finite and infinite, and the unity of opposites in the absolute. Vivekananda is also wedded to the pantheistic principle of "everything in everything." His doctrine of practical Vedānta interprets this principle as the basis of common responsibility for every individual, and likewise the responsibility of one for all, as well as a guarantee of the inalienability of human dignity by virtue of an unlimited potential of positive qualities behind any multitude of actualised negative manifestations.[2] At times Vivekananda translates into Vedānta the famous formulae of Nicolaus Kusanus. For instance, he compares God to a boundless circle whose centre is everywhere (whereas man is compared to a boundless circle with a fixed centre).

1. Swami Vivekananda, *The Complete Works*, vols. I-VIII, Mayavati, 1947-51, vol. II, p. 425.
2. Ibid., pp. 25-26.

Despite the strong qualities of Vivekananda's theory (e.g. objections to creationism), it fails to prove that Vedānta and science are in agreement over these problems. On the one hand, from the standpoint of Advaita, to which Vivekananda generally adheres, all his dialectical and anti-creationist generalisations remain on the level of *vyāvahārika,* while on the level of true knowledge (*pāramārthika*) the concepts of space, time and motion are inapplicable. On the other hand, even the concepts adopted by Advaita-Vedānta, on the level of *vyāvahārika,* are far from instrumental in drawing a scientifically realistic picture of this world. In Vivekananda's work the concept of *Īśvara,* which is the cornerstone of the Vedāntic scheme of things, is given a pantheistic interpretation as a spiritual element that combines individual and non-individual features. In science, however, the universe is regarded as material and impersonal. To tone down this discrepancy, Vivekananda tries to minimise the religious content of Vedānta. Like many other nineteenth-century reformists, he rejects certain traditional religious notions (heaven and hell, subordinate gods, etc.); God is regarded by him (although with some inconsistency) as above all an impersonal spiritual source. Nevertheless, despite this attempt, much of the doctrine is at variance with modern science. So is, for instance, the Vedāntic interpretation of the World Soul (*Hiraṇyagarbha*) as a form of subtly structured matter composed of innumerable particles (*sūkṣma śarīra*), which are necessary for metempsychosis.

Like other exponents of neo-Vedāntism, Vivekananda never denies the concepts of *karma, saṁsāra* and *mokṣa,* but, as has been mentioned earlier, he interprets them in a rather peculiar manner. Vivekananda himself seems to realise, to some extent, the contradiction between his own and a scientific approach to these problems. In one of his works he quotes objections to the transmigration theory, raised by some natural scientists who explain the innate properties of living organisms by heredity.[3] In reply to this, Vivekananda contends that to properly explain the said phenomenon, the hereditary mechanism alone is not sufficient, and that transmigration should be acknowledged as an additional property-transmitting "mechanism."[4]

Apart from all that, Vivekananda interprets certain *saṁsāra*-related mythologems in a naturalistic fashion and modernises them. For example, the Brāhmanical belief in "the path of the ancestors" (*pitṛ-yāna*) along which souls travel between the moon and the earth, is compared to the hypothesis of cosmic dissemination of life, which enjoyed great popularity at the turn of the century. Vivekananda makes more extensive use of certain originally naturalistic schemes, taken by Vedānta from the early Upaniṣads and from Sāṁkhya, to describe the evolution of the universe after it was brought into being by *Brahman*.

There are numerous allusions to the so-called scheme of the development of elements (from fine to gross), in which the process begins with cosmic ether (*ākāśa*), and ends with the earth (*pṛthvī*). Vivekananda likens this scheme to the late nineteenth-century physical theory of ether and even claims that the Vedāntic conception is more coherent. In actual fact, the conception of *ākāśa* was assimilated into Vedānta and revised by it very early; its evolution therefore was, from the very beginning, of an entirely different character than that of the physical theory mentioned by Vivekananda. To get an insight into its initial meaning we have to examine the aforementioned parallel contained in the Upaniṣads (particularly *ādhyātmika* and *ādhidaivata*), the

3. Swami Vivekananda, op. cit., vol. II, pp. 221-22.

4. Ibid., p. 89.

sophisticated process of gradual demythologisation of the cosmology in the Upaniṣads, and other problems. Naturally, all this has nothing to do with scientific experiment or scientific theory. For that reason, a comparative study of schemes that evolved in basically dissimilar historical backgrounds can only go as far as to advancing certain conjectures, such as the millennia-old concept of cosmic ether.

The tendency to modernise the naturalistic conceptions of the Upaniṣads, assimilated by Vedānta, has proved very persistent. In our time there are attempts to read into the Vedic canon and into Vedānta, elements of modern cosmology and cosmogony, Albert Einstein's theory of relativity, and so on. Very often such comparisons are grossly far-fetched. For instance, the special theory of relativity is compared to Advaita-Vedānta on the grounds that both deny absolute time and space, while no mention is made of the fact that Advaita also denies their objective nature on the level of *pāramārthika.*

Drawing a methodological parallel between Advaita and modern science is another device invented by Vivekananda, who believed that Vedānta is similar to science in its appeal to practical experience as a cognitive method and its inclination to see a hidden unity behind the diversity of phenomena.[5]

It should be pointed out that in this case Vivekananda abandons the traditional Advaitic approach, while according to Śaṅkara, intuition (*anubhava*) is the final stage of cognition rather than its source (in the conventional sense of the term *pramāṇa*), Śruti is the only source in the case of cognition of *Brahman*. It is, therefore, clear why Śaṅkara is strongly opposed to the interpretation of yogic experience as a

5. Swami Vivekananda, op. cit., vol. I, pp. 368-72; vol. VI, pp. 47-48.

legitimate source of cognition of supreme reality, whereas Vivekananda actually expounds this interpretation.

This deviation from orthodoxy, however, does not bring Vivekananda any nearer to scientific thinking. In his opinion, practical experience, being fundamental to Vedānta, is an ineffable experience of Unomnia in *turīya*. But by contrast with science, Vivekananda discards any correlation with the object, and the very idea of an object becomes meaningless. Experience is held to be absolutely (i.e. not relatively or just conventionally) direct and spontaneous.[6]

The thesis of the unity of the world in Vedānta and in science does not coincide either. Science refers to the unity of matter, which is proved by revealing the multiform and complex relationship between existing material objects, and not by reducing this complexity to some universal homogeneous entity, as stated in Vivekananda's works.

In the nineteenth century the west European influence on the formation of neo-Vedāntism was on the whole rather obscure. The observed alterations in Vedānta during this period had to do more with its social aspects than with the conceptual ones. But in the first two decades of the twentieth century there appeared attempts to analyse the interaction between the Indian and west European philosophies, and to revise certain Vedāntic doctrines for the sake of a cross-cultural synthesis.

Very important in this respect was the philosophical system enunciated by Bhagavan Das (1869-1958). Although his activity lasted a fairly long period of time, his principal ideas had been formulated within the first decade of this century in such fundamental works as *The Science of Peace* (1904) and *The Science of Social Organization* (1910).

---

6. Swami Vivekananda, op. cit., vol. VI, p. 430.

The title of the first of these two books is significant. In explaining it, Das points to such aspects of the sought-for "peace" as pacification of spirit, reconciliation of conflicting approaches to reality in general, and Eastern and Western thought in particular.[7] The last of these ideas is clearly neo-Vedāntic, while the others are traditional.

In the first six chapters of *The Science of Peace* he analyses the typical Indian and Western approaches to the principal (from his point of view) problem of philosophy — correlation of *singular* and *plural*. This fashion of formulating the problem slurs over the opposition between materialism and idealism, presenting materialism as just one out of many attempts to solve this problem, and an unsuccessful one at that. That is why his philosophical comparison of the East and the West boils down to singling out two kinds of idealism — Vedānta and classical German philosophy, especially as represented by Fichte and Hegel.

Das examines three different Indian approaches to this problem. All three have parallels in the West. In Indian philosophy these theories are Ārambhavāda (or in his interpretation, "the doctrine of a beginning"), Pariṇāmavāda (the doctrine of transformation) and Vivartavāda (the doctrine of reversal). Das describes the first theory as theistic and creationistic, the second as a complex of materialistic (and in the West also agnostic and positivist) doctrines, and the third as idealistic monism.

It should be observed that it is not quite correct to describe Ārambhavāda as theistic because in Vaiśeṣika some *sūtras* originally connect it with the creation of the world from atoms through the agency of *adr̥ṣṭa,* an invisible power (which was only later replaced by God). Das, however, neglects the materialistic and atheistic tendencies of early Vaiśeṣika.

7. B. Das, *The Science of Peace,* Adyar, 1948, pp. xii-xvi.

Das exemplifies the three said approaches by the classical Indian philosophies of Vaiśeṣika, Sāṁkhya and Advaita. In criticising the first approach, Das rejects the idea of the separation of God from the universe, and exposes the discrepancies of theodicy and the untenability of the thesis that the universe was created from nothing (as postulated in West European theology).

Turning to the second approach, he points to the complication arising from the dualism of Sāṁkhya and arbitrarily compares it to materialism in general, including European materialism (which, he alleges, invariably regards force and energy as independent elements). It is noteworthy that Das interprets the main anti-Advaita trends within Vedānta as modified versions of the aforementioned classical schools. Dvaita of Madhva, for instance, corresponds typologically to Ārambhavāda, and Rāmānuja's Viśiṣṭādvaita to Pariṇāmavāda. This explains why, from Das's point of view, Śaṅkara's Advaita is the most significant of the three main Vedāntic trends, as, unlike the other two, it evolved on its own, original basis. Nevertheless, this certainly does not make him concur with Śaṅkara's theories. Das holds that Śaṅkara's illusionistic approach contains a number of unremovable contradictions.[8] Thus, beyond demonstration remains the possibility of the emergence (even though illusory) of any entity from absolutely self-identical and non-differentiated source. Or beyond reconciliation are propertyless and all-exclusive *Brahman* and *māyā*.

Before offering his own view on these problems, Das turns, in *The Science of Peace* and *The Science of the Self* to classical German philosophy. More than others he favours Fichte, whose doctrine appears to Das to be closest in spirit

---

8. B. Das, *The Science of Social Organization*, Adyar, 1932, pp. 32-33.

of Vedānta. Das sees the three fundamental principles of Fichte's *The Science of Knowledge* as the most adequate expression of monistic idealism achieved in the West. At the same time he believes that these principles should be presented as merged together into one integral "act of consciousness." Besides, Das wants Fichtean and Hegelian *dialectics* to complement each other. He describes Fichte's dialectics as more *inward,* i.e. giving an insight primarily into the world's origin, while Hegel's dialectical method is held by him to be more *outward,* or concerned above all with the world's evolution and the self-recovery of the absolute idea after its self-alienation.

According to Das, the correlation of singularity and plurality is attained through his formula (logion) "I-This-Not" (*Aham-etad-na*), which, it is claimed, syncretises all the wisdom of the Upaniṣads, the whole of Hegel's philosophy and Fichte's three basic theses.[9] To Das, this logion is a transcendental logic, the highest form of logical description of the structure of the "all-embracing" (*saprapañca*) Absolute, in which all types of opposites are in unity, including (in consonance with Hegel and Vedānta) the ultimate opposition of "Being" and "Nothing";[10] for this reason there can never be any final description of the Absolute. The only adequate "description" is the infinite development of the universe, and Das logion is a clue to it.

The triple structure of the logion comprises *subject, object* and *interrelation* (the dialectical opposition "positive-negative"; the object is at the same time the subject and therefore a negation of itself). This basic triad is the first link in the long chain of subordinate triads. In constructing this chain, Das was influenced beyond doubt by classical

9. B. Das, *The Science of Peace,* pp. 117-19.

10. Ibid., p. 151.

German idealism. True, the "triad rhythm" in logic can be traced as far back as to early Vedānta (e.g. its "triple-structured" continuum *vyaṣṭi-samaṣṭi*), but in this tradition it only served as a "regulator" of a very general type and did not determine to any great extent the structures of Vedāntic philosophical schemes, whereas the whole of Das's system strictly abided by the triad principle.

Apart from the logion, Das's system involves the traditional triad of the attributes of *Brahman*: *sat, cit, ānanda*. Each of the logion's components can be correlated with one of the attributes of *Brahman*: *cit* — I; *sat* — this, *ānanda* — *is* not.[11] These attributes, in turn, correlate with the components of universal matter (*cit* — *sattva; sat* — *rajas; ānanda* — *tamas*); with the categories of quality, action and substance which are pertinent to particularised matter (*cit* — *guṇa, sat* — *karma, ānanda* — *dravya*); and also with the properties of individualised consciousness — knowledge, action and will (*cit* — *jñāna; sat* — *kriyā; ānanda* — *icchā*).

Along with these triads, which are related to "I" and "Not-I," of great importance in Das's system (especially in its natural philosophical part) are the categories which pertain to the relationship between "I" and "Not-I" (which Das also calls *śakti*, power). In the first place it is the triad "space-time-motion," every member of which entails a series of subordinate triads (the three spatial dimensions; the temporal aspects of the past, present and future; the beginning, interpenetration and termination in motion, etc). Of the same kind is the triad "action-counteraction-causality."

In *The Science of the Self* Das connects his system of triad categories with a classification of the sciences. (He made his first attempt to produce such a classification in *The Science of Organization*.) In conformity with his general scheme, he divides the sciences into three groups: (1) sciences of the

11. B. Das, *The Science of Peace*, pp. 237-38.

self; (2) sciences dealing with the relationship between the self and non-self; and (3) sciences of the non-self. What would be the purport of such a classification? Influenced by classical German idealism, Das defends his view of philosophy as "the science of all sciences," which is an obvious anachronism in the twentieth century, and attempts to squeeze science proper into his neo-Vedāntic scheme, referring to the latter as a metascience.

Yet, there is an echo of nineteenth-century Indian enlightenment ideas in his presentation of the hierarchy of scientific disciplines. Das, like Vivekananda, supported the movement for universal education. His classification is also a list of subjects that, he insisted, should be taught in India. Like many nineteenth-century Indian enlighteners, Das was concerned with the development of the natural sciences. He expressed some valuable opinions in this respect. He pointed to the growing role of mathematics, a tendency to differentiation and integration of diverse scientific disciplines, including integration of scholarly knowledge about the micro- and macro-cosmos.

For all that, Das's conception of science is essentially religious and parochial. He tries to present the latest achievements in physics (such as quantum mechanics and the theory of relativity) as proof of the verity of Hinduism in general and of Vedānta in particular. Sanskrit "terms" are coined for modern scientific disciplines, which are alleged to have analogues in ancient Indian culture (quite in the spirit of Dayananda); the basic conceptions of modern science "turn out" to be "codified" in traditional religious texts, and so on and so forth. Typical of Das is his shift from Vivekananda's notion of "scientific religion" to the watchword of "religious science."

Das's religious apologetics goes hand in hand with his political conservatism. Thus, while favouring ideas about

India's political independence, free economic development and literacy of the population, Das sees in the Laws of Manu the model for building a new society in India. Like most neo-Vedāntists he idealises *varṇāśrama-dharma* and, contrary to India's more radical-minded reformists, criticises the caste system (*jāti-vyavasthā*) only in general.

In the final analysis, Das's modernisation of Vedānta is not very radical. True, his Vedāntic scheme seems rather sound logically, but behind it one can discern the classical prototype, though somewhat blurred. One cannot but agree with P.T. Raju who says that Das's philosophy is typologically akin to *bhedābheda*.[12] Indeed, in both there are: (1) the all-embracing (*saprapañca*) Absolute, (2) its division into *Īśvara, jīva*s and cosmos, and (3) the contradistinction of the eternal and the transient, which goes with admitting the partial illusiveness of the multitudinous (not complete, as in Advaita). Characteristically, Das retains the traditional Vedāntic notion of the cyclical nature of the universe's evolution.

This traditional notion has been overcome in the essentially more radical, though formally less salient, version of Vedānta offered by Aurobindo Ghose, who put forward the concept of irreversible development of society and the world as a whole. The principal philosophical ideas of Ghose are expounded, above all, in his two-volume work entitled *The Life Divine*.[13] Quite traditionally, Ghose seeks a clue to the mystery of the universe in the human mentality, but he points to the need for a comprehensive approach, criticising one sided conceptions of human nature, namely as a purely biological entity (materialism), as a manifestation

12. P.T. Raju, *Idealistic Thought of India*, Cambridge: Harvard University Press, 1953, p. 320.
13. Sri Aurobindo, *The Life Divine*, Calcutta, 1944-47.

of the world life (vitalism), as a complex of ideas (subjective idealism), and as a spirit (spiritualism).

Here we see the famous Vedāntic teaching on the different aspects (*kośa*) of man, "divided" into several philosophical doctrines. It is remarkable, however, that in the very beginning of *The Life Divine* (chapters 2, 3) Ghose distinguishes between two diametrically opposite points of view, both of which he subjects to criticism. These are: ascetic spiritualism (roughly equivalent to Śaṅkara's Māyāvāda) and materialism.

The former, according to Ghose, is fraught with Oriental parochialism and the latter with occidental "one-sidedness." Like in Das's *Science of Peace,* the problem of a cross-cultural dialogue also comes up, albeit somewhat obscurely, in Ghose's theory. Ghose criticises both extremes from positions of axiology. In his words, they are two kinds of refusal to recognise the meaning and purpose of earthly existence. Ascetic spiritualism regards it as illusory and something to break away from into supreme being, whereas according to materialism, he maintains, earthly being is objective, but ephemeral and transient and therefore devoid of eternal purport.

To his axiological objections Ghose adds some ontological and epistemological arguments. For example, he denounces Māyāvāda (in Advaita) as inconsistent, because (1) it is essentially dualistic in spite of declared monism (*māyā* constitutes the second, after *Brahman,* universal principle); (2) *māyā* and *Brahman,* when compared, prove to possess properties opposite to those ascribed to them: impotent *māyā* appears omnipotent in creating the world, all-powerful *Brahman* fails to prevent *māyā* from so doing; and (3) the postulate that the relation between *Brahman* and *māyā* is inexplicable is nothing but an act of intellectual capitulation.

Significantly, in formulating his attitude to materialism Ghose follows the same scheme. He endeavours to reduce the materialist epistemology to the so-called theory of epiphenomena. As a result, Ghose obtains "the reverse" of Māyāvāda (matter is real, consciousness is unreal), to refute which the three above arguments, in modified form, would suffice. But, notwithstanding the formal likeness of these argumentative schemes, they are essentially different. In the first case, criticising a very special idealist school, Ghose involuntarily touches upon the weak points of idealism in general; in the second case, while attempting to criticise materialism as such, he in fact does not go beyond a critique of the vulgar and mechanistic forms of materialism. This gives Ghose the feeling of an easy victory, but dialectical materialism remains practically outside the field of his vision.

Then, what solution to the problem in question does Ghose himself suggest? He believes that to establish the right place for man in this world, it is necessary to consider the contrary processes of *involution* and *evolution*. In his system, the starting point of involution is *nirguṇa* (attributeless) *Brahman* — an indeterminate, indivisible and shapeless spiritual entity, an indiscernible unity of three infinite attributes: being (*sat*), knowledge (*cit*) and bliss (*ānanda*). This entity is similar to the one described in Advaita, but Ghose interprets it not statically (as Advaitists do) but dynamically, as possessing objective power (*śakti*), which endows *Brahman* with the faculties of self-manifestation, self-restriction and self-absorption. The universe comes into existence through the agency of these properties in the course of divine involution.

The first stage is connected with the manifestation of "super mind," which is the realisation of *Brahman*'s first faculty. Each of the three main attributes manifests itself as a unity of correlated principles: *ānanda* comprises love, joy and beauty; *cit* includes knowledge and will; *sat* appears as the Universal Self (*Puruṣa*), the World Soul (*Ātman*), and the Sovereign of the universe (*Īśvara*). These principles in turn give rise to subordinate categories. Love forms a triad which embraces loving, the beloved and the process of love; joy becomes a triad of the subject, the object and the process of joy, and so forth. This is the emergence of spiritual plurality, which (like Plato's *World of Ideas*) is analogous to material plurality. All the constituents of spiritual plurality are interpenetrating and inseparable, their emergence is a non-linear process. Ghose describes three stages of this process in the form of three "statuses" or "positions" of the supermind. At the first stage there is absolute identity of the subject and object, the second stage marks the beginning of their distinction, and at the third stage there comes a conscious self-identification of the subject with a multitude of spiritual objects.

Later, the second aspect of *śakti,* which is connected with *Brahman*'s faculty of self-restriction, becomes active. It results in the transition from the supermind to the so-called global mind, or overmind. The overmind singles out the emerging spiritual determinants of the world and arranges them in a special order.

The segregative function of the overmind produces three entities of the lower existential sphere: intellect, life and matter. It also produces the souls. These products of the overmind incarnate the four main principles of higher existential sphere (*sat, cit, ānanda,* and the supermind). Intellect corresponds to bliss (*ānanda*), which is held to be the supreme intellect of the soul; life corresponds to consciousness (*cit*); and matter to being (*sat*). The lower existential sphere is detached, or estranged, from the higher one as a result of cosmic ignorance (*avidyā*). The alienation reaches its culmination in matter, where all its intermediate stages are "dissolved," and matter becomes qualitatively homogeneous. This means that the initial stage and the final stage of the alienation process coincide. In the first case the inner homogeneity is caused by absence of limitations, and in the second case by utmost self-restriction. This is the third aspect of *śakti*, which determines *Brahman*'s faculty of self-absorption and completes the process of involution.

Clearly, Ghose's scheme of this process does not overcome the difficulty of deducing the world from the spiritual absolute. In the final analysis, the division of integral *Brahman*, the emergence of ideal plurality in the supermind and the following self-alienation of the spirit are as inexplicable as the creation of plurality by *māyā* held in Advaita.

Although Ghose's scheme of involution is quite original as a synthesis of the emanational principle with that of logical evolution (the latter was first employed by B. Das at the turn of the century), his approach to *evolution* is even more innovatory. One of his early articles, which appeared in *Arya* in 1915 and was entitled "Evolution," was devoted to criticism of Herbert Spencer's theory of evolution, which Ghose mistakenly identified with the materialist approach to evolution. He negated the concept of gradual rectilinear development picturing development as a spasmodic and interruptive process, with qualitative and quantitative changes, with alternating advancements and recessions, a process which on the whole is more similar to a spiral than a straight line.

This concept is also expounded in *The Life Divine*, where Ghose describes three main principles of the evolutionary process: ascent, expansion and integration (part II, chapter 18). In the course of evolution are observed: (1) quantitative complication (the emergence of ever more complex material structures, which is a step towards the germination of life); (2) qualitative transformation (transition from inorganic structures to organic ones, the inception of thinking, etc.); and (3) transformation of inferior forms and incorporation of them into superior existential forms, which determines the cyclical character of the whole process.

In the article "Evolution," Ghose does not consider the struggle of opposite tendencies of development as a separate subject. But in *The Life Divine* and some other works he deals extensively with this question. He believes that everything in the world (and perhaps the world itself) was brought into being by the confrontation of material and non-material powers. The conflict of diverse powers, trends, principles and phenomena is the motive force of universal evolution; it destroys the old and gives rise to the new.

In 1916 and 1917 Ghose published in *Arya* a number of articles on Heraclitus of Ephesus, in which he dwelt on Heraclitus' conception of the correlative aspects of opposites — identity, conflict and transition. Ghose concurs with Heraclitus in this, but with a number of reservations. According to Ghose, conflict is the initial, not the final stage of development. Love supplants conflict, which helps the supreme spiritual motive power rise over the "blind mechanism" of development. Ghose interprets the struggle of opposites only as the "mechanism" of evolution, not as its source. It should be remembered that it is exactly over the question of the source of development that the metaphysical and dialectical approaches to evolution become antagonistic. Notwithstanding the indisputable dialectical element found in Ghose's theory of evolution, the metaphysical tendency prevails, which fact is directly connected with his spiritualism and with the mystical quality that he ascribes to the nature of development.

First, Ghose regards evolution essentially as the

evolution of consciousness. The sequence (reverse to involution) of the progressive stages of evolution — matter, life and intellect — is presented correspondingly as the unconscious, the subconscious and the conscious. Further development, through change of attitude to the subliminal and the transconscious, leads to the superconscious.

Second, evolution is treated theologically. Its source and aim is the supermind.

Third, in the course of evolution there is interaction of the pure aspects of being (which are formed during involution) with the mixed, matter-born aspects. Thus appear peculiar modifications: the sensual mind, the vital mind, and so on.

Fourth, evolution is accomplished with the supermind's descent to the lower sphere of being and its supramentalisation.

This is the beginning of the last stage of evolution, which results in the transformation of humanity into superhumanity, a society of "gnostic beings" who "implement" the Divine on earth. This ideal has something in common with that proclaimed by Vivekananda, an ideal of general emancipation and a society of *jīvan-muktas* (the emancipated). But, in contrast to Vivekananda, Ghose's "gnostic beings" are physically immortal, and transformed matter reaches the summit of the evolutionary spiral, which is an *irreversible* process (i.e. not repeated in the cosmic cycles). In this lies the essential difference between Ghose's integral Vedānta and the classical teachings as well as the other neo-Vedāntic doctrines, including Vivekananda's and Das's philosophies.

Ghose believes that the highest stage of evolution can be achieved not individually, but by *the whole of humanity.* That is why the theory of social (and cultural) development constitutes an organic part of Ghose's philosophy. The main principles of this theory are presented primarily in two of his works: *The Human Cycle* and *Ideal of Human Unity.*

The first edition of *The Human Cycle*, published in *Arya*, was entitled *The Psychology of Social Development*. The principal stages of history are treated in it with regard to changes in mass psychology which, Ghose holds, determines the character of any historical epoch. Like K. Lamprecht, a prominent German representative of the so-called cultural-historical school of the late nineteenth century, Ghose names five such epochs — symbolic, typal, conventional, individualist and subjective. Characteristically, Ghose omits the first and final phases of the historical cycle as described by Lamprecht, namely "natural consciousness" and "nervous irritability." The scheme therefore gains a meaning radically different from that intended by its inventor. Lamprecht sought to show the origin, development and decline of religious consciousness, whereas Ghose regards the crisis of religion as only a transitory episode in human history; he believes that religious ideas triumph at the beginning and end of history. Incidentally, Ghose sees history as a spiral rather than a circle, because it moves on from the infra-rational stage to the rational and then to the supra-rational stage. The initial and final stages, however similar, are far from being coincide. According to Ghose, along with the mentioned socio-psychological evolution there goes on the process of humanity's cohesion (which he examines in *Ideal of Human Unity*). The first, second and third stages are represented by pre-national cultures, the current, the fourth one, by national cultures, and the final (fifth) by super-national civilisations leading to a harmonised humanity.

In characterising the above stages, Ghose turns extensively to the history of India. In the first, "symbolic" era, dominated by the most primitive, pre-rational forms of consciousness, solitary sages (especially the Vedic *ṛṣis*) had profound revelations. These revelations, however, were expressed in symbols hardly comprehensible to the common people and primitively interpreted by them.

In order to enlighten people and to enable them to grasp the meaning of the symbol, there were attempts to reorganise the ordinary tenor of life with emphasis on moral and psychic perfection. Thus began the second, "typal" era, characterised in India by the setting up of a system of *varṇas* and *āśramas*. Reforming mass consciousness, however, proved no easy undertaking, for it was obstructed by inertness and egocentrism in individuals and groups. As a result, the ideals of this era were deformed, while social relations ossified during the era of "conventionalism."

That is how a hierarchical caste system took shape in India. It served the purpose of preservation of privileges rather than spiritual progress. The social system became increasingly rigid, which also told on culture: formally refined and exquisite, it lacked spontaneity. Escapism and asceticism grew rife. (Ghose cites Advaita as a glaring example of this.) But the more inflexible society and culture became, the nearer was their decline.

According to Ghose, reason is the power which puts an end to stagnation. The role of reason slowly but steadily grows even during the first three historical stages. Finally, in the era of "individualism," it comes into its own and breaks antiquated traditions.

Ghose illustrates the collapse of conventionalism, using for the most part examples from European history: the elimination of class privileges, the fall of certain "sacred" political (the monarchies) and religious (the church) institutions, the renunciation of centuries-old creeds. Ghose's attitude to these sweeping transformations is on the whole positive. He regards as important accomplishments of the contemporary epoch the eradication of superstitions, economic and scientific development, the triumph of democratic principles, the growth of national consciousness and other signs of progress. Yet he does not consider reason to be capable of achieving humanity's desired goal — that of building a harmonious society. The way out would be a transition to a supra-rational mentality at the last historical stage conducted with the help of spiritual mentors who would lead to a fraternity of "gnostic beings."

This is Ghose's general scheme of social evolution. Although it reflects some features of Indian social and cultural history, Ghose, in trying to deduce the social from the spiritual, in the final analysis misinterprets both. His approach to the development of society is purely ideological (in terms of the historical period in question) and therefore uncritical, whereas in his treatment of spiritual life he disregards its social basis and for this reason errs historically.

These traits are found in the majority of neo-Vedāntists, who tend to idealise the ancient period of Indian history (the "symbolic" and "typal" eras), criticise the feudal past (unlike B. Das's works, Ghose's criticism is expansive, versatile and often quite radical). Like most other neo-Vedāntists, Ghose favours anti-feudal reforms, while emphasising the importance of cultural tradition for avoiding contradictions in the new era.

The development of nations and their aspiration for independence are viewed by Ghose as the main positive result of the "individualist" epoch. This point of view is very characteristic of him, especially considering his early activities. Speaking of prospects for the future, Ghose sharply criticises the capitalist system ("commercialism" in his terminology), but refuses to accept socialism as a feasible historical alternative.

He presents the struggle between capitalism and socialism as resulting from the absolutisation of the ideas of freedom on the one hand, and of equality, on the other. In addition, he regards anarchism as an absolutised notion of "fraternity." To revive the once-integral formula *"liberté, egalité, fraternité"* is possible only by changing over to a supra-rational mentality. Therefore, according to Ghose, the contradictions inherent in capitalist society can be overcome not through economic and political restructuring, but by reforming mass psychology.

In Ghose's opinion social reforms depend on recasting the *human nature.* Historically, he believes, different aspects of human psychology have improved under the influence of various forms of culture which contributed to the development of man's will (morality), his emotional vision (art), his mind (science and philosophy), and his spiritual perception (religion). But these achievements have been only partial.

Only *yoga* can bring an adequate solution to the problem of man's perfection. Ghose's conception of *yoga* in a broader sense is this: *yoga* is life, and life is *yoga*. Historical (and even cosmic) development is a way which leads to superman and to a "gnostic society." In a narrow sense *yoga* is a complex of specialised methods applied for the accomplishment of this historical (and cosmic) goal.

By analogy with the denomination of his general philosophical teaching of integral Vedānta, Ghose defines his *yoga* as "integral" or "complete" (*pūrṇa*). Many of his works describe *pūrṇa-yoga,* the most noteworthy of them being a series of articles published in *Arya* between 1915 and 1921 under the title *The Synthesis of Yoga.*

Let us now examine the distinctive features of integral *yoga*. First, it incorporates the main types of the Vedāntic school of Yoga, outlined in the *Gītā* (viz. *karma-yoga, bhakti-*

yoga, and *jñāna-yoga*). The author of the *Gītā* accentuates, above all, the intrastructural integrity of these methods and their inter-reflectivity, while the later commentaries on the *Gītā* attempt to select one principal type of *yoga* and classify these methods in order of subordination. Contrary to this, Ghose points to their mutual complementarity. He deems all three methods equally vital for accomplishing the intended aim. They ought to be applied all together, none of them being treated as auxiliary or preliminary. These methods are meant to reform the chief aspects of man's psychology: *karma-yoga* — the will, *bhakti-yoga* — the emotions, and *jñāna-yoga* — the mind.

Second, Ghose sees the aim of his *yoga* not in *mokṣa* alone (as in the traditional yogic schools), but in a peculiar fusion of *mukti* (emancipation) and *bhukti* (pleasure), as "gnostic beings" shall not renounce the material world, but fill it with new spirit.

Third, integral *yoga* incorporates three stages of man's remaking — psychological, spiritual and supramental. The first consists in a breakthrough from the empirical self to the spiritual (subliminal). The second stage is the ascent of the spiritual self to the supreme sphere of being. The third is the descent of the supramental self to the lower sphere of being in order to transform it. This descent is described by Ghose in the fourth *yoga* (the *yoga* of perfection), which he adds to the three traditional Vedāntic methods. It is interesting to note that Ghose's vision of human personality contradicts the mainstream of traditional Vedāntic thought. Man in Ghose's theory is not an impersonal spirit (as held in Advaita) and not a static spiritual entity that has temporarily lost its identity in the world's flux (as in Viśiṣṭādvaita), but a dynamic personality.

Fourth, and this is perhaps the most significant distinction — integral *yoga*, unlike all the traditional *yoga*s, is an instrument for reforming the whole of society by reforming people individually. Ghose assigns a cardinal role to the cloister (*āśrama*), which is a practical, though mystical, embodiment of his philosophy. Ghose's philosophy, intended as a synthesis of Eastern and Western philosophical thought, is indeed a blend of several traditions, but all these traditions are idealistic. He certainly did not embrace the whole cultural heritage of the East and the West, as the publishers of *Arya* considered. In framing his system Ghose made use of the diverse trends of Vedānta, Yoga and Tantrism.

Of particular interest to us is his effort (following Vivekananda) to integrate the three main varieties of classical Vedānta. Ghose considered himself a disciple and follower of Vivekananda. But while Ramakrishna and Vivekananda envisaged such a synthesis on a cognitive-psychological plane (with reference to the stages of yogic experience and of advancement to the ultimate truth), Aurobindo Ghose added to this an ontological basis (with reference to the three phases of the supermind). This obvious difference shows how markedly Ghose departs from the traditional Vedāntic schemes.

The novelty of Ghose's and Das's theories is undoubtedly connected with the interaction between the Indian and European idealistic traditions. But the European influence in Ghose's works is by far less evident than in those of Das. Although familiar with Western philosophy, Ghose seldom refers directly to European thinkers, which can be explained by his "Asia-centrism." Charles Moore holds, not without grounds, that Ghose was largely influenced by the philosophy of Hegel, by his ideas of the self-alienation of spiritual being in material existence and its return, at the supreme stage, to cognised truth, as well as of the special role that human history plays in this respect in the cosmic process; of the leap from necessity to freedom as the meaning and purpose of history; of national spirit and the spirit of historical epochs (*Zeitgeist*), the realisation of the "absolute idea" in the development of various forms of social consciousness (art, religion, philosophy). The influence of Hegel's dialectical method can also be traced in Ghose's philosophy.

At the same time, the philosophies of Hegel and Ghose are different in a number of ways. Hegel absolutises human thinking, expounding a doctrine of the primary existence of logical categories. Ghose underlines the super-logical and conceptually inexpressible nature of the absolute. Hegel criticises the metaphysical deficiency of rational cognition and counterposes to it dialectical thinking. Ghose counterposes intuition to reason. Hegel seeks to make philosophy a science, Ghose considers a scientific approach useless in solving philosophical problems. All these liken Ghose's teachings to the views held in the English neo-Hegelian school of philosophy of the late nineteenth century (Thomas Green, Edward Caird, Francis Bradley), which, incidentally, promoted the spread of Hegelianism in India.

Ghose's teaching on evolution is in some points similar to various versions of the west European doctrines on "creative" and "emergent" evolution. Noteworthy is the interest that some scholars specialising in the studies of Aurobindo Ghose's legacy display today to the comparison of his philosophy with Bergson's teaching. Ghose's notes on Bergson saw the light of day for the first time in the jubilee edition of Ghose's collected works. In these notes Ghose favours Bergson's critique of the intellect and his conception of the advantages of intuitive knowledge. He writes with appreciation of Bergson's concept of the priority of power over inertia, life over death, and freedom over fate. Ghose also concurs with Bergson in criticising (from a spiritualist standpoint) the theories of mechanism and reductionism and in extending the concept of "life" (in his principal work Ghose distinguishes between life as a stage of evolution and "life" as a universal cosmic entity contained in all matter). They both emphasise the hopelessness of any scientific analysis of the creative aspects of evolution.

Some scholars draw curious parallels between Ghose's and Teilhard de Chardin's theories of evolution. These are just parallels, however, for any influence either way is absolutely out of the question (not like in Bergson's case). Tielhard himself, on reading *The Life Divine,* after Second World War, was amazed to discover that Ghose's train of thought was "just like his own, but in an Asiatic manner." Indeed, disregarding the dissimilarity of the traditions, backgrounds and scholarly interests of both thinkers, the likeness of their teachings is striking. In both cases the purport of cosmic evolution is seen as the perfection of consciousness, and this process is interpreted teleologically; both thinkers point to three similar stages that precede evolution (Teilhard's "prelife-life-thought" and Ghose's "matter-life-consciousness"); and finally, the whole process results in an eternal union of individuals (Teilhard's "superlife," Ghose's "supramentalised" humanity). This resemblance is in no way a coincidence; it can be explained, by the common philosophical task of the two thinkers — to bring the modern concepts of evolution in harmony with the spiritualistic traditions. In seeking to resolve this task, Teilhard moves from creationism to pantheism of a mystical kind, while Ghose embraces the Oriental variety of pantheism and modernises it, rejecting the archaic conception of closed cosmic and social cycles.

Of all the social undertakings connected with the name of Aurobindo Ghose, perhaps the most remarkable is the project of Auroville, the City of the Future. In conformity with the resolution of UNESCO, the project was inaugurated on 28 February 1968.

The project of Auroville bears an unmistakable imprint of Ghose's religious Utopia. The city is designed as a centre for integral *yoga*. For this purpose Matrimandir, the Temple of the Mother, is erected in the heart of the city. But the goal of the project goes far beyond these intentions. Ghose often confessed that he dreamt of a fraternal unity of all nations. The Auroville project, approved by representatives of many states, envisages this city as a centre for extensive study of diverse cultural traditions for the sake of bringing nations closer together, for acquainting various nations with one another's life and culture. This objective makes the city of Auroville an embodiment of the noble aspiration for world brotherhood.

CHAPTER FOURTEEN

Muhammad Iqbal
As an Islamic Reformer

MARIETTA STEPANYANTS

ACCEPTANCE of religion as the most perfect form of social consciousness constitutes Iqbal's philosophical world outlook. "Philosophy," he wrote, "must recognise the central position of religion and has no other alternative but to admit it as something focal in the process of reflective synthesis."[1] Iqbal did not deny the importance of science and philosophy in the process of cognition, but he held that ultimately only religion can save unfortunate mankind from all calamities. Among all religions he gave preference to Islam as being the most perfect.

Recognising that "conservatism is as bad in religion as in any other department of human activity," Iqbal admitted the need to "reconstruct" the religious teaching of Islam.[2] Although he took into full account the "philosophical tradition of Islam," he tried very hard to reform Islam in the light of more "recent developments in the various domains of human knowledge."[3] Of the philosophical heritage of Muslim thinkers Iqbal was most of all attracted by the philosophy of the medieval mystics.

---

1. Iqbal, *The Reconstruction of Religious Thought in Islam*, Lahore, 1962, p. 2.
2. Ibid., p. 183.
3. Ibid., p. 51.

The influence of Sūfism had a great influence on Iqbal's theory of knowledge and concept of personality. To a large extent Iqbal assimilated the Sūfi interpretation of intuition and its role in the process of cognition. His understanding of the relationship between man and God, his concept of the "perfect man" and ways of achieving this perfection largely derived from the ideas of Ibn al-Arabi, Rumi and al-Jili.

However, it is noteworthy that Iqbal never accepted the Sūfi world outlook as a whole. He adopted a critical attitude toward Muslim mysticism, and as the years passed the criticism became increasingly sharper. For example, he did not subscribe to the view of those who regarded intuition in isolation from reason. For Iqbal, intuition and thinking were two inter-connected and necessary processes of cognition.[4]

Struggle: The Essence of Man

Iqbal vehemently criticised Sūfism for its advocacy of shunning everything that links man with the mundane world and thereby achieving, through the release of the particle of the divine essence contained in man, his merger with God. Iqbal perceived in Sūfism the danger of reducing all human activity to passive mystical contemplation. Criticising Sūfism, he wrote:

> The ultimate aim of the ego is not to *see* something, but to *be* something. . . . The end of the ego's quest is not emancipation from the limitations of individuality; it is, on the other hand, a more precise definition of it. The final act is not an intellectual act, but a vital act which deepens the whole being of the ego, and sharpens his will.[5]

---

4. Iqbal, *The Reconstruction of Religious Thought in Islam,* p. 196; Vahid, *Iqbal: His Art and Thought,* L. 1959, p. 76.
5. Iqbal, *The Reconstruction of Religious Thought in Islam,* p. 198.

Muhammad Iqbal, expressing the spirit of the new times, championed creative activity and struggle as the true expression of man's essence, being convinced that the "world is not something to be merely seen or known through concepts, but something to be made and re-made by continuous action."[6] He maintained that mysticism "destroyed the ego's creative freedom" and therefore "medieval mystic technique" could no longer serve as a method for cognising truth.

In order to arrive at a new method Iqbal turned to the experience of the West. "With the reawakening of Islam," he wrote, "it is necessary to examine, in an independent spirit, what Europe has thought and how far the conclusions reached by her can help us in the revision and, if necessary, reconstruction of theological thought in Islam."[7] Iqbal borrowed from the West the intellectual tools most appropriate for his philosophical concepts.

His main aim was to construct a philosophic system that would be based on a "modernised" religious philosophy of Islam. He sought to demonstrate that Islam had not become obsolete and that its precepts had only to be expressed in the terms and concepts of the new age. Hence Iqbal strove to find points of contact between Muslim philosophy and contemporary Western philosophy. For example, he was especially drawn by the epistemological concepts of Kant and Bergson because, as he believed, they could be enlisted as proof of the "correctness" and "modernity" of the philosophy of Islamic Sūfīsm. (The Sūfīs claimed that the possibilities of reason were limited and that "ultimate problems" could be cognised only with the help of mystic experience.)

6. Iqbal, *The Reconstruction of Religious Thought in Islam*, p. 198.

7. Ibid., p. 8.

It was no accident either that Iqbal turned to Fichte's philosophy. In the latter's interpretation of the concept of ego he found definite points of contact with the philosophy of Muslim medieval mystics who claimed the inseverable connection of the human "I" with divine substance. Moreover, in the pluralism of Leibniz, Iqbal saw a similarity with the pluralistic concept of the philosophy of *kalām*.

In short, Iqbal accepted from Western philosophy ideas which could be reconciled or in some way "combined" with the Muslim philosophical traditions. However, his attitude towards the philosophy of Nietzsche has become controversial. Some students of Iqbal claim that his entire philosophy is a kind of repetition of the Nietzschean philosophy — E.G. Browne, for instance, defines Iqbal's philosophy as mainly an adaptation of the Nietzschean philosophy.[8] A diametrically opposed view is held by others who deny the influence of Nietzsche on Iqbal, asserting that there is nothing in common between their philosophies.[9]

Both views seem to miss the point. Iqbal undoubtedly felt the influence of Nietzscheism but, far from becoming its follower, he sharply criticised it. To a certain extent the attraction of Nietzscheism was determined by another, no less important, premise (mentioned earlier), from which Iqbal proceeded to work out his philosophical system: the need, in pragmatic terms, to create *a philosophy of action* in a period of incipient national liberation movement in India. That is why Iqbal was drawn by the ideal of the Nietzschean superman, a personality of strong will capable of "heroic existence."

8. E.G. Browne, *A Literary History of Persia*, IV, Cambridge, 1924, IV, p. 41; Radhakrishnan, *History of Philosophy: Eastern and Western*, I, p. 512; P.T. Raju, *Idealistic Thought of India*, p. 393.

9. Vahid, *Iqbal, His Art and Thought*, p. 97.

Nietzsche's criticism of Christian asceticism which dooms man to slavish passivity appealed to Iqbal because he himself was bitterly opposed to the asceticism preached by Muslim mystics. Iqbal borrowed some images from Nietzsche, including those of diamond and coal, as symbols of firmness and lack of will.

Although attracted by Nietzsche's philosophical writings and literary talent, Iqbal never did accept the very essence of Nietzscheism. He admitted that Nietzsche had the ability of "divine seeing," and in this sense the ability to become a prophet. But Nietzsche, maintained Iqbal, could not become one, because he relied solely on his own faculties and did not have in his spiritual life "guidance from without." Moreover, the principles of his philosophy could be carried out only by the elite, by strong personalities, as opposed to the "herd."[10] Nietzsche's atheism and cynical aristocratism made his doctrines unacceptable to Iqbal, who based his entire world outlook on faith and believed in the inseverable connection of man with God and society.

After examining the main spiritual sources of Iqbal's philosophical views, an analysis of some aspects of his world outlook is in order. In constructing his ontological conception, Iqbal tries critically to revise the philosophical doctrine of *kalām* "to turn the Asharite scheme of atomism into a spiritual pluralism."[11]

He regarded in a positive light the *mutakallimūn* (dialectical theologians) idea of being as a whole, especially stressing its dialectical nature. Iqbal regarded as "dialectical" the postulate of *kalām* about the unlimited number of atoms constantly created by God, as also the proposition about accidents, the attributes of substances created each time anew

10. Iqbal, *The Reconstruction of Religious Thought in Islam*, p. 195.

11. Ibid., p. 72.

by God. He saw in all these assertions an expression of the idea that everything in the world is in constant flux and subject to change.

However, Iqbal strongly objected to the *mutakallimūn* proposition that all atoms and all substances are similar, and that reason or the soul is nothing but one of the accidents of substance. His criticism of this proposition was evidently determined by two causes. In the first place, he acted here from a consistent position of monistic idealism. Second, he believed that the *mutakallimūn,* by recognising the soul (*nafs*) as only one of the attributes of substance, assumed a position of "pure materialism" and thereby "oppose[d] the real trend of their own theory."[12]

Indeed, the *mutakallimūn* interpretation makes it possible to draw a conclusion regarding the existence of two substances: one possessing the aperception of reason (that is, the spiritual), and the other devoid of it (that is, the material). Iqbal opposed this dualism. "Reality is essentially spirit," he asserted. "The whole world is an expression of the Ultimate Reality — of God."[13]

God is the Ego which engenders a plurality of egos, each of which is His self-expression. "The world in all its details, from the mechanical movement of what we call the atom of matter to the free movement of thought in the human ego, is the self-revelation of the 'Great I am.'" Egohood is most perfectly expressed in man. "That is why," Iqbal concluded, "the *Koran* declares the Ultimate Ego to be nearer to man than his own neck-vein."[14]

Assertion of various levels of substance enabled Iqbal to revise one more proposition of the *kalām*. According to

---

12. Iqbal, *The Reconstruction of Religious Thought in Islam,* p. 70.
13. Ibid., p. 71.
14. Ibid., p. 72.

the Asharite interpretation, all bodies are composed of identical atoms and differ from one another only by accident. Thus man consists of the same substance as a worm. Man, like everything else in the world, possesses no internal potential and does only what is pre-ordained by God. For Iqbal such an interpretation of man's place and role in the universe was unacceptable. He believed (as noted before) in the creative activity of the human ego and in man's definite freedom of choice and action. That is why Iqbal claimed that the ego's substances differ, depending on the degree to which they express the Divine Ego.

"Man," Iqbal stated, "in whom egohood has reached its relative perfection, occupies a genuine place in the heart of Divine creative energy and thus possesses a much higher degree of reality than things around him. Of all the creations of God he alone is capable of consciously participating in the creative life of his Maker."[15] Iqbal admitted that in his criticism of the Asharite philosophy he was guided by the traditions of Muslim thought. This statement undoubtedly contains a measure of truth, and apparently the pantheistic school of Sufism exerted here a great influence on Iqbal. But, in the opinion of this author, Iqbal's main reasons for revising the *kalām* theory of being were the *new socio-political* conditions demanding fresh approaches to many philosophical problems, including the position of man and his role in society.

The form in which Iqbal's concept of being was expressed resembled in many respects Leibniz's monadology. This similarity is very clearly visible in Iqbal's followers, who include Pakistani philosophers, especially Khalifah Abdul Hakim, M.M. Sharif, and others. Iqbal's interpretation of the essence of being was the basis on which he and his followers developed their epistemological and ethical concepts.

15. Iqbal, *The Reconstruction of Religious Thought in Islam*, p. 72.

In the philosophy of the Muslim mystics (especially in the thought of al-Ghazzali) Iqbal found the most suitable approach to the problem of knowledge. What attracted Iqbal to al-Ghazzali was that his philosophic aim in the medieval world of Islam was similar to Iqbal's own, namely securing for religion the right to exist independently of science and metaphysics.

In his lectures, *The Reconstruction of Religious Thought in Islam,* Iqbal compared al-Ghazzali with Kant, saying that the mission of both was "apostolic," in the sense that both proceeded from positions of scepticism in the period of the greatest advance of rationalism and eventually succeeded in restoring religion to its rightful position. From Iqbal's viewpoint there was, however, an important difference between al-Ghazzali and Kant. "Kant, consistent with his principles, could not affirm the possibility of a knowledge of God," whereas al-Ghazzali, "finding no hope in analytic thought, moved to mystic experience, and there found an independent content for religion."[16]

Although Iqbal had high regard for al-Ghazzali's philosophy he nevertheless pointed to an essential shortcoming in his philosophical world outlook — his failure to understand that thought and intuition are organically related. Iqbal believed that thought and intuition were non-contradictory:

> They spring up from the same root and complement each other. The one grasps Reality piecemeal, the other grasps it in its wholeness. The one fixes its gaze on the eternal, the other on the temporal aspect of Reality.[17]

In contrast to most religious philosophers, Iqbal considered

16. Iqbal, *The Reconstruction of Religious Thought in Islam,* p. 5.
17. Ibid., pp. 2-3.

it necessary to subject the "data" of mystic experience to an intellectual and pragmatic test. He asserted that "critical interpretation" or the "intellectual test" by philosophers "leads us ultimately to a reality of the same character as is revealed by religious experience."[18] As for the "pragmatic test," it is a function of prophets.

Iqbal was primarily a religious thinker; simultaneously, his philosophy reflected the tendency of renouncing blind adherence to religious dogmas and developing the creative activity of man's reason. This tendency was further developed in Iqbal's ethical concepts.

Man, The Partner of God

Iqbal, poet and philosopher, advocated recognition of man's freedom of will. He regarded man as a creator, as a partner of God the Maker. In his poem, "Conversation of the Creator with Man," man speaks to his Maker as an equal:

God

I made this world, from one same earth and water
You made Tartaria, Nubia, and Iran.
I forged from dust the iron's unsullied ore,
You fashioned sword and arrowhead and gun;
You shaped the axe to hew the garden tree,
You wove the cage to hold the singing-bird.

Man

You made the night, and I the lamp,
And You the clay and I the cup;
You — desert, mountain-peak, and vale;
I — flower-bed, park, and orchard; I
Who grind and mirror out of stone,
Who brew from poison honey-drink.[19]

18. Iqbal, *The Reconstruction of Religious Thought in Islam*, p. 27.

19. Kiernan, *Poems from Iqbal*, L., 1955, pp. 93-94.

The recognition that man is a creator who transforms the world left to God only the role of the prime impulse, which created the world and then gave man full freedom of action. Seeking to resolve this contradiction, Iqbal asserted that God in this way consciously limited His omnipotent will. "It (this limitation) is born out of His own creative freedom whereby He has chosen finite egos to be participators in His life, power and freedom."[20] For Iqbal recognition of the freedom of the will was a prerequisite for the awakening in people of faith in their powers and potentialities. Describing man as a co-worker of God the Maker, Iqbal sought to convince his compatriots of the need for action and energetic intervention in the reconstruction of social life.

Iqbal accepted in his own way the Sūfī interpretation of the relationship between good and evil. In contrast to the *Koran*, which states that whatever good falls to the lot of man comes from Allah and whatever evil befalls man comes from himself (*Sura*, IV.79), medieval Sūfīs asserted that both good and evil in the world come from God. The Muslim mystics held that evil was objective and necessary for the realisation of good. Just as a bird can fly only by overcoming the resistance of the air, so man can become pious only by overcoming evil. That is why man has no right to complain about the existence of evil, but must accept it as necessary.

Borrowing this concept of evil from the Sūfīs, Iqbal transformed it into a contingency for realising good. But the spirit of pessimism and passivity underlying the writings of the medieval mystics was abhorrent to him. Also, in order to solve the problems of relationship between good and evil, Iqbal was attracted by the romantic and dynamic European philosophy of the seventeenth and eighteenth centuries.

20. Iqbal, *The Reconstruction of Religious Thought in Islam*, p. 80.

As a poet Iqbal perceived Western philosophical ideas chiefly through literature. That is why, for example, he borrowed the dialectical concept of good and evil from the poetry of Goethe and Milton. The problem of the relationship between good and evil is solved by reinterpreting the biblical legend (*Sura*, VIII.10-24) about the fall of man and his eviction from paradise. In contrast to the traditional religious interpretation of the legend, Iqbal welcomed the fall of man as a manifestation of the first act of his free will. "Man's first act of disobedience," he wrote, "was also his first act of free choice."[21] Since good is a product of free choice, it may be said that evil creates good. Iqbal's Iblīs-Satan, like Goethe's Mephisto, is a part of "the eternal force always striving for evil which created only good." Without it life would be devoid of dynamism, and dead passivity would prevail in this world. As in Milton's *Paradise Lost*, Satan in Iqbal's *Javid-Namah* (*The Book of Eternity*) is more attractive than God because he symbolises a more dynamic and creative spirit. Addressing God, Iblīs says:

> You created the stars, but they owe their movement to me.
> The world's hidden life comes from me, not from you.
> You breathed life into man's body, but it owes its dynamism to me.
> You followed the road of passivity, while I urged all to act.
> This Adam wrought of clay, devoid of vision and of narrow horizon
> Was begotten by you, but he will mature under my guidance.

---

21. Iqbal, *The Reconstruction of Religious Thought in Islam*, p. 85.

The revolutionary spirit of Iqbal's concepts of good and evil corresponded to the sentiments of many Muslims. Recognition of the objective existence of evil was of interest to them. This made it possible to explain all social difficulties and hardships not in terms of subjective causes, but in terms of existing objective evil personified by colonialism. By advocating the close connection of good and evil and their transmutation it was possible to substantiate and justify action against the social and political order of the day. Disobedience, active protest, and even violence, regarded by the prevailing morality as evil, were pictured as forces creating good.

CHATPER FIFTEEN

The Philosophical and Socio-Political Views of Maulana Abul Kalam Azad

MARIETTA STEPANYANTS

THE history of Indian Muslims — since the 1857-59 Uprising against British Rule, the first major anti-colonialist action in India, and up to the victorious outcome of the National Liberation Movement in 1947 — is characterised by a great variety of religious, philosophical, social and political trends. Politically, they embraced a religious-separatist movement which resulted in the formation of Pakistan, on the one hand, and a movement for unity of Hindus and Muslims in their struggle against British colonialism, on the other. During the concluding stage in the struggle for political independence, these two trends were personified by two political leaders: Mohammed Ali Jinnah, who led the Muslim League and the communal movement, and Abul Kalam Azad (1888-1958), an outstanding Muslim figure in the National Congress Party, who stood for the unity of Hindus and Muslims.

Revivalism was one of the leading trends in the religious-philosophical thinking of Indian Muslims, providing a framework for expression of ideas both by those who called for a return to medieval ways and who opposed the development of capitalist relations (the ideology of the Jamat-i-Islam Party), and by those who, like Abul Kalam Azad, sought to interpret Islamic precepts according to the requirements of the rising national movement.

The views of the ideological proponents of "Muslim nationalism," Jinnah in particular, have been considered in works by Russian and foreign Indologists. As for Abul Kalam Azad, until now Russian scholars have portrayed him primarily as a political figure, and his philosophical and social views have not received proper scrutiny. This paper purports to dwell on precisely these aspects.

Abul Kalam Azad's philosophical and socio-political views are inexorably linked with religion. This link was conditioned above all by the features characteristic of India's historical and socio-economic evolution in the nineteenth and early twentieth centuries. Another significant factor was Azad's background as a member of an Ulema family and his education in the Muslim tradition. Like many of his compatriots, he held religious faith to be an indispensable part of the life of every individual and of the social organism as a whole.

Azad sought answers to general philosophical questions in religion, believing that neither science nor philosophy could provide them. And when he entered the arena of political struggle, he sought in religion guidance for dealing with concrete political problems of the day.

Dissatisfied with the traditional interpretation of the *Koran*, Azad looked for new ideas. This he did not by trying to modernise Islamic dogma, but through reviving what he considered the original teaching. Thus he wrote in 1913 that Muslims did not need to lay down a new foundation or exhibit their ingenuity. Instead, they should revive and reconfirm what the *Koran* prescribed. There is no need, he maintained, to build a new house; one has only to come back to the one that was abandoned. Therein lies the fundamental difference between Azad's ideas as to what was to be done and the methods used by his contemporaries.[1]

1. See *Al-Hilal*, vol. 2, no. 21, Calcutta, 1913.

First in his articles and letters, and later in his translation of the *Koran* into Urdu and his commentaries, Azad presented his interpretation of Islam. According to him, the authors of previous commentaries "did not aim at representing what the *Koran* actually states." Every commentator had some view to advance and he used the sacred text to lend support to this view.[2] Moreover, the spirit of the *Koran* was distorted when its ideas were interpreted with the help of philosophical methods as well as by attempts to fit the *Koran* in the framework of Aristotelian logic. As a result, "the beauty and attraction of the Koranic method of argument and of demonstrating its truth was lost in a network of dialectical disquisitions. In fact, the truth had already been lost . . .".[3] He disproved the idea that the "Koran should support and endorse every new discovery in scientific knowledge."[4]

Azad saw his mission in helping the faithful to interpret the holy scripture in the way it was understood at the time of Muhammad. He believed that "the first generation of people among whom the *Koran* was delivered was not a sophisticated race. Their mind was not cast in any artificial or conventional mould furnished by civilisation. It was content to receive a simple thought in its plain simplicity."[5] Thus, he explained the origin of the word "Allah" as a reflection of the ecstasy and admiration experienced before the Almighty Creator, expressed in the exclamation *Illāh*, indicating wonder and the humbleness of man.

He did not try to go into a logical explanation for the

---

2. A.K. Azad, *The Tarjuman al-Koran*, vol. I, Bombay, 1965, p. XXXIX.
3. Ibid.
4. Ibid., p. XXXVI.
5. Ibid.

existence of God. He held that it was unnatural for man to doubt, or to reject, the existence of God because the "sense of God is inherent in human nature,"[6] a sense that cannot be effected by man's intellect or his environment.[7] According to Azad, it is as natural for man to anthropomorphise divine attributes as to have an unshakable faith in God's existence. Whenever man tries "to visualise a thing unseen or unfelt, he inevitably conjures up its qualities and feelings of which he is aware in his own mundane life . . . whenever man attempted to carve out an image of God, he gave to Him his own shape."[8] Consequently, only the *Koran* shows the middle way between the transcendentalism of the Upaniṣads which leads, in the final analysis, to rejection of all divine attributes and of anthropomorphism.[9]

Though the *Koran* recognises individual divine attributes (God is living, all-powerful, creating, merciful, all-seeing, all-hearing, all-knowing, etc.), none of them is similar to human attributes: "And when there is none like unto Him, it follows that whatever attributes that might be assigned to Him cannot be assigned at the same time to any other."[10]

Azad's interpretation of divine attributes formed the basis of his ontological views. He considered four main divine attributes, which in the first *Sūra* of the *Koran* are determined as *Rabbul-i-Alamin*, *Al-Rahman*, *Al-Rahim*, and *Malik-i-Yawmiddin*. The first attribute was interpreted as divine providence, thanks to which the world follows the laws of expediency and harmony. The world was created so that "whatever is needed for the existence and

---

6. A.K. Azad, *The Tarjuman al-Koran*, vol. I, p. 36.
7. Ibid., p. 102.
8. Ibid., p. 105.
9. Ibid., p. 127.
10. Ibid., p. 136.

sustenance of every being is provided at appropriate time and in appropriate quantity."[11] To illustrate his point, the commentator reminds us how water, drop by drop, reaches all the corners of the earth during definite seasons and in definite amounts. However, he chooses not to answer the question why divine providence deprives many of his compatriots of water while sending floods to others subjecting all to hunger as a result.

God's mercy is expressed, according to Azad, in the harmony of his creation. Philosophy falls short of explaining its proportion and beauty. The *Koran*, on its part, explains that the divine attribute of mercy, as well as other attributes, seeks its earthly embodiment, and finds it, in making each and everything appearing in the world good and beautiful.[12] This attribute also manifests itself as ". . . the law of gradualness or of steady movement," according to which violence should not be employed immediately against something which disrupts harmony and is evil.[13]

Azad also considers the social aspect of mercy and maintains that the *Koran* does not isolate the notion of mercy from that of justice: "The *Koran* . . . regards justice as mercy itself. It states that one cannot display in his life the sense of humanity, unless at the same time one sets one's face against every form of cruelty."[14] It is divine justice that preserves order in the world and ensures the ultimate triumph of good at all times.

Azad's emphasis that the *Koran* regards justice and punishment not as whims of God, but as an outcome of individuals' actions, is noteworthy. The struggle for justice lies, in Azad's view, at the core of one of the chief precepts

11. A.K. Azad, *The Tarjuman al-Koran*, vol. I, p. 25.
12. Ibid., pp. 48-49.
13. Ibid., p. 68.
14. Ibid., p. 84.

of Islam — *jihād*. All work and hardship for the sake of justice, all pain and suffering, spiritual and physical, endured on this sacred path, all struggle, each instance of the giving up of life or property, and all service in word or pen for the sake of truth and justice — all this is *jihād*, he maintained.[15]

Azad allowed for the use of violence in this struggle. An active participant in Gandhi's non-cooperation campaigns and non-violent resistance, Azad, nevertheless, thought it necessary to stress the difference between Mahatma Gandhi's views and his own. The observance of non-violence was in the nature of a religious precept for Gandhi; it was only a matter of political tactic for Azad. "Unlike Mahatma Gandhi my belief is not that armed force should never be opposed by armed force," Azad stated at a court hearing in 1921. "It is my belief that such opposing of violence with violence is fully in harmony with the natural laws of God in those circumstances under which Islam permits the use of such violence. . . ."[16]

The sociological inferences arising from Azad's interpretation of divine attributes are rather contradictory. On the one hand, by accepting the expediency and harmony of the universe, which are seen as an expression of divine providence and mercy, man is reduced to a passive existence in this beautiful and harmonious universe, and consequently any action by man to reorganise this world becomes senseless and irrelevant. But, on the other hand, by conceding divine justice to reward or punish the actions of man, Azad holds man responsible for his actions.

Azad recognised God as the guiding force in the process of cognition. Divine guidance (*hidāyat*) manifests

15. See *Al-Hilal*, vol. 2, no. 3, 1913.
16. M. Desai, *Maulana Abul Kalam Azad: A Biographical Memoir*, Agra, 1946, p. 56.

itself in the ability of human beings to have instinctive, sensitive and rational knowledge. But even the highest form of knowledge is imperfect, since, according to Azad, "what is beyond our senses, reason can scarcely comprehend. . . . Even in the sphere of mundane activity, which may be regarded as its field of operation, reason or intellect cannot always give us an effective lead."[17] But there is a force, he maintains, that can correct the mistakes of the intellect and show men the right way, and this force is divine revelation (*Al-Huda*), or, in other words, religion.

To the extent to which a man possesses instincts, feelings and intellect, he also is given the universal guidance of divine revelation.[18] This revelation, Azad held, was not a blessing confined to one individual, but was given to mankind in general, without any discrimination, through a number of prophets, whose teachings did not contradict each other, but aimed at uniting all peoples in their belief in the *oneness* of God.

Azad made a distinction between the spirit of religion and its outward expression. The *Koran* teaches, he maintained, that the specific features inherent in individual religions are not the distinctive features of the spirit (*dīn*), but of the outward expression of religion, of the ways and methods of worship (*shara* and *minhaj*). These distinctions are natural as they are determined by the different social conditions and times. "Every religion," he admitted, "has had to evolve its own ritual as demanded by its environment. The thing that matters is devotion to God and righteous living."[19]

Azad saw the main objective of religion to lie in bringing people together.

---

17. Azad, op. cit., p. 151.
18. Ibid., p. 152.
19. Ibid., p. 159.

> The message which every Prophet delivered was that mankind were in reality one people and one community, and that there was but one God for all of them, and that on that account they should serve Him together and live as members of but one family.[20]

The notion of one God for adherents of all religions and the ensuing notion of the unity of humankind worshipping one Supreme Lord was the nucleus of Azad's religious-philosophical system. This conception determined his political position *vis-à-vis* the Indian National Liberation Movement.

Beginning around 1911, he emerged as a champion of Muslim nationalism and an opponent of British colonial rule. His philosophical and socio-political views of that period were vastly covered by the two journals he published: *Al-Hilal* (from July 1913 to November 1914) and *Al-Bilagh* (from November 1915 to April 1916).[21]

He resolved to publish a journal to promote the formation of Indian Muslim public opinion after he had spent two years in Islamic countries such as Iraq, Egypt, Syria and Turkey (1907-09). The young Azad's political views were shaped, to a considerable degree, under the influence of his acquaintance with Iraqi revolutionaries, leaders of the Young Turk movement, and followers of Mustafa Kemal Pasha. Though the need to change the attitude of Indian Muslims towards the colonial regime became apparent to him earlier, as a result of the 1905 Partition of Bengal and subsequent events, it turned into a firm political conviction after this tour. Azad saw the involvement of his compatriots and fellow Muslims in political activity and struggle against the British as the chief task of his weekly.

---

20. Azad, op. cit., p. 168.
21. H.R. Bedar, *Abul Kalam Azad* (in Urdu), Rampur, 1968, p. 117.

Al-Hilal challenged participants in the Aligarh Movement who, following Syed Ahmed Khan, advocated co-operation between the Muslim community and the British, seeing in it the way to greater prosperity for Indian Muslims. Azad's resolute rejection of any collaboration with the colonialists was the first step towards breaking with the Aligarh school. It took him 10 years to prepare for the next and no less important step — renouncing the narrow religious nationalism that led to communalism and weakened the National Liberation movement. In the meantime, using *Al-Hilal* as his mouthpiece, he acted as a Muslim nationalist who insisted on unbreakable ties between politics and religion.

Of interest in this respect is Azad's interview published in the 29 December 1912 issue of *Al-Hilal*. "You have suggested separation of politics from religion," he said. "But if we do this what, then, is left with us? We have developed our political thinking from religion. . . . We believe that every thought which draws inspiration from any institution (including politics) other than the Koran is *kufr* (infidelity)."[22]

At that time, Azad did not think that Hindus and Muslims should pool their efforts in the struggle against the colonial authorities; moreover, he actually called upon his fellow Muslims to pursue what can be described as political separatism. "Islam," he insisted, "is such a perfect religion that its followers need not imitate Hindus in moulding their party. . . . The Muslims must not join any political party. They were the leaders of the world. If they submit to God, the whole universe will bend to their will."[23]

---

22. Quoted from A.W. Khan, *India Wins Freedom: The Other Side*, Karachi, 1961, pp. 22-23.
23. A.K. Azad, *Muzamin* (*Essays*) (in Urdu), Delhi, 1944, p. 25.

In opposing religious unity to national unity, he saw in each Muslim, first and foremost, a citizen of the world Muslim brotherhood. These ideas of Azad clearly bore an imprint of pan-Islamism, which was widespread in the late nineteenth and early twentieth centuries.

Azad was a more consistent proponent of the pan-Islamic theory put forth by Jamal ad-Din al-Afghani than any other Indian Muslim. Thus, unlike Muhammad Iqbal, who also came under the considerable influence of Afghani, but who did not deduce from the idea of pan-Islamism defence of the Khilāfat, Azad believed that political loyalty to the Khalif, the rallying of all the world's Muslims under him and complete subordination to him should become the main principles of a pan-Islamic society.

According to Azad, the subordination of the Muslim community to the Khalif should be political, not religious in nature, since religious guidance is the sole prerogative of God and His Prophet. To this he added a most important condition — political loyalty to the Khalif should be absolute only so far as he acts in strict observance of the precepts of the *Koran* and the teachings of the Prophet.[24]

What won Azad his popularity, however, were not his ideas of religious nationalism or even Islamic separatism, but the militant, anti-colonialist stance of his journals. It was not surprising, therefore, that *Al-Hilal* was closed down in 1915 and *Al-Bilagh,* which attempted to pursue the same line, had to stop publication in 1916. The publisher, Abul Kalam Azad, was banned from Calcutta under the Defence of India Regulations. The authorities in Punjab, Delhi, the United Provinces and Bombay also deprived him of the right to enter these cities and provinces, following which he was interned in Ranchi from autumn 1916 till the end of 1919.

---

24. A.K. Azad, *Mosaida-e-hilafat aur jazira-e-alarab* (Problems of the Khilāfat and Arabian Peninsula) (in Urdu), Lahore, pp. 20-25.

These years of internal exile proved decisive for Azad, who undertook a serious review of his positions. The primary motivation for this was apparently the rapid progress made by the country's National Liberation movement. But it was the backing given by the Indian National Congress to the Khilāfat movement that opposed the predatory policies of the imperialist powers against the countries of the Ottoman empire which compelled Azad to give up extreme Muslim nationalism and to champion joint opposition to British colonialism by Muslims and Hindus. Following Mahatma Gandhi's initiative, the Indian National Congress proclaimed its solidarity with the Khilāfatists and launched a sweeping agitation campaign in defence of Turkey and other Islamic countries.[25]

The evolution of Azad's views from religious nationalism to secular nationalism was largely dictated by the developments in Turkey and countries of the Arabic Orient, such as the elimination of the institution of Khalifs by Ata Turk and the growth of Arab nationalism based on the common territory and linguistic, historical and cultural background of various Arab peoples.

Having become a member of the Congress Working Committee in 1920, Azad remained for the rest of his life one of the party's most prominent leaders and a consistent champion of Muslim-Hindu co-operation. He was President of the Congress (1940-46), Minister of Education and then Minister of Natural Resources and Scientific Research (1947 58). Between 1951 and 1958, he was Deputy Leader of the Congress Party in parliament.

Encouraged by the progress of the liberation movement in India, Azad became convinced that success in the struggle

25. Congress backing was due not only to the anti-imperialist nature of the Khilāfat movement, but also to the fact that it helped rally the Muslim and Hindu communities in the struggle against colonial rule.

for national independence depended on the unity of all Indians, irrespective of their religious or linguistic background. He justly maintained that the so-called community issue should and could be resolved only after the attainment of political independence.

He held that the division of the country on the basis of religious affiliation, far from resolving Hindu-Muslim contradictions, would only exacerbate them. The creation of two states opposed to each other would not solve the problems of the minorities in either of them, he believed. Further, instead of allaying religious-communal fears, Partition would consolidate them for ever, by creating two separate states on the basis of religious and communal animosity. In fact, Azad came to realise that the Hindu-Muslim conflict, as any communal strife, stemmed not from religious, but from socio-economic causes. He said that the real problems of the country were economic, not communal; the differences related to classes, not to communities. Once the country became free the Hindus, Muslims and Sikhs would all see the true nature of the problems facing them and communal differences would be resolved.

He also foresaw the international consequences of the Partition and opposed it precisely because he did not want to see the integrity of the Indian state sacrificed for the sake of political independence.

> If an angel were to descend from the high heavens and proclaim from the heights of the Qutub Minar, "Discard Hindu-Muslim unity and within twenty-four hours Swarāj is yours," I will refuse the proffered Swarāj, but will not bulge an inch from my stand. The refusal of Swarāj will affect only India while the end of our unity will be the loss of the entire human world.[26]

---

26. Quoted from *Maulana Abul Kalam Azad: A Memorial Volume*, ed. Humayun Kabir, New Delhi, 1959, p. 49.

Azad upheld the concept of a mixed nation against the demand for Partition and the underlying theory of two nations championed by the leaders of the Muslim League. In his younger years he had written and spoken emphatically for the isolation of the Muslim community and the advantages of Islam over other religions, in particular Hinduism, calling upon his followers to take the special Muslim road. But after the 1920s, he consistently upheld the inseparability of the destinies of Hindus and Muslims and of their main social and political interests.

In his presidential address at the Ramgarh session of the Indian National Congress in 1920, Azad stated:

> Our language, our poetry, literature, society, our tastes, our dresses, our traditions and the innumerable realities of our daily life bear the zeal of a common life and a unified society . . . our social intercourse for over 1,000 years has blended into a united nationalism.[27]

It might be worthwhile to compare the above statement by Azad with that of Mohammed Jinnah, leader of the Muslim League, who said that Muslims and Hindus are two different nations in the full meaning of the word. The Muslim nation is a nation of one hundred million and, more importantly, a nation with its own culture and civilisation, language and literature, art and architecture, names and place-names, values and laws and moral norms, as well as customs, calendar, history, traditions, affinities and ambitions, in a word, a nation with its own, special view of life.[28]

Those criticising Azad often accuse him of being contradictory.[29] In fact, his philosophical and socio-political views in later life were very different from those he held in

27. Quoted from A.W. Khan, *India Wins Freedom*, p. 27.
28. Quoted from A. Beg, *The Great Revolution*, Karachi, 1959, p. 13.
29. See A.W. Khan, *India Wins Freedom*.

his youth. However, this contradictoriness is not evidence of his inconsistency, it only shows the logical evolution of Azad's views in the course of the historical development of Indian society. Having once revised his former convictions, Azad firmly, even courageously, advocated his new views prompted by his experience of the struggle for liberation.

Azad based his conception of nationalism on the common territory, history and culture of the peoples of India. Nationalism, according to this rather ambiguous definition, is "a special state of belief in the collective life of man,"[30] one of the highest stages in the development of human relations and collective feelings. It is a higher stage, he claimed, than the awareness of family or kinship ties, than the feeling of community shared by the inhabitants of a village, town or district. Azad linked nationalism to a common country, a definite and common territorial and historical background.

It is important to point out the distinction that Azad made between different kinds of nationalism — the "aggressive" and "defensive" types, those of oppressing and oppressed nations respectively. Referring to the history of European nations, he stated that though "nationalism was born to defend the freedom and the rights of man, later on it became the greatest impediment to their achievement."[31]

According to Azad, Islam does not reject nationalism unless it is of the aggressive type, but it values it less than affiliation to one's religion, a sentiment which unites peoples from different countries, to say nothing of the awareness of belonging to a world of human brotherhood. Although the ultimate goal of Islam consists in achieving this highest stage, only the one-before-last — or religious stage has been reached

30. A.K. Azad, *Masaida-e-hilāfat aur jazira-e-alarab* (in Urdu), p. 151.
31. A.K. Azad, *Islam aur Nationalism* (in Urdu), Lahore, 1929, p. 37.

so far. What is referred to in this passage are the medieval Khilāfats. It is noteworthy that the pan-Islamic movement drew inspiration from an essentially identical ideal.

During the last decade of his life, Azad often elaborated upon the idea of world citizenship, especially while addressing international gatherings. He held that the methods of teaching geography and history should be reviewed so as to "bring out the unity of the world . . . and the unity of man."[32] In his speech of welcome at the Second Session of the Indian National Commission for Cooperation with UNESCO, he said:

> We must have new maps for children in the elementary stages *in which the world* will be painted in one colour; we must teach the child that he is a citizen of the world first and foremost, and then go on to tell him that just as a town is divided into different wards for purposes of convenience . . . so the world is divided into segments . . . but such divisions do not disrupt the unity of the world.[33]

This notion of world citizenship in effect stemmed from his concept of one God and religious pluralism. It reflected his hopes that reforms in education and a synthesis of culture could resolve both political and social conflicts.

The above also underlay his conception of the mitigation of the so-called conflict between the West and the East. He argued for the compatibility of Western and Eastern cultures, the differences between them being, in his view, an outcome of placing emphasis on different aspects of common problems.[34] It is of interest in this context to examine Azad's interpretation of the "Occidental" and "Oriental" concepts of man.

---

32. *Speeches of Maulana Azad 1947-55*, Delhi, 1956, p. 152.
33. Ibid., pp. 150-51.
34. Ibid., p. 180.

Azad maintained that in the West from the earliest times (that of the Greeks) philosophy devoted far greater attention to what man does rather than to what man is. With the advent of Aristotle, a trend was firmly established to focus attention on man as a rational animal, a tendency which ultimately led to Darwinism, Marxism and Freudianism.[35] Conversely, in the East, the focus of attention was directed at man's inherent spirituality. According to Oriental teachings, an individual cannot be comprehended unless he is regarded as divine emanation, and man is looked upon as the supreme expression of God's being.

Both the "Western" and "Eastern" concepts of man, however, suffer from a certain one-sidedness in interpreting the essence of man, which has ruinous consequences for mankind. The "Eastern" concept raises man to the level of deity (the *Koran* goes as far as to see in man God's regent on earth) and makes him superior to all creation, master not only of animal life, but also of the forces of nature itself.[36] Azad admits, however, that this concept also implies an element of fatalism, for since man is an emanation of divinity, whatever he does is due to the will of God. From this it is but another step to think of man "as a mere toy in the hands of fate."[37]

Another weakness of the "Eastern" concept, according to Azad, consists in that too much emphasis on the unity of man and God prompts indifference to human suffering, regarded, therefore, as illusory. The outcome is, to quote Azad, that "Eastern societies have often been indifferent to the removal of the causes of social malaise,"[38] and the

35. *Speeches of Maulana Azad 1947-55*, p. 180.

36. Ibid., p. 183.

37. Ibid., p. 184.

38. Ibid.

concept was often "an impediment to human progress."[39]

Conversely, the "Western" concept is distinguished by its heeding the need for social progress, which can be achieved as a result of the individual effort of each and every member of human society. At the same time, it underestimates the spiritual element in man. If man is seen as a rational animal, "there is nothing to prevent his using science to further interests based on the passions he shares in common with animals."[40]

Mankind's salvation can be achieved, according to Azad, through a synthesis of the "Western" and "Eastern" concepts:

> If . . . the achievements of Western science can be utilised in the Eastern spirit of man's affinity with God, science would become an instrument not of destruction, but for the establishment of human prosperity, peace and progress.[41]

As a matter of fact, these concepts are an attempt to reconcile idealism and materialism and to find a middle course between them. For Azad, to conclude the necessity of such a "synthesis" amounts, in our opinion, to evolution of his views from his unqualified adherence to a religious world outlook to the understanding that religion is incapable of resolving some of the most crucial problems of living.

Although he remained a religious man to the last, his faith in the power of religion as a progressive social factor, near fanatical at first, was severely shaken. During a conversation with Mahatma Gandhi's secretary Mahadev Desai in 1936, he admitted:

---

39. *Speeches of Maulana Azad 1947-55*, p. 184.
40. Ibid., p. 185.
41. Ibid., p. 187.

> Religion is a force whose power it is impossible to gauge. A bullock cart in charge of a stupid driver may at the worst cause an accident resulting in some injury to the driver and one or two people. But we know what happens when there is a railway accident. Hundreds of lives are lost and untold damage is done. Religion is like the mighty steam engine which needs to be in charge of a skilful and wide-awake driver. In the hands of an unworthy driver it can cause untold misery. To our great misfortune religion has fallen into unworthy hands. They have turned it into irreligion, and I do not know where we are going.[42]

Thus, having set himself, at the start of his career, the task of reading the *Koran* through the eyes of the first faithful Muslims, he hoped to uncover the genuine meaning of the Holy Book which could guide his contemporaries in dealing with problems posed by life. However, if we accept Azad's own just observation, made in the Foreword to his *Commentary on the Koran*, that "in every age, the author of a work is normally the product of his intellectual environment,"[43] adding to this that the environment is a product of concrete historical and socio-economic conditions, it becomes obvious that the task Azad set himself was unattainable. A man of the twentieth century could not afford to view the world through the eyes of people belonging to the ninth or tenth century. Although he excluded from this rule "those who are gifted with vision and insight," apparently including himself among those, he failed to avoid in his *Commentary* subjectivity in the interpretation of Islamic precepts. Despite his intentions, he interpreted the *Koran* as a man of his epoch, and of concrete historical and social circumstances.

---

42. Quoted from M. Desai, *Maulana Abul Kalam Azad*, p. 83.
43. Azad, *The Tarjuman al-Koran*, p. 31.

CHAPTER SIXTEEN

Philosophy of Non-violence
Lessons of Gandhism*

MARIETTA STEPANYANTS

> His voice may not be heard by many in the tumult and shouting of today, but it will have to be heard and understood some time or other if this world is to survive in any civilised form.
> — *Jawaharlal Nehru*

EVERY culture has its own scale to measure moral values. This, however, does not exclude its essential oneness with the value systems of other cultures. Proof of this is provided in particular by the eternal search for a higher ideal, the way to which is endless, like the ever-receding horizon. The summit of perfection, of moral height, towards which people aspire, is called by different names by different people. In India, one who "possesses a divine nature, has attained the highest perfection" and is no more subjected to rebirth is called a Mahatma — a great soul.[1]

How did it come about that this name was given in the twentieth century to a small-statured, frail-looking man with a long nose and thick lips — an ordinary-looking man, Mohandas Karamchand Gandhi, born in the state of Gujarat?

---

* Revised version of the text translated from Russian (Moscow 1992) by Ravi M. Bakya and published in Marietta Stepanyants, *Gandhi and the World Today: A Russian Perspective*, ed. Bimal Prasad, New Delhi, 1998.

1. *Bhagavadgita or the Song Divine* IX:13, VIII:15, Gita Press, Gorakhpur, 1958.

Why was it that this man — condemned by his enemies and ill-wishers variously as "an agent of British imperialism", "a servitor of the Indian bourgeoisie" and "a naked fakir" — found a place in history as a Mahatma? What is the explanation of the fact that of all the leaders of the Indian freedom movement it was to Gandhi alone that the people gave the name of a Great Soul?

Gandhi himself seems to have provided an answer to this question in a statement he made in 1929, in which he said that man's achievement consists in harmonising "*dharma* and the ultimate aim of life, truth and *swarāj*."[2] Gandhi's greatness lies in the fact that he was more sensitive than all other leaders to the thoughts and feelings of his countrymen. By providing the national freedom movement a religious and ethical motivation, he was able to inspire millions of people to be ready for great heroic deeds and sacrifices for the sake of a sacred cause. Mohandas Karamchand Gandhi was of the view that popular awakening could be brought about only through political activity and if such activity was spiritualised, it could show the path to *mokṣa,* that is, salvation.[3] Gandhi became a Mahatma precisely because he directed his religious reformation, his thoughts and deeds towards national regeneration and building up an ideal society based on universal prosperity.

After a short period of practice as a lawyer in India, Gandhi set sail for South Africa. In Pretoria, he and his compatriots came face to face with the crudest manifestations of racism. In his first letter to Leo Tolstoy (whom Gandhi considered "the highest moral authority") written on 1 October 1909, Gandhi described the situation

2. *The Collected Works of Mahatma Gandhi,* vol. XLI, Delhi, 1970, p. 211.

3. Ibid., vol. XIV, Delhi, 1965, p. 201.

in Pretoria in these words:

> There is in that colony a British Indian population of nearly 13,000. These Indians have for several years laboured under various legal disabilities. The prejudice against colour and in some respects against Asiatics is intense in that colony. . . . The climax was reached three years ago, with a law which I and many others considered to be degrading and calculated to unman those to whom it was applicable.[4] I felt that submission to a law of this nature was inconsistent with the spirit of true religion. I and some of my friends were and still are firm believers in the doctrine of non-resistance to evil. I had the privilege of studying your writings also which made a deep impression on my mind. British Indians, before whom the position was fully explained, accepted the advice that we should not submit to the legislation, but that we should suffer imprisonment or whatever other penalties the law may impose for its breach.[5]

Gandhi's proposed campaign of civil disobedience came to be known as *satyāgraha* which, translated from his native Gujarati, means literally "insistence on truth." What made Gandhi select such a method of struggle?

There is a widely held view that in his student years, Gandhi was subjected to such a strong Anglo-Saxon influence that he always remained British to the core, that the idea of *satyāgraha* was basically Christian and was borrowed by Gandhi from the Bible, from the Sermon on the Mount. This made one of the researchers into Gandhi's

---

4. The reference is to the so-called "Black Law" of 22 August 1906 which limited the right of Indians to live and travel in South Africa and put them virtually in the state of slaves.
5. *The Collected Works of Mahatma Gandhi*, vol. IX, Delhi, 1963, pp. 444-45.

life state: "*Satyāgraha* is a new Indian word for same old ways of Western thinking."[6]

There is also the opposite viewpoint, namely that Gandhism is an exclusively Indian phenomenon, which has grown from the cult of non-violence which is characteristic of Indian religions and of the Indian philosophical spirit.[7] Gandhi himself repeatedly acknowledged the influence of three Western writers on himself — Henry David Thoreau, Leo Tolstoy and John Ruskin. But he also constantly spoke about the Indian sources that formed his views. His acquaintance with the spiritual wealth of his ancestors began with the reading and learning by heart of the *Rāmāyaṇa,* while he was still in his pre-school years, and later the *Bhagavad-Gītā.* Later in life, he called this book "Mother Gītā" and sought guidance from it every time he was in need of help or advice. For Gandhi, the war between the Kauravas and the Pāṇḍavas was not of historical but of a symbolic significance. The call "Stand up and flight" he understood as a call to defeat evil in oneself.

The fact that Gandhi was brought up in an atmosphere where Hindus, Jainas, Muslims and Parsis lived peacefully side by side and where *ahiṁsā* was acknowledged as a principle of life, also played no mean role. It is therefore not fortuitous that the following line from a didactic poem in his native Gujarati, which he once came across, forever won his heart and his mind: "But the truly noble know all men as one. And return with gladness good for evil done."

---

6. A.L. Hermann, "Satyāgraha: A New Indian Word for Some Old Ways of Western Thinking", in *Philosophy: East and West,* Honolulu, vol. XIX, no. 2, April 1969, pp. 123, 125, 139.
7. See N.W. Ross, *Three Ways of Asian Wisdom: Hinduism, Buddhism, Zen and Their Significance for the West,* New York, 1966.

Persistence in Truth

Why did Gandhi call his method "insistence on Truth"? What did Truth mean to him? Researchers have spared no effort to unravel the meaning hidden in the basic Gandhian axiom "Truth is God."[8] A key to this riddle may be found in a letter that Gandhi wrote on 9 July 1932. In this letter, he spoke of the formula "God is Truth," which Gandhi later referred to as "Truth is God." In this letter, he says:

> In "God is Truth," "is" certainly does not mean "equal to" nor does it merely mean "is truthful". Truth is not a mere attribute of God, but He is That. He is nothing if He is not That. Truth in Sanskrit means *Sat*. *Sat* means "is." Therefore Truth is implied in Is. God is, Nothing else is.[9]

Gandhi's idea of Truth cannot be explained by a metaphysical description. It is not realisable by the mind, it is existential. "God is Truth and Love; God is ethics and morality; God is fearlessness. God is the source of Light and Life and yet He is above and beyond all these."[10]

In the statements quoted above, there clearly exists a pantheistically tinted vision. God-realisation is understood as realisation of Truth. That is precisely why Gandhi revised his previous formula. He attached tremendous importance to this and considered it the most significant of his theoretical discoveries. Thus Truth appears before us as a basically ethical category.

Gandhi considers absolute Truth (that is, God) unrealisable. At the same time he holds that the meaning of human existence lies in the effort to realise it. He further observes:

---

8. M.K. Gandhi, *Autobiography or the Story of My Experiments with Truth*, Ahmedabad, 1927, vol. I, p. 88.
9. *The Collected Works of Mahatma Gandhi*, vol. L, p. 175.
10. M.K. Gandhi, *All Men are Brothers*, Paris, 1958, p. 58.

> But as long as I have not realised this absolute Truth, so long must I hold by the relative Truth as I have conceived it. That relative Truth must meanwhile be my beacon, my shield and buckler.[11]

It is prompted by the "inner voice," in other words, conscience. One must live according to one's conscience, constantly striving towards perfection, towards the realisation of Truth in oneself and in society.

Such statements are possible only for one who takes a non-orthodox view of traditional religious precepts. In fact, Gandhi was convinced that man's ideas about religion are imperfect, and therefore they must constantly be the object of the process of evolution and reinterpretation. He considered a critical reading of the religious texts not only permissible but also necessary:

> Error no matter, however immemorial it may be, cannot derive sanctity, and even a Vedic text, if it is inconsistent with morality, with justice, will have to go by the board.[12]

Gandhi's own life was an example of an untiring, bold and decisive experiment with Truth. It is not fortuitous that his autobiography is called *Autobiography or the Story of My Experiments with Truth.*

Gandhi's experiments were basically different from those which are known in Hindu, Buddhist or Jaina traditions. They are not limited only to the internal world of man. They are conducted in the broad social context and involve not only individual but, of necessity, joint, collective efforts. We shall quote just one example. The main theme of Indian religious-philosophical thinking is the problem of suffering (*duḥkha*). Almost all Indian philosophical systems

11. See n. 8 above, M.K. Gandhi, op. cit., p. 8.
12. Mahadev H. Desai, *Day to Day with Gandhi*, vol.VI, Varanasi, 1970, p. 95.

are concerned with finding ways and means of ridding oneself of suffering. The causes of suffering are supposed to be bad behaviour in one's "former birth," that is to say, the blame for suffering falls on man himself because in his former life he was guilty of unworthy actions, was not pious, and so on. The solution suggested is either meek acceptance of the sufferings one is made to undergo and exemplary behaviour in the hope of a happier life in one's next birth, or snapping of the chain of *saṁsāra* through the achievement of *nirvāṇa.* Both these ways are meant for the individual and are marked by a certain egoistic and asocial character.

Gandhi also considers suffering to be "the law of human beings." He assumes that the guilt for this lies not only on the individual, but on society as a whole. And therefore freedom from suffering can be achieved only through efforts aimed at improving both the individual and the society. Gandhi's arguments often appear paradoxical. Thus, he avers that suffering can be overcome by suffering, which "is more than a tool of conflict resolution, it is a way of changing reality."[13]

In Gandhi's view the main source of suffering lies in violence which manifests itself in various forms. Therefore, one can get rid of suffering by responding to violence by non-violent suffering.

Violence is seen by Gandhi as the presence of the animal spirit in man whereas non-violence, in his opinion, is a sign of man's divine essence. This is why he asserts that non-violence is a synonym for Truth God, its "soul" and means of realisation. Hence, "*ahiṁsā* is one's highest religious duty." Gandhi admits that by itself the ideal of non-violence is not original. It is an "eternal truth." He sees his own contribution in that he tries to use eternal truths in everyday life.

13. See M. Chatterjee, *Gandhi's Religious Thought,* Notre Dame, Indiana, 1983, pp. 78-79.

The experiments conducted by Gandhi are virtually experiments with different forms of non-violence, which he carried out both on the individual and the social levels. Gandhi consistently followed the principle of *ahiṁsā* in his personal life. In 1906, at the age of 36, he took the vow to observe *brahmacarya*. However, renunciation of all forms of violence was nothing new. (It is well known that Jainas, for instance, observe strict *ahiṁsā*.) What was new was Gandhi's experiment in using *ahiṁsā* in the social sphere.

Satyāgraha in Action

The non-violent civil disobedience movement that Gandhi conducted in South Africa from 1908 to 1914 was very successful. The authorities had to make a series of concessions, which made life somewhat easier for the Indians. The *satyāgraha* attracted the attention of the international community. Among those who extended their support to Gandhi were Bernard Shaw, Albert Einstein, Bertrand Russell, Romain Rolland and Leo Tolstoy.

Gandhi returned to India in 1915. In May of the same year, he founded his Satyāgraha *āśrama* near Ahmedabad. His *āśrama* turned into a kind of laboratory for his social experiment of realising in practice the principle of non-violence in a collective manner. During this period, Gandhi's *satyāgraha* campaigns in India were conducted for protecting the rights of the peasants in Gujarat from being expropriated by planters and the British colonial exchequer.

The first all-India *satyāgraha* took place in April 1919. Gandhi later called it "a Himalayan miscalculation."[14] This was because it was not found possible to avoid violent actions. Gandhi saw his "grave error" in what had happened

14. M.K. Gandhi, op. cit., vol. II, p. 508.

in that he had called upon the people to launch civil disobedience prematurely.[15]

Gandhi looked upon *satyāgraha* as a method of meeting the just demands of the people. He considered it a *satyāgrahī*'s duty to act openly, refusing to be part of any kind of a conspiracy, plot, etc. A *satyāgrahī* must think not in terms of one or two, but in terms of 400 million people. No secret or underground movement could ever become a mass movement or awaken millions to mass action.[16]

A *satyāgrahī* is called upon to achieve his/her aims without causing physical or material harm to an "opponent." In case of punishment, he/she must accept it without a murmur, with utmost humility. Obviously, it is extremely difficult to conduct oneself in this manner. That is why it is necessary to prepare very seriously for participation in *satyāgrahas*. Constructive work is what drill is for an army, which is meant to conduct a bloody war,[17] wrote Gandhi. He believed that this type of work ought to inculcate in a *satyāgrahī* consciousness of strength, calmness and firm resolution.

Thanks to the efforts of Gandhi and his associates, *satyāgraha* got acceptance and support from the Indian National Congress. An extraordinary session of the Indian National Congress held in September 1920 adopted a special resolution, drafted by Gandhi, adopting "progressive non-violent non-co-operation." This resolution acknowledged *satyāgraha* as a national method of struggle against colonialism. The resolution noted, in particular, that the

15. See M. Chatterjee, *Gandhi's Religious Thought*, Notre Dame, pp. 508-9.
16. See Pyarelal, *Mahatma Gandhi: The Last Phase*, vol. I, Ahmedabad, 1956, p. 37.
17. Ibid.

people of India had only one way open to them — to accept and adopt the policy of progressive non-violent non-co-operation. A call was issued by this session appealing to the people not to buy foreign goods, not to participate in elections to legislative bodies, not to join the army, to boycott British courts, schools and colleges, to turn down titles of honour and to resign from posts in the local administrative organs.

The most striking example of *satyāgraha* was the world famous "Salt March" which Gandhi organised with the aim of demonstrating open and all-round violation of the law which gave a monopoly for the manufacture of salt to the British authorities.

Pragmatic Idealism

Referring to the method of *satyāgraha,* Jawaharlal Nehru wrote that it was a striking, though non-violent, form of resistance. In fact, it should be regarded as a peaceful uprising, a highly civilised way of conducting a war. It became an effective method for rousing the broad masses of the people to action, a method which suited the psychological make-up of the Indian people. This was precisely what many of Gandhi's opponents and critics failed to comprehend. They saw in this position Gandhi's weakness, a tendency to subject the interests of the people to those of the colonisers. This was the opinion even of some of those who claimed to have made a careful study of Gandhism. Here is a typical statement:

> Gandhi's non-violence turned into a historical phenomenon only because it suited the interests of the Indian bourgeoisie. ... Non-violence is the product of a metaphysical, idealistic contra posing of the spirit to matter, an artificial separation of man from his environment.[18]

18. C.V. Martyshin, *Political Views of Mohandas Karamchand Gandhi* (in Russian), Moscow, 1970, pp. 167, 187.

In fact, however, Gandhi's choice of this tactic of political struggle was notable for its realistic nature, for its perceptive understanding of historical possibilities as well as of the national psychology of the Indian people. Gandhi's choice was dictated not only by high moral ideals, but also by objective realities.

The man who was accused of "idealism" was in reality a pragmatist (in the good sense of the word), who realised that calling upon an unarmed people to revolt against the colonial authorities who relied on a well-organised machinery of state force (police, army, and so on) was tantamount to sanctioning a massacre, condemning tens, perhaps hundreds, of thousands of people to death. Gandhi's realistic pragmatism was also derived from the fact that he acknowledged the need for an ethical motivation of action on the part of his countrymen, who were known for their deep religiosity — for them killing a person in a certain sense meant killing their own selves. This kind of "moral suicide" could weaken the "fighting spirit" of those who participated in the movement for national liberation, and deprive the movement of its moral and religious basis. Gandhi's adherence to non-violence was not a sign of weakness. On the contrary, it expressed an optimistic faith in man, in the strength of his spirit, his ability to actively influence the surrounding world. Gandhi did not consider that ideology, moral level and ethical values are entirely a product of material surroundings. On the contrary, surroundings become what we are. We alone are the cause and the creators of our surroundings, and no one else.

Salvation is Freedom

What kind of "surroundings" did the Mahatma want to create? In the first place, he wanted a free, independent environment. Gandhi dreamed of establishing Rām Rājya, a kingdom of God on earth, based on the principles of *swarāj* — non-violent democracy. As always, Gandhi formulated his ideas in simple language, adding the context of traditional culture, to make them comprehensible to the average Indian so that he could attract the masses to the realisation of his ideas. For him *swarāj* was *mokṣa* — the ultimate goal of Hinduism, Buddhism or Jainism.

Gandhi interprets *mokṣa* as self-control in the broadest sense of the word. This is, above all, freedom from passions, from sinful attachments, a freedom which is entirely personal to the individual. Not long before his death, Gandhi was asked to explain in more definite terms what he understood by *mokṣa.* He replied,

> the desire for *mokṣa* was indeed there, but it was not meant for anyone other than the individual himself. The world was interested in the fruits, not the root. For the tree itself, however, the chief concern should be not fruits, but the root. It was in the depth of one's own being that the individual had. He had to nurse it with the water of his labour and suffering. The root was his chief concern.[19]

Man is freed from everything that is false and superficial, at the same time strengthening his own real "I" by means of "patience, perseverance, ceaseless toil, courage and intelligent appreciation of the environment."[20] *Mokṣa* or liberation, is therefore the result of self-control, which is the "truest *swarāj.*"[21]

From the statements quoted above it becomes evident that Gandhi interprets *mokṣa* as the affirmation of life on healthy foundations. Moreover, he sees *mokṣa* not as an exclusively individual goal, but as a social objective since the freedom of the people as a whole is built from the

19. *Harijan,* 28 September 1947.

20. *Young India,* 27 August 1925.

21. *Young India,* 8 December 1920.

"liberation" achieved by separate individuals. *Mokṣa* or *swarāj*, on a countrywide scale means, according to Gandhi, self-rule, liberation from the dictates of the government, no matter whether it is native, or foreign, i.e. British.[22]

In Gandhi's view, *swarāj* should ensure India a non-violent political structure. For this, it should be a decentralised structure and India ought to be turned into a confederation of free and voluntarily interacting villages, each of them being a State unto itself, having full powers.[23] The village will undertake to provide the inhabitants food, clothing, the organisation of law and justice, education and culture (a village theatre, school, hall for meetings, and so on), and also protection from possible external foes. The government will be carried out through the *panchayat* — five men and women, elected by the villagers. The only electoral qualification, apart from age, is labour: the right to vote will belong to those who engage in physical labour. The society, which consists of a free confederation of village republics will, in Gandhi's words,

> not be a pyramid with the apex sustained by the bottom — i.e. not an hierarchical structure based on force — but it will be an oceanic circle whose centre will be the individual. The whole becomes one life composed of individuals never aggressive in their arrogance, but ever humble, sharing the majesty of the oceanic circle of which they are integral units.[24]

According to the Gandhian concept of direct democracy the people, through a system of multi-stage elections entrust their power to those whom they choose — members of parliament which by itself does not possess any power and does not exist apart from the people.

22. See *Harijan*, 25 March 1939.
23. See M.K. Gandhi, "Village Swaraj", *Harijan*, 26 July 1942.
24. M.K. Gandhi, "Independence", *Harijan*, 28 July 1946.

State law is not absolute, because natural law stands above it. Natural law is defined simultaneously as religious law dictated by a person's conscience. Gandhi believed in perfect democracy being based on personal freedom: an individual is the creator of his own government; both he and his government are governed by the law of non-violence; he and his villages are capable of challenging the whole world.[25]

The concept of natural law was not explained in detail by Gandhi. From several statements made by him one may draw the conclusion that he understood "natural" as something given by God to man. Man is obliged to listen to the voice of his conscience, and his conscience, in turn, presumes doing his duty, that which in essence, is termed *karma* in Indian religious tradition. The real source of laws is duty. This teaching was expressed by Kṛṣṇa as: "Only action belongs to you, its fruits do not depend on you." Action is duty. The result of action is law.[26]

Gandhi's acknowledgement of *karma* as duty is evidence of his belief in the legitimacy of the caste system. No matter how radical he was as a reformer, he cannot get away from what constitutes the fundamental basis of his religious belief. Otherwise he would cross the limits across which lies a phenomenon principally different from what he wishes to reform.

What in other languages is called religion is given the name of *dharma* in India. Literally (in Sanskrit) it means "that which holds." The semantic meaning of *dharma* is multifarious. It includes cosmic law, which determines the order of the universe and is the basis of morality, ethics,

25. See Gandhi, "Village Swaraj", *Harijan*, 26 July 1942.
26. See S. Abid Husein, *The Way of Gandhi and Nehru*, New York, London, 1960, p. 38.

manifestation of reality, the teaching of Buddha, and so on. *Dharma* in Hinduism considers an ideal society to be one in which every individual performs his duty, his obligations conforming to the four stages of life — *āśrama dharma,* and four *varṇa*s — *varṇa dharma.*

Gandhi does not question the importance of maintaining stability in society, which is achieved by division of labour, i.e. caste pluralism. But his outlook is vastly different from the traditional attitude to the institution of caste — he is categorically against caste discrimination. The Mahatma does not see man's duty in observing formal, predetermined norms of behaviour. He sees it in following the inner voice of conscience. Everyone must know what is *dharma* and what is its antithesis. For Gandhi, *dharma* means selfless service of others. The root of *dharma,* he affirmed, "is compassion."[27] *Ahiṁsā* and *satya* are two talismans of "the royal road of *dharma* that leads both to earthly and spiritual bliss."[28]

Gandhi does not look upon caste affinity as a sign of superiority of some over others. He says, for example, that all should strive to be śūdras. He affirms the unity of people, their interconnection with one another, which is the result of the divine nature equally manifested in every person. It would seem that Gandhi undertook an impossible task. He declared that the outcaste Indians — the untouchables — are "children of God." And he called them *Harijan*s. Gandhi often said that though he belonged to a higher caste, in his next birth he would like to be born an untouchable.

As always, the Mahatma did not limit himself to declaring his beliefs. He tried to realise them. He founded the weekly *Harijan* in order to start a mass movement to remove caste discrimination. Gandhi demanded the

---

27. See M. Chatterjee, op. cit., p. 16.

28. Ibid.

necessary changes in law and — even more — a change in the personal attitude of every Indian towards the most deprived among his compatriots. He set an example himself by inviting untouchables into his *āśrama*. He made it obligatory for all those who lived in his *āśrama* to take a vow to fight untouchability. Gandhi undertook fasts many times to protest against caste discrimination against *Harijans*.

Similarly, Gandhi's adherence to the idea of unity of all people determined his attitude to those belonging to other religions. He was categorically against discrimination based on religion, rightly calling it a manifestation of violence and therefore *harām* — a sin.

Gandhi's statements on the subject of religion and politics and their relationship may appear contradictory. In point of fact, Gandhi asserted that religion is a personal matter and it should have no place in politics.[29] But he himself had said, that those who say that religion has nothing in common with politics don't know what religion is.[30] Thus Gandhi speaks as a partisan of secularism in the first statement, while in the second he speaks as its opponent. To understand and correctly interpret such statements it is necessary to read them in their proper contexts. The Mahatma spoke from a secular position when it was a question of "exploiting religion" for narrow selfish political ends. For example, he does not accept the theory of "two nations," according to which religion is the main factor in the formation of a nation. This theory was utilised by the politicians to justify the Partition of India into two states and for whipping up confrontation between the Hindu and Muslim communities. At the same time, Gandhi

29. See *Harijan*, 9 August 1942.

30. Cited in S. Radhakrishnan, ed., *Mahatma Gandhi: Essays and Reflections on His Life and Work*, Allahabad, 1944, p. 14.

is an opponent of secularism if by this term one understands the negation of religion in the organisation of social life.

The real significance of Gandhi's position can be understood if we consider at least three most important points. Firstly, genuine belief in God and service to God in Gandhi's thinking is service to the people.

> I recognise no God except the God that is to be found in the hearts of the dumb millions, they do not recognise His presence; I do and I worship the God that is Truth, or Truth which is God, through the service of these millions.[31]

Secondly, the Mahatma looks upon religion as a basis for bringing together human society. Gandhi held that different religious teachings are beautiful flowers from a single garden or branches of a mighty tree: all of them are true in equal measure. The Allah of Islam, Gandhi said, is the same as God of the Christians and the *Īśvara* of Hindus. Real faith assumes equal respect for all religions. It would be the greatest expression of intolerance — and intolerance is another variety of violence — to think that one's own religion is more perfect than the religion of the other.[32]

And, finally, the third point. As has already been noted above, the Mahatma saw the path to the realisation of Truth-God in non-violence, and only non-violence.

Thus, while affirming the unity of politics and religion, Gandhi, in essence, insists on morality as an obligatory factor in political actions.

Spinning Wheel vs. the Big Machine

For Gandhi liberation of the Indian people from colonial oppression was not the final objective of struggle. In freedom he saw only the first step towards building a non-violent civilisation.

31. *Harijan*, 11 March 1939.
32. *Harijan*, 14 May 1938.

Gandhi explained his views on civilisation in detail in his paper *Indian Opinion* as far back as 1908, while he was in South Africa. This "dialogue" of the editor (Gandhi) with the reader was later published as a separate brochure called *Hind Swarāj* or "Indian Home Rule."

By civilisation (in Gandhi's native Gujarati the word is *sadācāra* which means "good conduct") he understood that mode of conduct which points out to man the path of duty.[33] Contemporary Western civilisation does not correspond to this understanding and is therefore the incarnation of "evil." "The chief symbol" of Western civilisation is the machine which "represents a great sin."[34] Gandhi was opposed to the big machine because in machine-production he saw the destruction of cottage industries and the traditional Indian way of life. "It is machine that has impoverished India. It is due to Manchester that Indian handicraft has all but disappeared."[35] Gandhi compared machine production with a snake-hole which may contain from one to a hundred snakes: "cities destroying villages, slavery of the workers, horrible exploitation of female labour, unemployment, sexual laxity, lack of faith in God, and mechanical means of transport which harm the health of the people." Violence permeates Western civilisation in all its spheres — in economics, in politics, in mutual relations between people, in international relations. "The greatest sin" of the civilisation was imperialism.[36]

Gandhi was repulsed by the machine-dominated West because of the destruction of man's links with nature.

33. M.K. Gandhi, *Hind Swaraj or Indian Home Rule*, Ahmedabad, 1938, p. 61.
34. Ibid., p. 94.
35. Ibid., p. 93.
36. Ibid., p. 96.

Gandhi's world outlook fully reflected the attitudes of European opponents of machine-civilisation, so well expressed by Nikolai Berdyaev:

> Technology radically changes man's relationship to space and time. It is inimical to all organic bodies. In the technological period of civilisation man stops living among animals and plants. He plunges into a new cold-metallic atmosphere, in which there is no more animal warmth, no blood. The rule of technology leads to the weakening of emotionality in human life. . . . Technology kills all that is organic in life. . . . [37]

True civilisation, in Gandhi's view, must be based on the principles of conscious and voluntary self-restraint. In the economic field, this means relying on the villages and cottage industries. It was no accident that Gandhi chose the spinning wheel as the symbol of the national freedom movement. He looked upon the spinning wheel as an instrument of national regeneration. The spinning wheel could revive handicrafts and free the Indian people from dependence on colonial imports of cloth, ensure mass employment, and in this way remove unemployment in the country.

The Mahatma supported decentralisation of production. He considered conditions which promoted the accumulation of capital ruinous for the country. In his opinion, concentration of industries in the cities was responsible for the ruin of the villages. Gandhi wanted the villages and the rural community to be revived by putting the towns at their service. He thought it necessary to retain only certain types of heavy industry which were absolutely essential. He said, moreover, that it was necessary to establish state ownership over all

37. N. Berdyaev, "The Spiritual State of the Contemporary World", paper read in May 1931 at the Congress of Leaders of World Christian Federation. Quoted from *Novy Mir* (in Russian), Moscow, no. 1, 1990, p. 219.

such industries. Through the state, people will be the owners of the products of their own labour.[38] In all other spheres Gandhi preferred co-operatives (though he did not rule out individual production. He believed that, to the extent possible, all types of work should be conducted on a co-operative basis.[39]

While wanting to remove exploitation which he considered as a form of violence Gandhi, at the same time, did not support forcible expropriation of property. When he was once asked what he thought about complete abolition of private property, he replied that by destroying the capitalists, the workers will deprive themselves of the hen that lays the golden eggs.[40] Similarly, he thought that it was more rational not to abolish landlordism. He wanted to improve it because, in his own words, "the man who supplies brains and money is as much a tiller as the one who labours with his hands."[41]

Gandhi was against expropriation not because he was an "agent" of the exploiting classes, as was often stated. He had different reasons for holding this opinion. In the first place, he took into consideration the low cultural level of the basic mass of the Indian working people, the majority of whom, being illiterate, could simply not become independent producers. Secondly, he was against any kind

---

38. See Nirmal Kumar Bose, ed., *Selections from Gandhi*, Ahmedabad, 1948, pp. 67-68.
39. See M.K. Gandhi, *Rebuilding Our Village*, Ahmedabad, 1951, p. 5.
40. See M.K. Gandhi, *Towards Non-Violent Socialism*, Ahmedabad, 1951, p. 150.
41. M.K. Gandhi, *Economic and Political Life and Relation*, Ahmedabad, 1957, vol. Ill, p. 179.

of violence, even if it was sought to be justified by noble aims. He considered the path of consistent reform, personal and collective improvement, superior not only from the moral point of view, but also more productive and effective. In the Mahatma's view, gradual removal of private property was possible through trusteeship. To his impatient opponents, who thought that this type of transformation was too slow, Gandhi replied,

> The way to make the *kisāns* happy and prosperous is to educate them to know the reasons of their present condition and how to mend it. We may show them the non-violent or the violent way. The latter may look tempting, but it is the way to perdition in the long run. Seemingly the longest process is often the shortest.[42]

In the same way, in relations between the workers and the employers, Gandhi preferred peaceful settlement of disputes instead of confrontation. This does not mean that he was opposed to strikes in general. But he held recourse to legal means and arbitration more desirable. He considered the possibility of a strike only in extreme cases.

The Mahatma led a few strikes which ended successfully. When resorting to this means, he was guided by definite rules: Do not start a strike without appropriate preparation and do not use it for purely political purposes.[43] The latter is considered by Gandhi's critics as evidence of his "bourgeois nature." However, it seems that here too the Mahatma was guided purely by his thinking (which does not mean that he could not be mistaken on occasions). He did not say that strikes cannot be used for political ends but Gandhi believed

---

42. M.K. Gandhi, *Economic and Political Life and Relation*, Ahmedabad, 1957, vol. Ill, p. 179.
43. See M.K. Gandhi's article on strikes in *Young India*, 16 February 1921.

that one does not need great intelligence to understand that it is extremely dangerous to use workers for political ends unless they understand the political situation in the country. The greatest contribution the workers can make to politics is to improve their own living conditions, to be informed, to insist on their rights and even to demand from the owners proper utilisation of the products in the manufacture of which they play such a vital role.

The main principles of the Gandhian concept of the ideal social order are non-violence and hard work. If the former is sufficiently well known, the significance of the latter is clearly underestimated. But it is precisely in his attitude to work that we see with special clarity the reformist — one may even say the revolutionary — spirit of Gandhism.

As we have already said, in traditional Hindu society, according to the Hindu religion, priests, warriors and traders belonged to the upper, twice-born *varṇas*. The śūdras, i.e. those who were engaged in physical labour, were considered representatives of the "lower" castes. Gandhi's dream, however, was that all should become śūdras. Referring to the authority of the *Bhagavad-Gītā,* Gandhi asserted that it "contained the teaching of labour, of *bhakti* or devotion, of *jñāna* or knowledge. Life must be a harmonious integrity of all three."[44] The Mahatma did not see any difference in principle between religious salvation and worldly occupations. He assumed that self-sacrifice is nothing but labour in the sweat of one's brow to earn one's daily bread. Thus, for the Mahatma, an ideal person is not one who is a *saṁnyāsī* or ascetic, a monk living outside the world on alms, but a toiler who labours to improve earthly life.

In Indian culture there is the term *tapas* (literally, penance), inspired by religious fervour. We find the first

44. *Young India,* 3 November 1927.

mention of this in Vedic literature, in the *Ṛgveda* in particular. An ascetic who takes such a vow subjects himself to inconceivable trials; he spends many days surrounded by a ring of burning fires or under the burning sun in the hottest season of the year, standing on his legs for many years, and so on. Gandhi calls upon people to undergo *tapas* of a new type, which would lead to individual perfection and to the transformation of society.

The Mahatma experimented with collective forms of *tapas*. The first experiment of this sort was the foundation by him of the Phoenix settlement (not far from Durban in South Africa).

The idea of founding this colony, in which collective self-restraint was expected to lead to common living, appeared to Gandhi under the "magic spell" of John Ruskin's book, *Unto This Last*. This work by the British art critic and publicist contained a romantic critique of capitalism, which could be overcome by means of aesthetic and moral education of man "in the spirit of religion and beauty." In this book, Gandhi — in his own words —"discovered" some of his deepest convictions. "That is why I was so captivated by it and why it brought about an instant transformation in my life."[45] This is how the Mahatma sums up the basic teachings of Ruskin's book:

1. That the good of the individual is contained in the good of all.
2. That a lawyer's work has the same value as the barber's, inasmuch as all have the same right of earning their livelihood from their work.
3. That a life of labour, i.e. the life of the tiller of the soil and handicraftsman, is the life worth living.[46]

45. M.K. Gandhi, op. cit., vol. II, p. 107.

46. Ibid., pp. 107-8.

Gandhi decided to start realising these principles. With those who shared his views — people who collaborated with him in his paper *Indian Opinion* published in Transvaal since 1904 — he acquired in Phoenix 100 acres of land. Each family of settlers received a plot of three acres so that they might have the opportunity of making their living through physical labour. The people gave their spare time to working in the press which published *Indian Opinion.* All those who worked for the paper, irrespective of their racial or national origin, received the same monthly allowance — three pounds. Life in the Phoenix settlement was simple, democratic, ascetic and full of intensive labour.

This experiment was further developed in the Tolstoy Farm founded in 1910. An important reason for its organisation was the need to support the families of the *satyāgrahīs* arrested in Johannesburg. The farm was bought by Gandhi's associate, the German architect, Hermann Kallenbach. It was named after Leo Tolstoy as a mark of their admiration for his religious and philosophical views. In Gandhi's own words, during the first years of his life in South Africa he made an "intensive" study of such of Tolstoy's works as *The Gospels in Brief* and *What to Do?* But it was the Russian writer's *The Kingdom of God is Within You* which made the strongest impression on him.[47] On 1 October 1909, Gandhi wrote his first letter to the great Russian writer. In this letter, he drew Tolstoy's attention to the movement of "passive resistance" in Transvaal and asked his opinion about the ethics of conducting a competition for an article on the effectiveness of passive resistance which could help popularise the aims and methods of the movement.

Gandhi's second letter to Tolstoy was dated 4 April 1910, which he sent along with his book *Hind Swaraj,* or

47. M.K. Gandhi, op. cit., vol. I, pp. 212, 373.

"Indian Home Rule." A note in Tolstoy's diary shows that this booklet left a positive impression on the Russian writer. On 19 April 1910, he noted in his diary:

> This morning two Japanese came, wild people, moved to rapture by European civilisation. But from an Indian I received a book and a letter which show an understanding of all the shortcomings of European civilisation, even all its worthlessness.[48]

In his reply, Tolstoy wrote from Yasnaya Polyana:

> I read your book with the greatest interest, as I think that the question that you discuss in it — passive resistance — is a question of vital importance not only for India but also for all mankind.[49]

And finally, Leo Tolstoy received letters from Hermann Kallenbach and Gandhi at the same time in August 1910. Kallenbach informed him about the founding of the Tolstoy Farm, given to the "head of the Indian colony in South Africa," i.e. Gandhi "for the needs of the non-resisters and their families" and promised "to make every effort to live up to the ideas which you (Tolstoy M.S.) have so fearlessly placed before the world."[50]

In his third and last letter, Gandhi wrote to Tolstoy that "no other writings have left such a strong impression on Kallenbach" as Tolstoy's and therefore he took the liberty, after consulting Gandhi, to name the farm in Tolstoy's honour as a stimulus to further efforts to achieve the same ideals "which the writer had put forward before the world."[51]

The correspondence ends with Tolstoy's letter of 7

---

48. *Literary Heritage* (in Russian), Moscow, vols. 37-38, p. 346.

49. Ibid.

50. Ibid., p. 348.

51. Ibid., p. 347.

September 1910 which Gandhi received a few days before the great non-resister's death. It says, in part,

> Your work in Transvaal, as it appears to me at this end of the world, is work which is the most central, most important of all causes which are at present being pursued in the world and in which the people, not only of the Christian but of the entire world will inevitably take part.[52]

In its organisers' conception, the Tolstoy Farm was to become a prototype of the social organisation of the future. It was a kind of a commune whose members carried out various experiments on themselves — experiments of self-denial — for educating and strengthening their spirit. Thus they observed all possible fasts in the belief that for those whose minds are working towards self-restraint dietetic restrictions are very helpful. In fact, without their help lust cannot be completely rooted out of the mind.[53] But the chief motive of abstention was the desire "to live the life of the poorest people."[54]

Another type of experimentation was Gandhi's experiments in the sphere of education. Gandhi believed that only parents can give their children ideal education. Therefore, he looked upon the farm as a kind of a "family" and upon himself as the father of the family. The fundamental thing in Gandhi's system of education was labour, physical labour in the first place. There were no servants in the farm. All work — beginning with cooking and ending with sweeping off dirt — was done by the farm inhabitants. Children took part to the extent possible in all types of labour. Gandhi later recalled:

---

52. *Literary Heritage* (in Russian), Moscow, vols. 37-38, p. 351.
53. M.K. Gandhi, op. cit., vol. II, p. 181
54. Ibid., p. 180

> On Tolstoy Farm, we had made it a rule that the youngsters should not be asked to do what the teachers did not do, and therefore, when they were asked to do any work, there was always a teacher co-operating and actually working with them.[55]

Not more than three hours a day was spent on subjects of general education. Moreover, teaching was mostly oral, because Gandhi believed that the teacher is the real "textbook" for his pupils.[56]

Spiritual education was a much more difficult matter. Gandhi was of the opinion that "To develop the spirit is to build character and to enable one to work towards a knowledge of God and self-realisation."[57] In contrast to the generally accepted tradition of giving oneself up to self-realisation during the fourth phase of life, that is, on the doorstep of one's death, the Mahatma believed that "those who defer preparation for this invaluable experience until the last stage of life, attain not self-realisation but old age, amounting to a second and pitiable childhood."[58] Gandhi emphasised the need to educate one's spirit from an early age through "exercises," the choice of which depended wholly upon the way of life and character of the teacher.

These experiments in educating the spirit and collective living were continued in the *āśrama* organised by Gandhi and his followers in different parts of India.

Gandhi gave a new meaning to an *āśrama*. His *āśrama* was a place for collective self-improvement which was practised in order to transform worldly life. The *āśrama* was looked upon as a model of an ideal social structure, where all were equal, where there was no violence and where love

---

55. M.K. Gandhi, op. cit., vol. II, p. 193
56. Ibid., p. 202
57. Ibid., p. 202
58. Ibid.

reigned. Here there were no teachers and no taught. Here "family" relations were the rule.

Gandhi practised collective prayers of universal significance. For example, during the evening prayers it was the practice to read the last nineteen verses from the second chapter of the *Bhagavad-Gītā,* which called for ascetic self-restraint, self-control and non-violence.[59]

All Wars are Evil

The ideal of a non-violent civilisation can be attained only if there is a fundamental change in the character of international relations. For achieving this, Gandhi dreamed of creating a world government — at least a world union of free nations which would put an end to colonial oppression, guaranteeing the equality of all nations by preventing aggression and exploitation of some nations by others, protecting national minorities and pooling the world's resources for the sake of universal well-being.[60] He stressed the need for creating a world order that would be free from exploitation, would be based on the principles of equality of rights, mutual respect and co-operation of all nations. There is no doubt that in such a civilisation there would be no place for any kind of aggression. Gandhi believed that any war, of necessity, is evil. At the same time, he acknowledged the necessity of making a distinction between aggressors and those who take up arms because of being victims of aggression.

It is extremely important to note the position Gandhi adopted when the atom bomb was dropped on Hiroshima and Nagasaki. He did not see any justification for this action.

59. M.K. Gandhi, op. cit., vol. I, p. 165.

60. M.K. Gandhi, "Atom Bomb and Hiroshima", in *Non-Violence in Peace and War,* Ahmedabad, 1949, vol. II, p. 97.

Japan was guilty of committing crimes to achieve its unworthy ambitions, "but the unworthiness conferred no right on the less unworthy (Gandhi has in view the USA) of destroying without mercy men, women and children of Japan." Gandhi sees the tragedy of what had happened and felt that the atomic bomb had violated "the laws of war" which had guided people for centuries, and more importantly, it "destroyed the soul" of Japan and the United States, because one cannot put down violence by counter-violence: counter-hatred only increases the surface as well as the depth of hatred.[61]

Gandhi spoke up for disarmament and called upon the great powers to set an example by deciding unilaterally to give up militarisation.

No doubt, preaching love as a norm of behaviour in international relations may appear naïve. The Mahatma himself admitted that a long time will be needed for the laws of love to be accepted in international affairs.[62] All the same, he predicted that people would gradually and definitely move towards acknowledging the truth that "force does not solve any problems."

Non-violent Civilisation: Utopia or Ideal?

Non-violence is the ideological credo of Gandhism. This credo is not limited to the task of achieving national liberation for India or the radical reorganisation of Indian society on the basis of a re-interpretation of religious traditions. It has a universal dimension as, in the final analysis, it is directed towards the achievement of a world-wide non-violent civilisation.

---

61. M.K. Gandhi, "Atom Bomb and Hiroshima", in *Non-Violence in Peace and War*, Ahmedabad, 1949, vol. II, p. 97.

62. See *Young India*, 23 June 1919.

Is the Gandhian project for the future then the brainwave of an Utopian or an insightful perception of a world order which may be far away, but still possible as a matter of principle?

There are many who think of Gandhi's scheme as a Utopian conception which is archaic for our times and which is oriented towards preserving pre-capitalist community relations. Such arguments are not without basis. There are more than enough reasons for such a view if one looks at the statements made by Gandhi about machine production, about modern means of transport and energy, about towns which Gandhi saw as nothing more than "appendages of the village," about the monetary system and trade which he wanted to be reduced to inter-community natural exchange, etc. In fact, Gandhi can appear as the precursor of a modern social phenomenon which has become especially evident during the last decade. We have in view "fundamentalism" or "revivalism" of the Islamic, Hindu or other varieties. It represents in the Third World countries not only a broad but often a dominating socio-political trend.

The crash of hopes about the possibility of rapid economic progress after the achievement of political sovereignty, the failure of attempts to raise the country to the modern level of production by imitating Western models of development, stimulate the search for "national" models of social progress, give rise to idealisation of the past and to hopes that success would be achieved through the re-establishment of traditional values and institutions. "Revivalism" is a kind of reaction opposed to Western-oriented modernisation. That is not all. It is also, in fact, a sign of the reformation process directed towards the expression of internal impulses of development which would allow traditional societies to attain modern levels of living. Everyone who loves India, Gandhi believed, must stick to ancient Indian civilisation, as a child to the mother's breast. Healthy growth is possible only when one has strong roots which are fed by the life-giving juices of one's own soil.[63] Gandhi's "revivalism," however, is different from the movements to which we have just referred.

Gandhi's revivalism is absolutely free of national egoism. The Mahatma considered only that to be morally justifiable which does not harm the interests of others. He said that when the interests of someone's country do not conflict with the interests of the world, serving the cause of his country leads a man to *mokṣa*.[64] Gandhi based his internationalism on his conviction that mankind is one. God is "the sum total" of all souls, "we have but one soul," he liked to repeat.[65]

One of the main features of Gandhi's reformism is the fact that — being born out of Indian reality — it is oriented towards the transformation of the human community as a whole. Looking at this "universal" nature of Gandhism, his first biographer wrote:

> I question whether any system can absolutely hold him. His views are too closely allied to Christianity to be entirely Hindu, and too deeply saturated with Hinduism to be called Christian, while his sympathies are so wide and catholic that one would imagine he has reached a point where the formulae of sects are meaningless.[66]

---

63. See n. 33 above, M.K. Gandhi, op. cit., pp. 87-89.
64. See *The Collected Works of Mahatma Gandhi*, vol. XXXII, p. 430.
65. Chatterjee, op. cit., p. 132.
66. Joseph J. Doke, *M.K. Gandhi: An Indian Patriot in South Africa*, Reprinted by Publication Division, Government of India, New Delhi, 1967, p. 106.

The Mahatma himself, in his outer appearance and in his use of terms, concepts and symbols of Hinduism, constantly demonstrated his inseparable link with Indian culture. At the same time, he never tired of insisting on the unity of mankind. Man's ultimate aim is the realisation of God, and all his acts, social, political, religious, have to be guided by the ultimate aim of the vision of God.

> The only way to find God is to see him in His creation and be one with it. This can only be done by service to all. I am a part and parcel of the whole, and I cannot find Him apart from the rest of humanity.[67]

Gandhi's view of the future is not a linear, hierarchical representation of progress. It is in harmony with the most contemporary ideas. Two years before his death Gandhi wrote:

> Life will not be a pyramid with the apex sustained by the bottom. But, it will be an oceanic circle, whose centre will be the individual always ready to perish for the village, the latter ready to perish for the circle of villages, till at last the whole becomes one life composed of individuals, never aggressive in their arrogance, but ever humble, sharing the majesty of the oceanic circle of which they are integral units.
>
> Therefore, the outmost circumference will not wield power to crush the inner circle, but will give strength to all within and will derive its own strength from it.[68]

What is this? Is it an Utopia or a prophecy? Was not his attachment to the ideal of non-violence the most tragic error committed by the Mahatma? Does not the history of India and Gandhi's own personal end, so full of drama, prove

---

67. *Harijan*, 29 August 1936.
68. *Harijan*, 22 July 1946.

the hopelessness of the non-violent method of attaining one's goal, which he always defended?

Let us recall the great price India had to pay for her Independence — the Partition of the country on a communal basis and the creation of Pakistan in 1947. The Partition was accompanied by cruel communal riots. Gandhi's calls for religious tolerance and brotherhood more and more often evoked the harsh slogan (from both the Hindus and the Muslims) *"Gandhi Murdabad!"* — Death to Gandhi! And then on 30 January 1948, when Gandhi came out to meet the people during his evening prayer, a man emerged from the crowd and pumped three bullets into him at point-blank range. Independence could not be gained without bloodshed.

The embitterment of the people led to raging communal riots and the death of hundreds of thousands of people. The preacher of *ahiṁsā* was himself assassinated.

Then were Gandhi's asceticism and the ideals he preached all in vain?

An answer to this question is important not only for an evaluation of the historical events of the past. Without an answer to this question, the present generation cannot live with a clean conscience.

Gandhi himself provided an absolutely clear and categorical answer. Foreseeing a tragic end, he wrote on 15 June 1947:

> There is no hope for the aching world except through the narrow and straight path of non-violence. Millions like me may fall to protect the truth in their own lives; that would be their failure, not of the eternal law.[69]

But are we really justified in considering the Gandhian experiment a complete failure? Did the Mahatma not awaken the self-respect of his compatriots? Did he not imbue them — those who were forgotten, disarmed and bereft of

69. See n. 60 above, M.K. Gandhi, op. cit., p. 266.

hope — with faith in their power, in their ability to overcome evil? Did he not succeed in uniting them into a mighty liberating force, irrespective of their caste, class and religion? Was he not able to disarm many of his opponents by the example of his "suffering without vengeance"? And finally, did he not provide inspiration to the non-violent anti-racist movements in the USA and Africa and to the struggle for peace in the East, West, North and South?

To those lacking foresight, Gandhi will remain a hopeless idealist. But a penetrating mind will judge him as a "dreamer with his feet firmly planted in the ground." Being a hard realist himself, the Mahatma acknowledged the unreality of the complete triumph of the idea of non-violence in the near future. "I know that the progress of non-violence is seemingly a terribly slow process," he wrote in 1939, "but experience has taught me that it is the surest way to the common goal. Violence, even for vindication of justice is almost played out. With that belief I am content to plough my lonely furrow, if it is to be my lot that I have no sharer in the out-and-out belief in non-violence."[70]

The "bankruptcy" (in Gandhi's own expression) of the politics of non-violence in India was in the Mahatma's view not due to any fault in the concept as such. It was due to the fact that "non-violence of India's struggle was only in name — in reality, it was passive resistance of the weak who were incapable of armed resistance."[71] Non-violent resistance will, in Gandhi's view, become "the strongest force in the world" when people take recourse to it out of conviction. It will then turn into the non-violence of the strong.[72]

70. See n. 60 above, M.K. Gandhi, op. cit., vol. I, p. 211.

71. M.K. Gandhi, "Two American Friends", *Harijan*, 16 November 1947.

72. M.K. Gandhi, op. cit., p. 265.

Gandhi also soberly assessed the prospects for realising his design of a non-violent civilisation. Two years before his death, he wrote, referring to *Rām Rājya:*

> I may be taunted with the retort that this is all Utopian and, therefore, not worth a single thought. If Euclid's point, though incapable of being drawn by any human agency, has an imperishable value, my picture has its own for the mankind to live. Let India live for this true picture, though never realisable in its completeness.[73]

A non-violent civilisation, in fact, appears to be a Utopia. The movement of history is irresistible. Conservation of the past (the village community, rural civilisation, patriarchal family, and so on), however strong the nostalgia for it, is neither possible nor desirable. In this sense *Rām Rājya* may appear to contradict social progress.

Notwithstanding all this, the Gandhian design has also its positive features. It touches on the "sore points" of industrial civilisation, it is imbued with a critical enthusiasm which exercises a sobering, healthy influence on those seeking ways of overcoming socio-economic backwardness by blindly imitating alien social models. The Gandhian critique can be fruitful also for those who live in materially prosperous countries but are still conscious of the need for improvement and for a movement for a better world, not only for the chosen few among nations but for mankind as a whole.

And, finally, what is most important, Gandhi discovered for himself and revived for others a universal value — respect for the sacred gift of life. A civilisation without violence is an ideal towards which we are all called upon to march untiringly, a lighthouse illuminating the path lest mankind perish in darkness.

---

73. M.K. Gandhi, op. cit., p. 112.

CHAPTER SEVENTEEN

Sarvepalli Radhakrishnan's Perennial Philosophy

ALEXEI LITMAN

THE cornerstone of the metaphysical system enunciated by the outstanding Indian philosopher Sarvepalli Radhakrishnan is known as "universal religion," also called "the religion of the spirit." It is based on the idea that religion is one of the most important factors that determine the life of man, and that humanity in general as well as every particular individual need faith. "Human societies like human beings live by faith and die when faith disappears," declared Radhakrishnan.[1] "Belief might be difficult, but the need for believing is inescapable."[2]

He explains this tenacity of faith by the notion that religion shows the right life-path, implying any form of life. Religion, being the quintessence of life, helps forward man's spiritual evolution. "Religion is not a movement stretching out to grasp something external, tangible and good, and to possess it. It is a form of being, having a mode of life. Spiritual life is not a problem to be solved, but a reality to be experienced."[3]

---

1. Sarvepalli Radhakrishnan, *Recovery of Faith,* London, 1956, p. 9.
2. *The Philosophy of Sarvepalli Radhakrishnan,* New York, 1952, p. 25.
3. Ibid., pp. 67-69.

According to Radhakrishnan, only religion gives an insight into the mystical unity of all beings, which accounts for the important role religion plays in the life of man. R.P. Singh, who studied Radhakrishnan's teaching, rightly observed that Radhakrishnan understands and describes religion as mysticism that is founded on the demonstrable truths of spiritual life, and above all, the unity of being. For Radhakrishnan, mysticism is a true religion, the foundation for a new civilisation, as it reveals the very essence of faith — the spirituality and unity of the world.[4]

If mystical experience is part and parcel of religion, and religion in turn is a form of being or "a mode of life," an important question arises: which of the existing religions can today meet the intrinsic human need for faith? Radhakrishnan shows no preference for any creed, believing them all to be permeated with dogmatic fanaticism and prejudice and disunited by outward differences which, when exaggerated, breed mutual hostility, ruinous to both society and the individual. It is therefore only natural that atheism should become so widespread. Atheism, however, is opposed to fanaticism, prejudice and superstition, rather than religion as such. Denouncing these evils, atheists in fact help to get rid of them and reveal the true nature of faith. For that reason, "atheism has often been the expression of the vitality of religion."[5] Incidentally, in one of his speeches, Radhakrishnan stressed that "what the atheist denies is an idea of God, not God Himself," i.e. the atheist rejects only an ideal distorted by fanatical adherence to dogma.[6] He concludes:

Atheism has been, both for the individual and the society,

4. See R.P. Singh, "Radhakrishnan and Emergence of a New Civilization", *The Aryan Path*, vol. 35, no. 12, 1964, pp. 530-31.
5. *The Philosophy of Sarvepalli Radhakrishnan*, p. 25.
6. Ibid.

> a necessary means for the achievement of the larger truth. Sometimes we may have to deny God in order to find Him. Though they may not be aware of it, even atheists' revolt is in the name of God.[7]

Radhakrishnan saw the purpose of religion as being to raise man's spirituality and achieve inner harmony, integrity and self-esteem, while dogmatism and fanaticism cause inner conflict and a split personality by opposing the divine to the mundane, the spiritual to the carnal, thereby clashing with humanistic principles. In Radhakrishnan's opinion, humanism is a legitimate protest against those forms of religion which separate the secular and the sacred, divide time and eternity and break up the unity of soul and flesh. . . . Every religion should have sufficient respect for the dignity of man and the rights of human personality.[8]
Another reason for the growth of atheistic sentiments is the anti-humanistic nature of contemporary religions. It is this that makes a great number of people become unbelievers, and particularly because the various churches seem to have lost all sense of vital problems, including social issues that have become a matter of great concern to people.

Ideally, Radhakrishnan believes, religion should be closely connected with the life of society. It is capable of giving man "a spiritual shelter" and protecting him against the miseries of life. "Religion is a social cement, a way in which men express their aspirations and find solace for their frustrations."[9]

All of Radhakrishnan's reasoning is focused on the idea of a universal religion, the so-called religion of the spirit, which was conceived as an alternative to dogmatic creeds.

7. S. Radhakrishnan, op. cit., 1956, p. 803.

8. Ibid., p. 49.

9. Ibid., pp. 23-24.

There are already elements of such a religion in every existing faith. To adopt the religion of the spirit, it is necessary first of all to comprehend the true meaning of every religion and to discover the elements which are common to all the doctrines. It is only after the disposal of hidebound religionism that a synthesis of all religions can be attained and the true essence of religion fully revealed, so that religion's historic mission will at last be fulfilled.

The **problem of man** is central to Radhakrishnan's perennial religion due to its essential humanism. Radhakrishnan acknowledges the fact that human nature is very complicated and should be studied from different viewpoints — biological, sociological and political. Moreover, every man is also to be studied as an individual.

In his doctrine, however, Radhakrishnan treats man only as the most advanced biological species. Even while realising that man is a very peculiar species, he explains this peculiarity by the unity of body, mind and soul, the last two attributes being the most important for distinguishing man from the rest of nature.

> Man is more than a physical being. Psychology is not a mere extension of physiology. There is a part in man's nature which is not merely objective; it is this non-objective aspect which gives man his uniqueness in the world of nature. Man is not merely a creature of instinct, not merely a centre of mind. His nature is not exhausted by that by which he becomes an object of psychology, physiology or sociology.[10]

This conception of man is opposed both to the mechanistic and socio-historical approaches to the problem. Radhakrishnan considered the view of man as an "intellectual animal" or a "thinking machine" to be

10. S. Radhakrishnan, op. cit., 1956, p. 92.

inconsistent, as it ignored the basic qualities of the human being. He vigorously rejected the standpoint of some of the "leaders of our age who are fascinated by the triumphs of science and technology and speak of man as a purely mechanical material being, a creature made up of automatic reflexes. They emphasise the more earthly propensities of human beings and seem to be unaware of the higher sanctity that lives in them."[11]

At the same time Radhakrishnan does not accept the socio-historical approach, according to which man's ability to make tools and use them in order to change the world to meet his needs is man's distinctive quality. Rightly criticising the mechanistic theory and emphasising that there is more to man's nature than just his physiology and anatomy, Radhakrishnan fails, however, to see the social nature of man. He never admits that any individual existence is a manifestation of social being. Radhakrishnan holds that "there is something of the divine in every man" and "man with his sense of value is the most concrete embodiment of the Divine on earth."[12] The divine in man does not develop in the course of his natural evolution, nor is it a result of social advancement; it is a permanent quality, inherent in man and irrelevant to the natural environment. "Man has the spark of spirit and is not a product of objective nature. He is an *aṁśa* or fragment of the Divine and is therefore a principle of light and power."[13]

Assuming that man's divinity is his distinctive quality, Radhakrishnan claims that human nature is of spiritual origin. "Human beings are original, unique and creative

---

11. S. Radhakrishnan, *East and West: Some Reflections*, London, 1955, p. 119.
12. Ibid., pp. 115, 120.
13. *The Philosophy of Sarvepalli Radhakrishnan*, p. 805.

spirits who are not bound by the necessities of the space-time world."[14]

This view on human nature preconditions the approach to the problem of freedom, which occupies an important place in the perennial philosophy. Radhakrishnan opposes freedom to causality and necessity in nature.

> Metaphysical thinking, which bases itself on experience, holds that nature is grasped with the concept of necessity and the nature of the self by that of freedom. Without this concept our understanding of man's nature will be deficient and distorted. While both man and nature are the creation of God, the being of man is made in the image of God and is therefore quite distinct from the being of nature.[15]

The belief that freedom is an essential component of human nature imparts a truly humanistic quality to Radhakrishnan's theory. He comes to the conclusion that capitalism does not create the necessary conditions for freedom, but on the contrary hampers it in a multitude of ways.

> The capitalist system of society does not foster healthy relations among human beings. When a few people own all the means of production, the others, though they may be nominally free in the sense that they are neither slaves nor serfs, have to sell their labour under conditions imposed on them.[16]

In his perennial philosophy Radhakrishnan attaches great importance to the **moral** aspect of human life. His morality is founded on the thesis that faith and behaviour go hand-in-hand. There should therefore be some universal code of morality to comport with universal religion. The framing

14. S. Radhakrishnan, *Recovery of Faith*, p. 95.
15. *Philosophy and Culture: East and West*, p. 259.
16. S. Radhakrishnan, *The Recovery of Faith*, p. 25.

of such a code, however, is impeded by lack of unity in a society with different classes and ethnic and religious groups. That is why, according to Radhakrishnan, the adoption of a universal ethic is a prospect for the remote future, whereas today there are temporary ethical systems, conditioned by the realities of class struggle.

Although in no way a recognition of the class nature of morality, this mention of class struggle is worthy of note. Radhakrishnan not only recognises the capitalist system as an obstacle to the development of social morality, but is even inclined to admit the necessity of fundamental change in social life. He writes:

> Humanism assumes that man is by nature good and that evil rests in society, in the conditions which surround man, and if these are removed, man's goodness will emerge and progress will be achieved.[17]

This insight, however, was not developed any further in Radhakrishnan's work, as he adhered mostly to moral and religious principles. The admission that universal morality can only be attained as a result of spiritual evolution is one of the most important points of his theory. Only by making use of man's spiritual potential, he insisted, can a new type of mentality be formed.

In consonance with Indian religious and philosophical traditions and influenced to some extent by Mahatma Gandhi's philosophy, Radhakrishnan assigns a special role to love and non-violence as the most significant principles of the future universal morality. Like Gandhi, Radhakrishnan proclaimed love to be the principal law of human life and explained social disasters in terms of violation of this law.

Though he regards religion as the domain in which the

17. S. Radhakrishnan, *The Recovery of Faith*, p. 44.

law of love manifests itself most vigorously, Radhakrishnan is strongly opposed to religious chauvinism and considers its eradication absolutely imperative. This is another humanistic streak in his teaching.

The law of love is closely linked with the humanistic principle of non-violence. Like Gandhi, Radhakrishnan derives this principle from the important ethical category called *ahiṁsā:*

> If we believe that each individual has the Divine in him, it follows that our attitude towards others should be one of non-injury. *Ahiṁsā* is *vaira-tyāga* — renunciation of hatred. There is no question that all those who are free from fear, who have attained *abhaya,* will act in the world in a spirit of love and compassion — *karuṇā.* Love is the basis of all civilised living.[18]

Radhakrishnan was aware of frequent violation of the principle of non-violence and the law of love.

> In this world it is not possible for us to abstain from violence altogether. . . . By our self-effort we must reduce the scope of force and increase the scope of persuasion. So *ahiṁsā* is the ideal which we have set before ourselves.[19]

In accordance with these principal ideas, Radhakrishnan defined the state of moral perfection in the following manner:

> The hero is the new individual, the new man who will be able to fight the enemies within himself: stupidity, folly, clinging to the past, non-recognition of the fact that the world is moving and he who does not move will be swept

---

18. S. Radhakrishnan, *Occasional Speeches and Writings,* Third Series, 1963, p. 263.
19. S. Radhakrishnan, *Occasional Speeches and Writings,* First Series, 1956, pp. 223-24.

> aside.... Man himself is an instrument of the evolutionary urge. He can develop from the intellectual to the spiritual level.[20]

If the goal of historical development is the oneness of humankind, its accomplishment will be determined by man's transition from the intellectual to the spiritual level. Radhakrishnan believes that people's integration on a world scale will proceed on the principles of universal morality and the religion of the spirit and this process will be nurtured by humanity's spiritual resources, including philosophy and the arts.

Morality, art and philosophy are interrelated and interdependent, and in exactly the same way they are related to the religion of the spirit. Their symbiosis lays the groundwork for humankind's spiritual cohesion.

Radhakrishnan enthusiastically presents the fundamental principles of the religion of the spirit and of universal morality in order to philosophically substantiate the system of the perennial philosophy. The philosopher states that religious belief, as one of the basic necessities of life, must be a corollary of the individual's world vision. He writes:

> The faith has to be sustained by metaphysical knowledge. We have to think out metaphysical presuppositions and attain personal experience of the religious a priori from which all living faith starts. We need intellectual effort and spiritual apprehension, metaphysics and religion. Only reasoned faith can give coherence to life and thought.[21]

He also points out that the only philosophy that gives an insight into faith is one that provides a comprehensive and profound perception of life and the world, a constructive theory that explains the final judgements about this world

20. *Philosophy and Culture: East and West*, pp. 756-57.
21. Ibid., p. 258.

and is obtained by vigorous effort of the mind. Faith, therefore, should be rational.[22] The perennial philosophy is a metaphysical system conceived to introduce into faith a rational element.

The idea that there should be a universal philosophy in addition to universal morality to form a universal religion is the bedrock of Radhakrishnan's theory. He states:

> In my writings my main contention has been to make out that there is one perennial and universal philosophy which is found in all lands and cultures, in the seers of the Upaniṣads and the Buddha, Plato and Plotinus. . . . It is this spirit which binds continents and unites the ages that can save us from the meaninglessness of the present situation.[23]

Radhakrishnan holds that philosophy as such should not keep aloof from the problems of everyday life. Various philosophies appear out of the necessity to cognise life and the world. Philosophy is largely a result of contradictions arising in reality, rather than of any historical study of such contradictions. With this idea in mind Radhakrishnan defines the tasks of philosophy. They are: to explain this world, to arrive at the truth that constitutes the essence of being, to grasp the universe in its entirety, and not only its parts, as done in science, and finally, to become "a way of life," to "harmonise the various aspects under which reality appears."[24]

Only an ultimate, universal philosophy is capable of achieving all these goals, and this, according to Radhakrishnan, is his religion of the spirit.

> I tried to show that my general position provides a valid interpretation of the world, which seems to be consistent

22. See S. Radhakrishnan, *The Spirit of the Metaphysical Quest*, Sinn und Sein. Ein Philosophisches Simposium, Tübingen, 1960, pp. 344-45 (in German).

23. *The Philosophy of Radhakrishnan*, p. 820.

24. Ibid., p. 816.

> with itself, to accord with the facts as we know them, and to foster the life of spirit.[25]

A consistent opponent of dogmatic religionism, Radhakrishnan points out the creative character of his philosophy and requires similar creative approach to it, so as to keep abreast of life and be able to amend the relevant principles according to new developments. Any authentic philosophy, Radhakrishnan asserts, proceeds from reality and is based on the empirical and logical analysis of real facts, not on abstract and inert tenets.

These are the underlying principles that Radhakrishnan seeks to apply in addressing diverse problems, above all, the fundamental question of philosophy, that of the relationship of consciousness to being. He adopts the notion of the primacy of being, but by "being" he implies some divine spirit, even *Brahman*, and not objective reality, which exists outside and independent of consciousness and is reflected by it. Reality is presented as secondary to *Brahman*, a derivative of it.

This objective-idealistic conception of being predetermined Radhakrishnan's approach to reality. He thinks it wrong to suppose that the world is an objective reality, as in this case it would be independent of any will or consciousness, whereas the universe has been brought into being by God, who is the unique objective reality. "The Absolute alone has non-created divine reality; all else is dependent, created reality. . . . The reality of the world is not in itself, but it is in the thought and being of the Creator. It is what God thought and willed it to be before it."[26] Radhakrishnan then proceeds to explain that the world is merely an expression of the Absolute, but neither the

---

25. *The Philosophy of Radhakrishnan*, p. 10.

26. Ibid., p. 41.

Absolute itself, nor its modification. He often describes the Absolute as the Primary Spiritual Reality, and the universe as a secondary derivative reality.

The problem of the relationship between being and reality prompted Radhakrishnan to approach the theory of cognition in a way which was to serve to substantiate the principles of perennial religion. Strongly opposed to peremptory dogma and any form of church fanaticism, he advocated an analytical approach to reality.

Radhakrishnan is optimistic about man's cognitive faculty. He rejects agnosticism and scepticism and regards being and reality as cognisable.

> Scepticism as a method is valuable, but not scepticism as a metaphysics. Doubt has been a great stimulus to inquiry, but it is not an end in itself.[27]

Radhakrishnan explains the necessity and possibility of knowing the world by man's inherent aspiration for freedom and happiness, since "man cannot be happy until he attains the truth."[28] He defines happiness as the attainment of moral perfection in a religious sense.

> The thirst for religion, the striving for integrity, the search for a different life show that man has to advance by way of consciousness.[29]

Moreover, Radhakrishnan justifies the necessity and possibility of cognition not only by an individual's needs and abilities, but also by humanity's striving for a perennial religion to unite all peoples into one family, which, ideally, would combine with the divine reality to form a whole.

> When mankind awakes to the Truth, universal

27. *The Philosophy of Radhakrishnan*, p. 817.
28. S. Radhakrishnan, *Fellowship of the Spirit*, 1961, p. 4.
29. *Recovery of Faith*, p. 99.

> brotherhood will follow the atonement with the great fountainhead of all creation.[30]

For this reason there is no question in Radhakrishnan's epistemological theory of subject-object relations.

> Truth is not the reflection of reality in sense and intellect. It is a creative mystery experienced by the soul in its deepest being. It is not a question of the subject knowing the object. It involves the realisation that subject and object are one in a deeper sense than any physical analogy can make clear.[31]

These are the fundamentals of the theory of cognition, on which the principal epistemic categories and types are based. Integral perceptiveness is considered to be the highest cognitive faculty of man, which, in Radhakrishnan's words, falls into three types: perceptual (*mānas*), intuitive (*ānanda*), and logical (*vijñāna*).[32]

All three types are interrelated, inseparable and function as an integral whole. Sense perception, however, is an inferior cognitive type, and it is therefore least discussed by Radhakrishnan. Intelligence, on the other hand, is discussed in great detail.

As noted above, Radhakrishnan's philosophy does not ignore the significance of the senses and reason. Preference, he insists, should be given to them, rather than the instructions of the scriptures. Otherwise philosophy is bound to slide into dogmatism and inconsistency. Moreover, Radhakrishnan stresses that religious faith, too, should be based on reason: "For us nothing is true by our faith if it is not true by reason."[33]

30. S. Radhakrishnan, *Occasional Speeches and Writings*, 1957, p. 236.
31. *Recovery of Faith*, p. 107.
32. *Occasional Speeches and Writings*, 1963, p. 263.
33. Ibid., p. 19.

These originally rationalistic ideas, however, were not elaborated by Radhakrishnan any further. Due to a clearly Vedāntic influence, Radhakrishnan imposes limitations on the functional capacity of reason and subordinates it to his ontological and epistemological theses. In conformity with his idealistic views on being and cognition, Radhakrishnan proceeds from the idea that to abide by reason does not always mean that the ultimate reality should be regarded only as an object of reason. He states:

> Though reason may not be adequate as an organ for the apprehension of the Divine, it is useful as a critic of claims to such apprehension.[34]

He deems the intellect to be "an indispensable aid to support and clarify spiritual experience," it is held to be an instrument of spirit. Although consciousness is man's distinctive feature, which has determined the special position he occupies in this world, reason alone does not suffice.

On these epistemic premises Radhakrishnan concludes that science, whose instrument is logic, does not bring one closer to understanding reality. Because the intellect prevails in scientific research, science cannot provide a basis for comprehension of the world's divine nature. It can only give an idea of the formal structure of existence, especially physical existence, but it is incapable of revealing the spiritual essence of being, the inner truth.

These essentially spiritualistic generalisations on reason and science are a prelude to presenting intuition as the main epistemic category. Radhakrishnan's interpretation of intuition is founded on the notions contained in the Indian philosophical tradition, especially in the school of Vedānta,

34. *Occasional Speeches and Writings*, 1963, p. 234.

and in Bergson's intuitionism. In distinguishing intuition from other cognitive methods, Radhakrishnan points out:

> Intuitive knowledge is a self-subsistent mode of consciousness, different from the intellectual or perceptual. Whereas perception gives us the outward properties of an object, discerns the law of which an object is an instance, intuition gives depth, meaning and character to the object.[35]

The grasping of an object's innermost nature by intuition is seen as a mystical insight into the nature of the Divine, and this insight, according to Radhakrishnan, leads to spiritual perfection and attainment of the ultimate goal of human life.

In this theory, where intuition plays the leading role in cognition (i.e. in cognising divine reality, not objective reality), the perennial philosophy finds the most distinct spiritualistic expression. Certain humanistic ideas contained in it are set forth by proclaiming the necessity of spiritual and moral perfection in order to gain freedom of spirit and unite humankind into a universal fraternity. This conception rests on a mystical-theological basis.

Rejecting all existing religions as inconsistent, dogmatic and parochial, Radhakrishnan offers as an alternative the perennial religion. Genuine practical humanism, however, presupposes social as well as spiritual liberation of man, and the eradication of prejudice and superstition.

Despite the fact that Radhakrishnan's teaching has not found a large following, or started a new trend in modern Indian philosophy, it has left a distinct trace in the history of Indian thought. Probably, more than any other system, Radhakrishnan's teaching is markedly social and humanistic.

Sarvepalli Radhakrishnan upheld noble moral ideals and egalitarian, secular and pacifist principles which contributed to the social and cultural advancement of his country.

---

35. *Recovery of Faith*, pp. 792-93.

CHAPTER EIGHTEEN

K. Satchidananda Murty
Sitting at the Feet of Śaṅkara

NATALYA ISAEVA

WHEN you are only starting to work in the vast field of Indian studies and yet entertain some hopes that one day you might reach your long sought goal, what you need most acutely is the help of a patient and knowledgeable master. You need not only the guiding thread of reliable texts but also somebody to actually lead you at least part of the way, someone to help you in determining your own path.

I was probably lucky in this respect, since one of the first books I read when I started to think about Śaṅkara's system was K. Satchidananda Murty's *Revelation and Reason in Advaita Vedānta.* To say that it was inspiring would be an understatement; it gave me much more than just a taste of brief exultations or emotional raptures: it supplied me with a necessary sense of perspective, and what is more — I truly believe it safeguarded me against usual pitfalls that are always awaiting a scholar when he is trying to apply his European culture and European modes of reflection to something which essentially needs a totally different kind of approach. After reading Murty's book I could not ever regard Vedic scripture as just an accidental and more or less optional envelope for really profound philosophical ideas of Advaita. I could not ever try to overlook the fact of an unswerving and steadfast connection between theoretical notions of Advaita and Vedic revelation.

While Murty himself was much too modest, insisting

that nowhere in his book *Revelation and Reason in Advaita Vedānta* were the personal views of the author explicitly expressed, in my opinion, the author's position is only too clear to the attentive reader, though, of course, it was intricately interwoven into the very texture of the monograph. To me, the key-words concerning the problem of religious symbolism run as follows:

> . . . the symbols are not to be taken literally; . . . the paradox and ambiguity in religious symbolism is the result of the difficulty of presenting the infinite in the forms of the finite; . . . the phrases used cumulatively convey some sense of the absolute significance, which never depends upon this or that way of speaking about *Brahman*; . . . words conjointly indicate a fact qualitatively other than the facts, of which they are usually used as symbols.[1]

Later in my life I had an opportunity to acquaint myself with other philosophical notions, expressed in various essays, books and lectures of Murty.

Gradually I became interested not only in the interpretation of Śaṅkara's system, but also in the methods and approaches, propounded by one of the most eminent present-day Indian thinkers. By that time I was already well aware of Murty's reputation as an original and highly competent scholar in the field of Vedānta studies.

In his address, delivered in September 1985, during the celebration of the Silver Jubilee of Shri Shankara Kripa, and entitled *The Advaitic Notion,* Murty lays bare his own principles of analysing Vedānta texts. Along the lines indicated by the famous Vedānta sage Śrīharṣa, he reminds that any knowledge, which dawned on a reflecting subject, is self-evident and naturally valid for him. There is no obligation and no need to plunge into the infinite regress

1. K. Satchidananda Murty, *Revelation and Reason in Advaita Vedānta,* N.Y., 1961, p. 287-88.

(*anavasthā*) of futile attempts to justify and demonstrate a chain of argumentation, since the crucial point, the point of support for every philosophical tenet is already preconceived and pre-settled by the absolute unity and self-luminosity of *ātman*.

This self-evident *ātman* lies at the source of every experience and every concept, it originates and it concludes the chain of reasoning, thus determining, in the ultimate sense, its very structure and reliability.

In this way, Murty finds a starting-point for his painstaking efforts to save Vedāntic ideas in our scientific and sceptical age. Indeed, having obtained an in-depth knowledge both of traditional, orthodox upbringing and of Western system of education, he is placed in quite a unique position, which allows him, so to speak, to embrace their respective shortcomings and advantages at a single glance. Hence, his approach to the role of Śruti, sacred scriptures is by no means the only, the absolute knowledge, which has to be accepted literally. Vedic texts constitute primarily the bridge between our finite world and the super-sensuous world of *Brahman*. Along with the self-evident revelation of *ātman*, the texts of Śruti supply at least a glimpse of eternal *Brahman* in our state of nescience.

In the same work *The Advaitic Notion*, Murty is summing up his explication of Śaṅkara's notions; he maintains that while self-awareness of *ātman* is absolutely self-proved, "Vedāntic sentences indicate its nature . . . in a secondary or indirect way."[2] It is fairly clear from the author's line of reasoning that Vedic scripture is not regarded here only as a holy revelation, which is definitely beyond any critique or discussion; the role of the scripture is

2. K. Satchidananda Murty, *The Advaitic Notion*, Sringeri, 1985, p. 17.

primarily a negative one: its main task consists in removing any arguments that might contradict the notion of the oneness and unity of the self (or *ātman*). This negative function, of course, is only relevant for our mundane plane of existence. As soon as the real knowledge dawns, all the finite instruments, including Vedic texts, become superfluous and have to be thrown away. As soon as the besieged fortress is conquered, the ladders that helped the warriors to climb the walls become of no use and might just as well be dropped to the ground. When Murty is reflecting upon this, he is surely reminded of the well-known thesis of Ludwig Wittgenstein, according to which all usual verbal statements about reality can be critically considered, understood or accepted only before the transition to some higher plane of existence; after that any word and any meaning should be thrown away as a used-up auxiliary instrument.

The ideas on the tradition of Advaita Vedānta, finding their place in various works of Murty, come to a clear focus in his Inaugural Address delivered for the International Congress of Vedanta, which was held at the Miami University, USA, in April of 1990. It is worth mentioning that the Congress itself was convened in order to celebrate Śaṅkara's anniversary (Murty was among those scholars who took the initiative of organising proper scholarly meetings and celebrations on the occasion of symbolic anniversaries of the Buddha, the Jina and, finally, Śaṅkara). It is really a lot that is demanded of a researcher who tries to tackle a trying problem of summarising his cherished ideas in just so many well-chosen phrases. One has to be brief but one cannot allow oneself to become flippant or even formal — the occasion is much too serious.

I remember how brilliantly the problem was solved in this particular case. To my mind, Murty used to full advantage the approach which proved so successful in his earlier works. I mean primarily his unique ability to combine Western analytical methods with traditional Indian education. He was both thoroughly logical and well-rooted in the ancient texts, painstakingly accurate in Sanskrit references and broad-minded in his evaluation of modern scientific ideas and superstitions. And he really succeeded in bringing Śaṅkara closer to the multi-cultural and multi-national audience, or, to be more precise, in bringing his listeners closer to Śaṅkara's tradition, Śaṅkara's destiny and Śaṅkara's own peculiar philosophy.

Taking as a starting-point for his exposition three well-known Sanskrit sayings: *nivartakam śāstram* (that which removes is a Śāstra), a text from Patañjali's *Mahābhāṣya; antyam idam pramāṇam ātmaikatvasya pratipādakam* (the ultimate *pramāṇa* is the one propounding the oneness of *ātman*), Śaṅkara's *Brahmasūtra-bhāṣya,* II.1.14; and *na tu brahmajñāne yatnaḥ atyantaprasiddhatvāt* (no effort is necessary for the knowledge of *Brahman,* since it is absolutely self-evident), an aphorism from Śaṅkara's *Bhagavadgītābhāṣya.*[3] Murty proceeds with his elaborate reflection on the whole of Śaṅkara's system.

If the exposition is started with clarifying the very roots of Advaita, which are deeply ingrained in the preceding tradition — firstly and foremostly in the tenets of the so-called "grammarians," there is a need to determine the role of words and sentences in particular, and the role of speech in general. Indeed, European philosophy has only recently become really interested in similar problems. Certain attempts by logical positivists (if I am to justify my somewhat arbitrary mention of Wittgenstein) were more or less

3. K. Satchidananda Murty, *Inaugural Address for the International Congress of Vedānta,* Miami University, Oxford, Ohio, USA, 1990, p. 5.

following the lines that had been exhaustively explored by early Indian thinkers belonging to the Grammar school. However, when I go through the notions minutely examined by Murty, I am more readily reminded of the theories of French semiotics, primarily of the ideas of Roland Barthes and Jacques Derrida.

According to the Indian grammarians, the words and the syllables of the sacred scriptures constitute the source of the universe and provide the empirical world not only with a deeper meaning but also with its innermost structure; in this respect one might well recall some of Derrida's singular interpretations, given to the phenomenological notions of Husserl. In Derrida's words,

> the phenomenological "voice" should be that spiritual body which continues to speak and to be presented for itself — which continues to understand itself — even in the absence of the world. And of course, what is acknowledged for the "voice," is also acknowledged for the language of words that could be considered as irreducible, indestructible. . . .[4]

And it is small wonder that one of Derrida's main books bears a significant title: *De la Grammatologie*, that is, "About Grammatology" (Paris, 1967), the fact, which might remind one of Bhartṛhari's words: "And the higher *Brahman* is only made known through the science of grammar (*vyākaraṇa*)" (*Vākyapadīya*, Brahmakāṇḍa, 22).

Anyway, as Murty aptly puts it, the "'science of grammar' does not derive or produce the word-form, but only removes the mistaken assumption about it."[5] In other

---

4. Derrida Jacques, "La voix et le phenomene" in *Introduction au probleme du signe dans la phenomenologie de Husserl P.*, 1972, pp. 15-16.
5. K. Satchidananda Murty, *Inaugural Address*, p. 6.

words, according to the Vedāntins, no Śāstra (including the Grammar school or Advaita itself), however right and correct it might be, generates any new knowledge, since all knowledge (*jñāna*) is already in existence — as the higher *Brahman*, as a self-evident *ātman* or as the ultimate language structure, which eventually shapes up all our notions and statements concerning the world. The whole of Advaita tradition is brought to light by Murty in order to substantiate this view. He is lavishly citing relevant passages from the works by Draviḍācārya, Gauḍapāda, Śaṅkara, from the texts of the later Advaitins — Ānandagiri, Prakāśātman, Vimuktātman, Jñānottama or Madhusūdana Sarasvati. The panoramic view, presented by this modern Vedānta scholar, is a clear enough demonstration of the main postulate: when any school of Indian thought offers its own solution or interpretation of a philosophical problem, the tenet itself should not be accepted as the ultimate, the only possible truth. It has to be regarded rather as a dialectical means of planting a doubt in the well-established set of empirical beliefs or superstitions, as an intricate and skilful way to remove all-too-familiar platitudes and ideas of ordinary life.

The second notion, or the second main principle of Advaita philosophy, singled out by Murty, is dealing with the concept of *antya pramāṇa*, the conclusive means of valid knowledge. In order to approach it, Murty refers to *Bhagavadgītā-bhāṣya* and *Brahmasūtra-bhāṣya* of Śaṅkara. According to the Advaitin, this *pramāṇa* is nothing other than the famous Śruti *mahāvākyas*, or "great sayings": *tat tvam asi* (That thou art) and *aham brahmāsmi* (I am *Brahman*). Providing his own interpretation to Śaṅkara's texts, Murty shows that this *antya pramāṇa* actually "removes the knowership (subjecthood, *pramātr̥tva*) of the Self; and even while so removing, it becomes a non-*pramāṇa*, just as a *pramāṇa* in a dream ceases to be so after awakening."[6]

So, contrary to the widespread and popular view, *ātman* is not a kind of a purified and absolute subject, nor is it a manifestation of some supreme knower. It is just impossible to apply this trash version of Hegel's *Absolute Geist* (Absolute Spirit) to the Advaitic concept of *ātman*, since in Śaṅkara's system, one cannot draw any distinctions between the cogniser, the act of cognition and the object of cognition. The opposition of the subject and the object, so dear to the classical, rationalistic trends within the scope of European philosophy, falls short of grasping the peculiar essence of *ātman*; preliminary approaches to this entity started to be outlined only after the emergence of Husserl's phenomenology, where one can already discern the concept of *transzendentale Ich* (transcendental I) which appears (or shines through) only after the removal (*phaenomenologische Reduktion*) of all empirical data and all empirical attributes. As Murty demonstrates with the help of Vedānta sources, the introduction of the *antya pramāṇa* abolishes any finite and paltry contraposition between the subject and the object of knowledge, thus clearing the way for less trivial suggestions and concepts.

The third main idea discernible in the foundation of Advaita is, in Murty's opinion, that of the right way of approaching *Brahman*. It is evidently closely connected with the principles discussed above, but now the emphasis of the investigation is slightly shifted, thus securing a different angle of approach. Śaṅkara's texts referred to in this connection are mostly taken from his *Bhagavadgītā-bhāṣya*. The whole of Murty's reconstruction and interpretation of Advaita started with the argument concerning self-luminous and self-manifest reality of *ātman*. Now he follows Śaṅkara in order to show how even the finite and relative

6. K. Satchidananda Murty, *Inaugural Address*, p. 12.

instruments of knowledge partake of this reality, which shines forth through them with its sheer presence and power. Actually, there is even a hint of some curious similarity between the notions of rigorously monistic Advaita and some tenets of rather more theistically biased systems (for example, Vijñānavāda of Rāmānuja — or even Thomistic versions of Christianity). Indeed, as Murty points out, "not only in the intellect, but also in the mind, senses and body also there is a semblance (*ābhāsatā*) of the consciousness of the Self, which is the reason for their being mistaken for the Self by some."[7]

Nevertheless, in spite of all the understandable and objectively justified reasons for mixing up *ātman* and its temporary outer sheaths, the only real spiritual task confronting an adept is his ability to distinguish and apprehend the Self. This culmination of knowledge (or, to put it in Śaṅkara's own terms, *jñānaniṣṭhā*) is possible only for diligent students well-versed in Vedānta, for assiduous disciples prepared to follow their *guru*, for those, who are prepared to leave for good the sphere of duality. As Murty puts it, "the removal of the notion of difference in external things alone is the cause of abiding in the true nature of the Self."[8]

So, the argumentation here has completed a full circle. Starting with the idea of self-luminosity and self-evidence of *ātman*, having discussed the role of Śāstra (both of sacred scripture and that of traditional philosophical speculation), a follower of Advaita comes to the conclusion that after the removal of the nescience obscuring the Self the validity of Śāstra itself vanishes, "and when the Real comes to be known, it is found there is no knower."[9] Thus a perfect

7. K. Satchidananda Murty, *Inaugural Address*, p. 14.

8. Ibid., p. 15.

9. K. Satchidananda Murty, *Inaugural Address*, p. 16.

balance is established between the validity of the sacred tradition and the demands of scholarly research, a gap between Vedic premisses and European philosophical approach is successfully bridged. I believe, the task which confronted Murty in his analysis of Advaita tenets was somewhat akin to the one that Śaṅkara was dealing with in his time. Indeed, after a long period of the Buddhist predominance, Śaṅkara could not be content with just referring to the validity and absolute authority of Śruti texts: he had to find a philosophical justification for choosing Śruti tenets as a foundation of his own system. Murty was hardly right when he disclaimed any originality of his interpretation of the ideas of the greatest Advaitins. The only way to develop and enrich ancient teachings is to follow them closely enough, while at the same time, trying to find a correspondence for every successive step within the realm of the present-day thought. And vice versa, when one is making an attempt to embrace modern philosophical trends, it might be worthwhile to take a short halt, sitting down at the feet of Śaṅkara. I can clearly discern both ways of approach in the enlightening works of one of my *gurus* (if he is prepared to acknowledge such a disciple), Murty.

If I am allowed just a couple of personal remarks, I might add that I had the pleasure of personally meeting Professor Murty on several occasions and in connection with different objectives. I have a deep conviction that a person remains basically the same whatever the demands of the specific situation might be. And even on those occasions when he was acting as a shrewd and able administrator, I had, I believe, a glimpse of the same bright fire illuminating the vast plains of Advaita, burning out ignorance, superstition or just pardonable human laziness.

CHAPTER NINETEEN

"Dialectical Dynamism" of D.P. Chattopadhyaya*

MARIETTA STEPANYANTS

THERE is a kind of *leitmotif* which goes through all the works written by Professor D.P. Chattopadhyaya. That is his approach to the relationship of tradition and modernity. In the introduction to his book published as the sixth volume in PHISPC series of monographs on history of philosophy, science and culture in India, he acknowledges:

> Many of our chosen ways of shaping the future are unnecessarily foreign. I do not even remotely suggest that all that is foreign is unwelcome. Many ideas and technologies of the foreign origin, because of their rational or beneficial character, are welcome. What I am suggesting is this. Even after the open conflict between our cultural identity and the identity of other culture subsides, the silent conflict (of interests, approaches and values) between the two persists.[1]

This quotation adequately sums up D.P. Chattopadhyaya's well balanced and realistic stand on the subject.

In my view D.P. Chattopadhyaya has laid a solid theoretical foundation under his stand by reflecting on the concept of development and progress as well as by

---

* Revised version of Marietta Stepanyants, *History, Culture and Truth: Essays Presented to D.P. Chattopadhyaya*, eds. Daya Krishna, S. Murty, New Delhi, 1999.

1. D.P. Chattopadhyaya, *Interdisciplinary Studies in Science, Technology, Philosophy and Culture,* New Delhi, 1996, p. xiii.

contemplating on the nature, formation and evolution of values. I would like to mention here some of his points which seem to be of great importance.

In D.P. Chattopadhyaya's understanding of "progress" the most essential are the following affirmations. First of all, though "the concept of progress is kindred to that of development . . . one must take note of the distinction between the two."[2] The main distinction is that "progress is basically cultural and not natural and that there is nothing like natural law of progress." Consequently, "our attention is likely to be focused on the human aspect of progress, on the factors underlying progress."[3]

Just because progress is basically a cultural phenomenon it is usually understood that progress and universal culture as such do not exist. D.P. Chattopadhyaya points out that culture, like language or morality, is universal only as a concept. Cultural, linguistic or moral *universale* are "intellectual constructions," they are "*universale* only by courtesy."[4] He does not deny that there are some generic characteristics which could be designated by terms, like "linguistic universals" (Chomsky), "cultural universals" (Lévi-Strauss), "biological universals" (Lenneberg) or "universal moral law" (Kant). He acknowledges common human roots. However, all those concepts are empty concepts having no objectual exemplifications. On that account, "cultural development or advancement does not necessarily entail universalisation or globalisation of some specific cultural achievements, artistic, legal or religious."[5]

---

2. D.P. Chattopadhyaya, *Interdisciplinary Studies in Science, Technology, Philosophy and Culture*, p. 276.
3. Ibid., p. 277.
4. Ibid., p. 279.
5. Ibid., p. 281.

Such universalisation is not only wrong, it is dangerous, and possesses "a dark implication." Referring to some examples, D.P. Chattopadhyaya reminds us that in the name of a universal religion "many unholy wars have been fought, resulting in the death of millions of human beings," and in the name of a universal science "pseudosciences have been promoted and different forms of science ignored or even crushed."[6] The point which is stressed upon in many of his writings is: "the recognition of difference between different forms of culture is unavoidable."[7]

D.P. Chattopadhyaya strongly opposes those who claim that "development . . . to be an invariant value of all cultures."[8] He realistically points out that "breakdowns of civilisation and sickness of culture are not accidents of history," they are "integral parts of it."[9] Here, like in many other cases, the student fully shares his teacher's (Karl Popper) observation: progress is not an inherent law of history. D.P. Chattopadhyaya calls to take a circumspect and critical view of history. "The easy option to establish objectivity in terms of linear progress or development," he states, "needs no modification, but rejection."[10]

Are we as human beings capable of preventing those breakdowns of civilisation and sickness of culture? Are we in power to shape our own future? What should be then our means and methods? The answer I have found in D.P. Chattopadhyaya's writings is: "Yes, we can, if the future is

---

6. D.P. Chattopadhyaya, *Interdisciplinary Studies in Science, Technology, Philosophy and Culture*, p. 281.
7. Ibid.
8. Ibid., p. 229.
9. Ibid.
10. Ibid.

not excluded from the present and from the past."[11] To include the present and in particular the past in our future means to take tradition as "a very important thing in the life of a nation."[12] However, it does not mean that tradition should be perpetuated or prolonged beyond a point of time since it would inhibit freedom and creative genius of the people concerned:

> Repetition of history is not the lesson of history. The lesson of history is to change and to enrich it by discoveries, inventions and innovations.[13]

D.P. Chattopadhyaya refers to and shares Gandhi's approach to tradition and modernity which is against a "discontinuous and violent change."[14] Gandhi instead suggested non-violent revolution like *sarvodaya* which literally means all-round development by a peaceful method of social change found in *satyāgraha*. D.P. Chattopadhyaya believes that non-violent *satyāgraha* aims "to maintain the inner continuity between tradition and modernisation."[15] Being truthful to the critical nature of his mind, D.P. Chattopadhyaya in spite of all his great respect for Gandhi, dares to mark the point of disagreements with Mahatma in this particular case. In his view,

> most of Gandhi's ideas and actions in respect of *satyāgraha* can be satisfactorily explained without using the God-in-Man hypothesis. The question of God has remained a favourite subject of philosophical disputes from the very dawn of human civilisation and culture. The results of

11. D.P. Chattopadhyaya, *Interdisciplinary Studies in Science, Technology, Philosophy and Culture*, p. 214.
12. D.P. Chattopadhyaya, *Environment, Evolution and Values*, New Delhi-Madras, 1983, p. 195.
13. Ibid.
14. Ibid., p. 203.
15. Ibid.

> human reason and experience accumulated and assimilated over the centuries have left behind enough of norms and forms to minimise conflicts . . . enabling mankind to discover and establish numerous modes of conflict, co-operation and integration. Some of the noblest teachers of mankind like Buddha and Marx who worked so much for human unity and progress were atheists. Some of the most well-known and influential followers of Gandhi like Nehru did not share their master's faith in God. *Satyāgraha* is a noble principle. But its metaphysical foundation seems to be questionable and dispensable."[16]

Thus, changes are inevitable and needed. D.P. Chattopadhyaya tries to develop the general thesis that the main dynamics of social change is man[17] with reference again to the ideas of Gandhi. However, he goes much further beyond the latter in his elaboration on the subject by bringing up his own evolutionary theory of values.

The prime point D.P. Chattopadhyaya states is: "whatever man makes, inherits, or needs — theory, values, or social institutions — is questioned, enriched, or impoverished, and, in the process, changed."[18] The evolutionary character of theory, value, institutions, etc., rightly understood, means the necessity of the human intervention in the process. "Transformation of both nature and culture is brought about by human ideas and actions."[19] Chattopadhyaya joins philosophers like Karl Popper who argue that values are basically human products and subject to the extremely complex laws of cultural evolution. In that process the role man plays is not of a copyist but of a creator.

16. D.P. Chattopadhyaya, *Environment, Evolution and Values*, pp. 203-4.
17. Ibid., p. 160.
18. Ibid., pp. 158-59.
19. Ibid., p. 159.

> Man can initiate thought and action processes. In other words, he creates values both as a part of nature and a partaker in a cultural process.[20]

In a number of his writings D.P. Chattopadhyaya points out shortcomings of the universalist theories of values with reference to different spheres of art, ethics, religion, sciences, etc. He believes that it is not only unwise but also dangerous to affirm the existence of so-called universal values and to impose, dictate them disregarding differences of culture, time and needs. He strongly insists on "the futility of search for values which are not culture-bound."[21]

To "law-oriented universalism" which goes along with "static structuralism" D.P. Chattopadhyaya opposes what he calls "fact-oriented particularism," "dialectical dynamism." Yet it does not mean that he does not realise that both approaches create certain difficulties. In fact, he is against both extremes:

> Emphasis on laws, whether these are construed in pro-naturalistic or anti-naturalistic ways, tends to berate the importance of the uniqueness of praxiological actions. Denial of laws in order to vindicate not only the unique character of valued actions but also the freedom of man as the author of those actions gives one the impression that values, strictly speaking, are neither objective nor universal.[22]

D.P. Chattopadhyaya looks critically into different efforts of reconciling the two opposite attitudes and in the long run finds out Ernest Cassirer's approach "very promising"[23]

---

20. D.P. Chattopadhyaya, *Environment, Evolution and Values*, p. 224.
21. Ibid., p. 295.
22. D.P. Chattopadhyaya, *Historicality of Human Practices: Art, Ethics and Religion*, Calcutta, 1989, p. 2.
23. Ibid., p. 17.

referring to his *The Philosophy of Symbolic Forms* where it is shown how symbolic representations of different forms of experience, despite their ontological regionalism or relativism, have transcendental and intelligible appeal. However, generally speaking, to reconcile historical or sociological practicalism with transcendentalism does not prove easy. D.P. Chattopadhyaya is of the opinion that different forms of metaphysical essentialism, anthropological structuralism and law-governed historicism which have been resorted to to deal with this disturbing situation retain the basic shortcomings: they are distant from and artificially related with actual practices, wide and disparate variety of practical examples.[24]

Though D.P. Chattopadhyaya straightforwardly affirms that he has not "the slightest sympathy either with any kind of universalism or with historicism of all varieties (Hegelian, Marxian, Spenglerian, Sri Aurobindian, Sorokian)," and he has "full sympathy with those who treat them with contempt,"[25] yet he feels that they indicate some problems which stay unsolved. D.P. Chattopadhyaya indicates one of those unsolved "riddles" in the domain of art.

In his view neither history nor sociology of art forms of different ages and cultures show any uniformity of laws and patterns. The diversity of art forms is boundless and their relativistic character is undeniable. How then to explain that certain works of art appeal to people belonging to widely separated cultures and epochs? In short, how to explain undeniable transcultural or objective appeal of art? Chattopadhyaya is sure that "enlarged and shared world

24. D.P. Chattopadhyaya, *Historicality of Human Practices: Art, Ethics and Religion*, Calcutta, p. 17

25. Ibid., p. 4.

of beautiful is not a matter of a priori or instant achievement," and it cannot result from some transcendental unity. It is the outcome, variable outcome, of experience, of what is experienced, of the will to experience and of the joy borne out of it."[26]

I am very much in agreement with D.P. Chattopadhyaya's general position on the subject. However, that latter solution of "the riddle" does not look to me clear enough. Since he considers that his basic argument could be extended to the spheres of ethics, religions and sciences, I wish his argumentation concerning how universal principles prove to be true of or establish its applicative credentials in relation to peculiar facts would be more precise and convincing.

One of the most thought-provoking statements of D.P.Chattopadhyaya is made in connection with the problem of conflict in the cultural development. There is no doubt that different and active cultures often prove conflicting. Cultural pluralism implies conflicts as well as conflicts imply cultural pluralism. Chattopadhyaya warns against condemning these elements of conflict without understanding their "functional import."[27] He affirms that "a culture which knows no conflict or does not allow any scientific or ideological controversy within it, slowly degenerates into a totalitarian form, a sort of uncriticisable tribalism."[28] In general, conflict plays a very important role within the evolutionary process:

---

26. D.P. Chattopadhyaya, *Historicality of Human Practices: Art, Ethics and Religion*, Calcutta, pp. 15-16.
27. See D.P. Chattopadhyaya, *Interdisciplinary Studies in Science, Technology, Philosophy and Culture*, pp. 282-90.
28. D.P. Chattopadhyaya, *Historicality of Human Practices: Art, Ethics and Religion*, p. 283.

> Unity of opposites, conflict and harmony and similar other paired concepts bring out the dynamic character of social development. Freedom of man is the root of this social dynamics.[29]

It is because of the latter that D.P.Chattopadhyaya makes his choice. As he acknowledges: "My approach is basically freedom-related."[30]

Now, after all that has been said, I would try to see to which trends of thought in the contemporary East D.P. Chattopadhyaya belongs. The first, in fact superficial, look at his writings may give an impression that he is a typical modernist-Westerniser. Such impression appears at the examination of the list of references he gives, which is commonly full of the names of Western philosophers. Further, the problems he deals with are very much those which are mostly under modern discourse. At least, Chattopadhyaya does not correspond to the image of a thinker-reformer. The latter generally tends to revise or reconstruct the traditional values and notions in response to the challenges coming from the West. Say, for example, a distinguished poet-philosopher both of India and Pakistan Muhammad Iqbal being aware of Asian and African young generation's demand for a fresh orientation of their faith (as a Muslim, he kept in mind here Islam), had come to the conclusion that it was "necessary to examine, in an independent spirit, what Europe has thought and how far the conclusions reached by her can help . . . in the revision and, if necessary, reconstruction of theological thought in Islam." In Iqbal's view, it was high time to look into the essentials of Islam and therefore he undertook "a

29. D.P. Chattopadhyaya, *Historicality of Human Practices: Art, Ethics and Religion*, p. 286.

30. Ibid., p. 287.

philosophical discussion of some basic ideas of Islam"[31] (essentials and basic ideas are also taken as Islamic universals).

In spite of all this Chattopadhyaya is undoubtedly a philosopher-reformer. He uncompromisingly adheres to an evolutionary way of bringing changes, to social dynamism and freedom. He seems to focus his attention not so much on the deliberation and revision or reconstruction of national values and notions as on the critical examination of Western way of thinking, Western ideas and Western world outlook. In doing that he warns his compatriots about the shortcomings (sometimes, even evils) of the Western civilisation and thus prevents them from following wrong directions.

I sincerely believe that Chattopadhyaya's "warnings" are of no less significance for my own compatriots.

The present stage through which Russia nowadays is passing is often called *"Perestroika,"* which means "reconstruction." However, it seems it would be more precise to describe it as the condition of being "at the crossroads," since the Russian "architects" and "constructors" do not have a plan of action for the realisation of any particular project. It is true that among them there are those who strongly believe that they need to build a "skyscraper," while others "prefer to construct an *Izba* — a traditional Russian village "log-cabin." As for the majority, they wish for themselves, and especially for their children and grandchildren, just to have a comfortable house where well-being and justice could reside.

In short, the controversy between so-called *zapadniks* (Westernisers) and *slavophiles* (a kind of Russian fundamentalists) which took place in the second half of the

---

31. Allama Muhammad Iqbal, *The Reconstruction of Religious Thought in Islam*, Lahore, 1996, p. 15.

nineteenth and the beginning of the twentieth centuries and was broken by the Russian October revolution of 1917 has been back nowadays. As it was in the past, the public opinion is divided between those who share Peotr Chaadaev's conviction: "it is impossible to become civilised without following a European model,"[32] and those who follow Konstantin Leontiev, who insisted: the main task of Russia is not to submit to Europe but "to preserve its particularity." Only future can give a final response to the question: who is right in this controversy? Yet in order not to repeat the mistakes of the past and to avoid new ones we are to participate in the dialogue of cultures, because "individuals and peoples get self-conscious only through comparing themselves with the others."[33]

While reflecting on the problems which are of vital importance for Russia we are inclined nowadays either to take the West as a certain *beau idéal* which can give us the right direction, or to rely exclusively on our own historical experience. In fact, the experiences of non-Western countries are completely ignored, though many of them have passed or are passing through the same period of "the reconstruction" like us.

Russia might learn a lot not only by taking into account the political experience of non-Western nations, in particular, those who possess a rich cultural heritage of their own. We can and I believe we should be more attentive to the voices of philosophers from those countries, to the voices of those who independently and creatively reflect on the

---

32. P.Y. Chaadaev, "Philosophical Letters. The First Letter" in P.Y. Chaadaev, *The Collected Works* (Russian edition), Moscow, 1989, p. 28.

33. K.D. Kavelin, *Collected Works* (Russian edition), St. Petersburg, 1898, vol. 1, p. 674.

problems of common vital importance. D.P. Chattopadhyaya is undoubtedly one of them. I wish my compatriots could follow his advices in many cases. At least the following statement by D.P. Chattopadhyaya is quite relevant to the modern Russian situation:

> There are certain basic human rights and . . . every civil society must recognise and wherever possible, enforce the same. The main difference arises on the question of practice or determining the enforcement conditions. . . . The principles of the basic human rights should not be formulated in an abstract manner, disregarding the conditions, the social context, of the concerned human beings.[34]

34. D.P. Chattopadhyaya, *Environment, Evolution and Values*, p. 225.

CHAPTER TWENTY

Leo Tolstoy Reads Shri Ramakrishna[1]

SERGEI SEREBRIANY

THIS paper is but a humble preliminary attempt on my part to approach the complicated and rather delicate theme which has been already touched, in one way or another, by some eminent authors. It is quite well known that the names of Tolstoy and Ramakrishna came together in the works of the famous French writer Romain Rolland who wrote first (in 1911) a biography of Tolstoy and later (in 1929-30) biographies of Ramakrishna and Vivekananda. But, for his purposes as a biographer, it was sufficient for R. Rolland just to mention the fact that Tolstoy knew about Ramakrishna.

Next comes my compatriot Dr. A.I. Shifman (Alexander Shifman, b. 1907). He is a distinguished Tolstoy scholar and has been for many years associated with the Tolstoy Museum

1. This paper was originally written by the end of 1986 and presented in January of 1987 at a conference in Calcutta, at the Ramakrishna Mission Institute of Culture. It was first published (under the title *Leo Tolstoy and Sri Ramakrishna*) in the *Bulletin of the Ramakrishna Mission Institute of Culture* (vol. XXXVIII, no. 7, July 1987, pp. 163-69; vol. XXXVIII, no. 8, August 1987, pp. 196-202) and later as a booklet: S.D. Serebriany, *Leo Tolstoy and Sri Ramakrishna*, Calcutta: The Ramakrishna Mission Institute of Culture, 1987, pp. 44. Since then I have not been able to continue this particular line of research. So for this publication the paper has been only slightly revised. Some notes have been added or enlarged.

in Moscow. Shifman has written in Russian a book under the title *Tolstoy and the East* (Moscow, 1960; 2nd enlarged edn., 1971).[2] A part of this work (in a somewhat modified version) has been translated into English and published in India, by the Sahitya Akademi, as a separate book under the title *Tolstoy and India*.[3] This was in many ways a pioneering work. Shifman investigated Tolstoy's archives and brought to light many facts, many bits of information, not known before and not presented in a better way so far. No study of Tolstoy's relations with India can do without Shifman's books. But they should be used critically. Their author is not an Indologist and therefore these books contain, as far as things Indian are concerned, a number of inaccuracies both in facts and judgements,[4] though on the whole Shifman has demonstrated an enviable scholarly acumen and a very strong common sense.

Another compatriot of mine, Dr. A.P. Gnatyuk-Danil'chuk (1923–2008), delivered a lecture in Bengali on "Tolstoy and Vivekananda" at the Ramakrishna Mission Institute of Culture in December 1985. An English version of this lecture (translated by Harish C. Gupta) appeared first in the March and April 1986 issues of the Institute's *Bulletin* and then as a separate booklet.[5] Quite naturally, Gnatyuk-Danil'chuk has

2. A.I. Shifman, *Leo Tolstoy and the East*, Moscow: "Nauka" Publishers, 1971. Now an electronic version of the book is available at the address: http://marsexx.narod.ru/tolstoy-vostok
3. Alexander Shifman, *Tolstoy and India*, tr. from Russian by A.V. Esaulov, New Delhi: Sahitya Akademi, 1969; 2nd edn., 1978. (Further references to this edition in the text of the paper.)
4. In the Indian version some but not all of these inaccuracies have been corrected.
5. A.P. Gnatyuk-Danil'chuk, *Tolstoy and Vivekananda*, Calcutta: The Ramakrishna Mission Institute of Culture, 1986. (Further references to this edition in the text of the paper.)

paid some attention to the Tolstoy-Ramakrishna theme as well.

The lecture is an admirable piece of scholarship and has, to my mind, only one flaw: Gnatyuk-Danil'chuk wants to prove by all means that Tolstoy absolutely admired Vivekananda or rather ought to have admired him and all his ideas without exception. And Gnatyuk-Danil'chuk does his best to explain away whatever evidences to the contrary there happen to appear. The underlying assumption seems to be something like the well-known dictum that "all great minds meet." But I think that this dictum should not be understood too literally, should not be pushed too far. Otherwise we may get to the notorious style of writing when all more or less eminent persons are decorated with the same labels like "humanist," "democrat," and "progressive." Great minds do differ quite often, especially if they belong to different cultures, to different traditions. And the differences between great minds are not less interesting and enlightening than their meeting points.

Contacts between the minds of Tolstoy and Vivekananda, of Tolstoy and Ramakrishna are parts of larger intercultural contacts which are by no means facile or free from problems and difficulties. The American scholar Dr. Mary M. Lago, who has edited the correspondence between Rabindranath Tagore and his British friend William Rothenstein, has called her book *Imperfect Encounter*.[6] And this is a very apt title indeed, not only for the case of R. Tagore and W. Rothenstein, but for other similar cases as well. When I read the correspondence between Romain

6. *Imperfect Encounter: Letters of William Rothenstein and Rabindranath Tagore*, ed. with an Introduction and Notes by Mary M. Lago. Cambridge (Mass.): Harvard University Press, 1972.

Rolland and Rabindranath Tagore, between R. Rolland and M.K. Gandhi, and even between M.K. Gandhi and L.N. Tolstoy, I could not help recalling that expression: "Imperfect Encounter." And this applies to the case of Tolstoy and Ramakrishna, too.

They were contemporaries. Ramakrishna (1836-86) was about eight years younger than Tolstoy (1828-1910), but died about twenty-four years earlier. A hundred years ago our world was not as united by informational networks as it is now. If Tolstoy and Ramakrishna had lived today and had been as famous in their respective countries as they were in their own time, they would have at least heard about each other. But in the nineteenth century a Russian writer, very famous in his country, and an Indian saint, very famous in his land, could be ignorant about each other.

By the middle of the 1880s Tolstoy had already become famous in English-speaking countries (first English translations of his works having appeared as early as the 1860s). For instance, Indian National Library in Calcutta has a copy of *My Religion* by Tolstoy published in London in 1884, a copy of the *Childhood, Boyhood, Youth* (i.e. the autobiogra-phical trilogy of Tolstoy) published in London in 1886, and one of the first English translations of Tolstoy's *War and Peace* also published in London in 1888.[7] In 1889, only three years after Ramakrishna's death, Rabindranath Tagore, in a letter to his niece, Indira Devi, mentioned — rather unfavourably — Tolstoy's *Anna Karenina*.[8] So it is quite probable that in Ramakrishna's lifetime some educated people in Calcutta already read Tolstoy's works in English.

---

7. See: *Leo Tolstoy, 1828-1978: A Book Exhibition*, Calcutta: National Library, 1979.

8. Rabindranath Tagore, *Chinnapatrāvali* (in Bengali), Calcutta: Viśvābharatī Granthālaya, 1960, p. 14.

But Ramakrishna himself hardly heard about Tolstoy. Moreover, he would have hardly appreciated, say, the *War and Peace* or *Anna Karenina*. Probably, Tolstoy's later religious-philosophical works would have appealed to him more. But I would not dwell further on such guesses.

Neither did Tolstoy hear about Ramakrishna in the latter's lifetime. The Russian writer got to know about his Indian contemporary only by the end of his own long life. How did Tolstoy get to know about Ramakrishna? What exactly did he get to know? What was Tolstoy's reaction to this knowledge? Answers to such questions we can get from several sources: Tolstoy's diaries, Tolstoy's letters, his later works, and, last but not least, from notes of Tolstoy's friend and personal physician, D.P. Makovitsky (the notes were taken from, 1905).[9] It must be stressed from the outset that the information yielded by these sources is rather meagre, fragmentary, incomplete, and sometimes rather contradictory. Further research may add to our knowledge and understanding, but the margin seems to be not too large. Besides, in interpreting Tolstoy's later works, notes, and remarks some exegetical and hermeneutical problems are involved which require a very special qualification, a special skill, which I cannot claim to possess. With all these reservations, I will try and present the pieces of information available to me now.

It was on 12 February 1903 that Tolstoy wrote down in his diary: ". . . [I] read an excellent theosophical journal;

9. D.P. Makovitsky, *Notes from Yasnaya Polyana*, vols. 1-4, Moscow, 1981. Hereafter Mak. Further references in the text of the paper. Selections from these "Notes" are now available on the Internet: http://marsexx.narod.ru/tolstoy/tolstoy-makovickii.html

there is much in common with my understanding."[10] From the extensive and very informative commentaries which accompany Tolstoy's writings in the volumes of his *Complete Works* we learn that Tolstoy read some issues for 1902 and 1903 of the journal *Theosophischer Wegweiser* (i.e. "Theosophical Guide")[11] which he had received from Germany. The issues contained a number of sayings and parables of Ramakrishna, and Alexander Shifman (p. 27) informs us that Tolstoy, while reading the journal, underlined some of them. So we may indeed presume that Tolstoy's words "there is much in common with my understanding" referred at least partially to the German translations of Ramakrishna's sayings. This guess is supported by the fact that in the book *Thoughts of Wise Men for Every Day,* compiled by Tolstoy in 1903, we find five sayings and parables of Ramakrishna taken from the German journal. In any case we may surely date (as Gnatyuk-Danil'chuk does) the first acquaintance of Tolstoy with Ramakrishna's name and ideas at least as early as 1903.[12]

10. L.N. Tolstoy, *Complete Works* in 90 volumes, Moscow–Leningrad, 1928-1964, vol. 54, p. 155. Hereafter *CW*. (Further references in the text of the paper.) All translations from Russian into English in this paper are mine — *S.D.S.*

11. The full title of the journal is remarkable: "Theosophischer Wegweiser zur Erlangung der göttlichen Selbsterkenntnis. Monatsschrift zur Verbreitung einer höheren Weltanschauung und zur Verwirklichung der Idee einer allgemeinen Menschenverbrüderung auf der Grundlage der Erkenntnis der wahren Menschennatur." It was published from Leipzig in 1898–1907.

12. A.P. Gnatyuk-Danil'chuk, op. cit., p. 9. Alexander Shifman writes (op. cit., pp. 25-26) that as early as 1896 Tolstoy read Ramakrishna's *Discourses.* But no references are given, and it is not clear what book is meant. Probably, this statement of Alexander Shifman is a result of a misunderstanding.

Next references to Ramakrishna in Tolstoy's writings and talks appear in 1906. Thus in a letter to his acquaintance (and his biographer) P.A. Sergeyenko on 13 February 1906 Tolstoy wrote:

> Thank you, my dear Pyotr Alexeyevich, for your letter and for your excellent excerpts. Ramakrishna I know. And I have got many excerpts from him. . . . I know Ramakrishna from theosophical journals. [But] those excellent thoughts that you have copied out are not there. Where did you take [them] from? — *CW*, vol. 76, pp. 98-99

D.P. Makovitsky records that on 17 February 1906 Tolstoy said, among other things: ". . . Sergeyenko has sent me excellent excerpts from Buddhist books and from Ramakrishna. It was a Brahmin who died recently . . ." (Mak., vol. 2, p. 53). And again on 27 February 1906: "Sergeyenko has sent me excerpts from Müller's book *Ramakrishna*,[13] — said L[ev] N[ikolayevich]. — He has copied out wonderful sayings. Ramakrishna died about 50 (!?) years ago. A most remarkable wise man." D.P. Makovitsky adds : "L.N. read aloud some [of the sayings] . . ." (Mak., vol. 2, p. 64).

Commentaries to the quoted passages tell us that P.A. Sergeyenko had indeed sent to Tolstoy some excerpts from Max Müller's book on Ramakrishna, but Tolstoy later misplaced them and so they are not available now. But from two other entries in D.P. Makovitsky's *Notes* we may infer what impressions and what ideas Tolstoy might have got while reading those excerpts. On 2 December 1906, in a

13. Obviously, the following book is meant: F. Max Müller, *Ramakrishna, His Life and Sayings*, London, etc.: Longmans, Green, and Co., 1898 (or some later edition). Now the book is available on the Internet: http://www.sacred-texts.com/hin/rls/index.htm

conversation with a guest, Tolstoy said: ". . . We do not know about [other peoples'] religious movements, about Baba,[14] about Ramakrishna (he lived in the 40s). The fundamentals of all religious teachings are the same, only they are encumbered" (Mak., vol. 2, p. 317). On 15 January 1907 Tolstoy had a talk with another guest, a Russian aristocrat who had become an Orthodox Christian monk. Tolstoy said: "Ramakrishna — he was an Indian saint, he lived in the last century, his sayings are very good." The guest expressed his surprise that an Indian should be called a saint. He obviously meant that saints could be only Christian. Tolstoy retorted: "Indian and Chinese religious-ethical teachings teach the same as the Christian one" (Mak., vol. 2, p. 353).

So we see that in both cases the references to Ramakrishna are connected in Tolstoy's talks with the idea of equal value of different religions, with the idea of religious universalism. It is quite probable that similar ideas were expressed in those extracts from Ramakrishna's sayings which P.A. Sergeyenko had sent to Tolstoy.

But, having misplaced those extracts, Tolstoy, it seems, never used them in his works. All actual quotations or paraphrases from Ramakrishna in Tolstoy's texts go back to that German theosophical journal.

During the last years of his life (from 1903 to 1910) Tolstoy compiled several books for everyday readings, meant mostly for the common people, though not only for them. In Indian terms, those books might be called Nīti-śāstras, or Dharmaśāstras, or perhaps even Jñāna-śāstras, as Tolstoy strove to encompass in them both worldly and religious

14. Here Baba Premananda Bharati (Surendranath Mukherjee, 1857–1915) is meant who corresponded with Tolstoy for some time.

wisdom. The first book in this series was titled *Thoughts of Wise Men for Every Day* (first published in 1903). The second is known as the *Circle of Reading* (first published in 1906). The third book was called just *For Every Day* (compiled in 1906-10, but first published in full only in 1929, in the *Complete Works*). And the last book in the series was *The Path of Life* (compiled in 1910). These books contain aphorisms, sayings, parables, and even short stories culled from various sources, Eastern and Western, ancient and modern, well known and rather obscure. In many cases Tolstoy rewrote original pieces. Some entries were written by Tolstoy himself.

The first book, *Thoughts of Wise Men for Every Day* (1903), contained, as has been already said, five entries by Ramakrishna. More exactly, they were Russian renderings of those German versions that Tolstoy had found in the *Theosophischer Wegweiser*. It remains to be investigated to what extent the resulting Russian texts convey the original words and ideas of Ramakrishna.

The text that comes first, for 22 February, reads:

> God lives in all people, but not all people live in God.
> This is the cause of people's sufferings.
> As a lamp cannot burn without fire,
> so man cannot live without God.
>
> — *CW*, vol. 40, p. 90

Another text, for 2 March, is a parable:

Brainwork cannot satiate.

> Into a garden there came two persons: a scientist and one who lived in accordance with God. The scientist began right away to check the number of trees, to count fruit and determine the price of the garden. But the pious one got right away acquainted with the master of the garden, came up to one of the trees and satiated himself with its fruit.
>
> Make use of fruit. The counting of leaves and idle

> calculations will not satisfy your hunger. Not the activity of reason, but life in God gives you the fullness of supreme bliss.
>
> — *CW*, vol. 40, p. 94

The third entry signed "Ramakrishna" (for 29 April) is again a parable:

> A learned brāhmaṇa once came to a wise king and said: "I know well holy books and therefore would like to teach you truth." The king answered to him: "I think that you yourself have not yet sufficiently fathomed the meaning of holy books. Go and try to reach true understanding and then I will accept you as my teacher." The brāhmaṇa went away. He re-read once more "holy books" and again came to the king. But the king sent him back again. For the third time the brāhmaṇa did not appear before the king because he, the brāhmaṇa, realised the futility of worldly gains and the supreme necessity of "self-perfection." So in the end the king himself came to the brāhmaṇa, knelt before him and said: "Now I see that you have reached the real understanding of the meaning of the scriptures, and now, if only it pleases you, I am ready to be you pupil."
>
> — *CW*, vol. 40, p. 105

The fourth entry, for 19 September, consists of two sayings:

1. When rainwater flows down some gutters,
   it seems to us that it flows out of them,
   whereas in reality water falls down from the sky.
   The same with the holy teachings
   which are told to us by godly people.
   It seems that the teachings come from them,
   but in reality they come from God
2. In order to extract a splinter that has got into one's foot, one takes another splinter to oust the first one; but when this is done, one throws away both splinters. Exactly in the same way reason is needed only in order to remove the unreason which

> darkens the vision of the divine "I," but, verily,
> both reason and unreason do not constitute the
> true revelation.
>
> He who has reached the true revelation can be called neither a man of reason, nor a man of unreason, because he has liberated himself from any duality, from any relations. —*CW*, vol. 40, p. 177

The fifth and the last entry signed "Ramakrishna" in the book (for 30 November) is one more description of a person's spiritual development:

> The leaves [petals] of a flower fall down,
> when the fruit begins growing.
> In the same way your weaknesses will
> fall down from you,
> when there begins growing in you
> the consciousness of God.
>
> Even if during millennia darkness
> has been filling space,
> it becomes immediately lighted,
> when light penetrates into it.
>
> The same with your soul: however long it
> might have been enveloped with darkness,
> it will immediately be lighted,
> as soon as God opens in it his eyes.
> — *CW*, vol. 40, p. 204

Two more extracts from the *Theosophischer Wegweiser* remained in the preparatory drafts for the book and were used by Tolstoy later.

The second Jñāna-śāstra by Tolstoy, the *Circle of Reading*, contained only three sayings of Ramakrishna, all taken from the first book in the series (with some slight verbal changes here and there):

1. "God lives in all people . . ."
   (moved to 14 May; *CW*, vol. 41, p. 325)
2. "When rainwater flows down some gutters . . ."
   (moved to 1 July; *CW*, vol. 41, p. 461)
3. "The petals of a flower fall down . . ."
   (moved to 18 October; *CW*, vol. 42, p. 153)

The third Jñāna-śāstra, *For Every Day*, contained again five entries going back to Ramakrishna. Some of them had been rewritten by Tolstoy and marked with the words "After Ramakrishna." Thus the entry for 2 January reads like this:

> As a candle cannot burn without fire,
> so man cannot live without spiritual force.
> Spirit lives in all people, but not all people know it.
> Joyful is the life of a person, who knows it, and
> unhappy is the life of a person who does not know it.
> —*CW*, vol. 43, p. 5

As we see, the word "God" has been replaced here by the word "spirit." Probably, this replacement reflects the evolution of Tolstoy's religious thinking in his last years. He must have found the word "God" not universal enough to be accepted as a designation of a supreme value by all cultural traditions of mankind. And it is exactly the all-embracing universality that he strove to achieve.

To come back to the book, *For Every Day*, its entry for 11 March, signed again "After Ramakrishna," is a parable about a monk, a wise old man, and a peasant. The parable begins thus:

> A monk was seeking salvation in a hermitage. And he incessantly read prayers, and would get up twice at night to pray. Food was brought to him by a peasant. And there came a suspicion to the monk, if such a way of his life was good. And he went for advice to a wise old man.
> —*CW*, vol. 43, p. 137

In the end of the parable the "wise old man" demonstrates to the monk that the peasant's way of life is in a sense superior to his.

This parable deserves a special study. In the original it tells about the sage Nārada, God Viṣṇu, and a peasant. But Tolstoy from the very beginning, so to say, de-Indianised it. There are at least two versions of the parable written by Tolstoy, and the final version included in the book, *For Every Day*, must have rather a remote resemblance to the Indian original. But it seems that the central idea — of a pious common man's superiority to a "religious professional" — had been already there in the original.[15]

The entry for 4 May in the book, *For Every Day*, is signed just "Ramakrishna" and reads thus:

> As long as a person sings, cries out, says:
> "O, Lord, Lord!" you should know
> that he has not found the Lord;
> he who has found Him, keeps silent.
> — *CW*, vol. 45, p. 67

The entry for 1 June (signed again "After Ramakrishna") is a version of the saying already quoted ("When rainwater flows down some gutters . . ."), but with a very interesting addition. Here the final phrase reads thus:

> . . . The same with the teachings of saints and wise men
> *such as Christ and others* (emphasis mine – *S.D.S.*):
> it seems to us that the teachings come from them,
> but they come from God. — *CW*, vol. 43, pp. 306-7

The words "such as Christ and others" are very significant. They put Christ on one level with other "saints and wise men." A devout Christian would never do this. But I believe

15. See the comparison of the version that was the "original" for Tolstoy with his various renderings: *CW*, vol. 44, pp. 470-71; Alexander Shifman, op. cit., pp. 27-29.

Ramakrishna would agree with this addition, with this specification, as it were, of his words.

Now we come to the last entry signed "Ramakrishna" in the book, *For Every Day,* the entry for 6 June. It is again one of the sayings already quoted: "The petals of a flower fall down, when the fruit begins growing . . ." But again there is a significant change at the end:

> . . .The same with your soul . . .,
> it will immediately be lighted,
> as soon as spirit opens in it his eyes.
> — *CW*, vol. 43, p. 313

The word "God" is once again replaced by the word "spirit."

During the very last year of his earthly existence Tolstoy compiled one more Jñāna-śāstra called *The Path of Life* (in Russian: *Put' zhizni,* which might be translated into Sanskrit as *jīvana-patha*).

Here we find three already familiar sayings of (or after) Ramakrishna (in this book entries are arranged not according to dates, but thematically):

1. When rainwater flows down some gutters . . .
   — *CW*, vol. 45, p. 31

   But the reference to Christ is deleted.
2. As a candle cannot burn without fire, so man cannot live without spiritual force . . . — *CW*, vol. 45, p. 33
   This is taken without changes from the book *For Every Day*.
3. As long as a person sings, cries out, says in everybody's presence: "O, Lord, Lord ! . . ."
   — *CW*, vol. 45, p. 67

   This too is taken with a slight verbal change from the book *For Every Day*.

So, I have practically exhausted the list of sayings and parables which go back to Ramakrishna and have been used by Tolstoy in his works. For the time being I have to leave it to those who know the legacy of Ramakrishna better than I, to judge how adequately the feelings and thoughts of Ramakrishna have been reflected in the passages that I have quoted. I would only risk suggesting that the acquaintance of Tolstoy with Ramakrishna through the medium of the German theosophical journal was bound to be rather incomplete and, so to say, selective. It would be interesting and even necessary to find out what other sayings and parables of Ramakrishna, if any, there were in that theosophical journal and what kind of secondary selection was done by Tolstoy himself.

But now let us analyse further Tolstoy's own sayings about Ramakrishna.

On 14 May 1908 Tolstoy recorded in his diary that on the previous day he had worked at his, by now famous, article "I cannot be silent,"[16] and immediately after this note there come the following words:

> [I] walked by foot, thought well. How wonderfully simple is the solution of life's riddle: the life of an individual — of a Lev, a Pyotr, an Ivan — is an absurd error. It is God that lives in me, and I am His organ. "God lives in everyone, but not everyone knows it." Yes, my soul feels wonderfully well. —*CW*, vol. 56, p. 118

Thus in his diary entry for 14 May 1908 Tolstoy quoted for himself the saying of Ramakrishna which he, Tolstoy, had included in his *Circle of Reading* (1906) exactly under the date "14 May." D.P. Makovitsky in his *Notes* also recorded on 14 May 1908:

---

16. Cf. http://en.wikisource.org/wiki/I_Cannot_Be_Silent

> L. N. said that God lives in all people, but not all people know him (Today's entry in the *Circle of Reading*).
>
> —Mak., vol. 3, p. 88

In Tolstoy's article "On the Annexation of Bosnia and Herzegovina by Austria," finished on 5 November 1908,[17] the seventh part begins with the following words:

> The doctrine, teaching that every human being has in himself the common spiritual principle striving to unity through love, this doctrine has been proclaimed many times and among various peoples: by Confucius, by Lao-Tzu, by Jewish prophets, by the Greek Socrates, by the Buddha, by Ramakrishna, by the Romans Epictetus and Marcus Aurelius, and, in a particularly clear and well-argued way, by Jesus Christ. —*CW*, vol. 37, p. 233

Again, Tolstoy must have had in mind the same saying of Ramakrishna. And this passage is the only one in Tolstoy's published works, other than the Jñāna-śāstras, where Ramakrishna is mentioned by name.

1908 seems to have been the heyday of Tolstoy's interest in Ramakrishna and Vivekananda. D.P. Makovitsky records that on 26 May 1908, having read two volumes of Vivekananda, recently received, Tolstoy said:

> Wonderfully profound: about God, soul, man, unity of religions. He is Ramakrishna's pupil, and died in 1902.
>
> —Mak., vol. 3, p. 96

But further reading of Vivekananda and Ramakrishna evidently disappointed Tolstoy and introduced certain ambivalence in his judgements about them. Unfortunately, he said and wrote very little about Ramakrishna, but there

---

17. This article was published in English in the 1960s under the title *The Crisis of Civilisation* (tr. R.V. Sampson). Cf. http://www.manasjournal.org/pdf_libraryVolume XX_1967/XX-02.pdf

are some passages about Vivekananda that are worth considering in this context. In these passages, written entirely for himself, Tolstoy judges Vivekananda rather harshly, but I am going to quote them not for the sake of their harshness, but because they throw some light on the reasons of Tolstoy's disappointment with Vivekananda and, indirectly, on the reasons of his disappointment with Ramakrishna, too.

On 29 June 1908 Tolstoy wrote in his diary:

> [I am] reading the Hindu (i.e. Vivekananda – *S.D.S.*). Very witty, verbose, and empty. He wants to justify their beliefs in objective beings and their doubts in them.[18] And all this is empty chatter. One thing is and one thing is beyond doubt: *my life and my* possibility and necessity to decide how to spend it. This alone, this alone is the basis of all religions, of all philosophies. And this alone is there.
>
> — *CW*, vol. 56, p. 364

Gnatyuk-Danil'chuk (p. 16) tries to explain away this passage as a sheer misunderstanding of Vivekananda on the part of Tolstoy. But I believe Alexander Shifman (p. 34) is nearer to truth when he comments:

> These critical remarks refer to Vivekananda's affirmation that soul is immortal, that man never dies, because his soul merges with the imperishable world soul — Brahma.

Indeed, the ontological aspects of Vivekananda's philosophy must have been alien to Tolstoy. Moreover the passage just quoted shows that Tolstoy disliked the very style, the very manner of Vivekananda's philosophising. This manner may be called "objective": a philosopher presents statements and arguments about what the world is, what God is, what man is, and so on. Tolstoy, on the other hand, mostly felt like

18. This sentence (being part of a private note, not intended for publication) in the Russian original, too, is rather obscure and, perhaps, needs a kind of deciphering.

philosophising in what may be called a "subjective" manner. In this respect he was akin to some of the existentialist philosophers. This is quite clear from the diary entry quoted above. This becomes even clearer from another entry in Tolstoy's diary of 4 July 1908.

On that day Tolstoy wrote down:

> [I] have read a superb article by Vivekananda about God. It must be translated. I myself thought about this: (1) His criticism of Schopenhauer's "Will"[19] is perfectly right. One thing is wrong: that he starts with an (objective) reasoning about the world (Universe).[20] Reasoning about this is not given to us. And all such reasonings, however important they might seem, are twaddle. Sensible reasoning always may and must start only with the individual, with oneself. To reason about the external, about the world, without having said about oneself, about him who sees the world, is the same as to begin a story like this: "because when he raised his hand against me" etc., i.e. to tell a story without mentioning who, where and to whom speaks.
>
> — *CW*, vol. 56, pp. 138-39

I have dwelt at some length on this point in order to show that Tolstoy's criticism of Vivekananda was not always caused by misunderstanding. Sometimes there were real differences of opinion and outlook. And the same applies to the case of Tolstoy and Ramakrishna.

But, in spite of some disagreements with Vivekananda and Ramakrishna, all through 1909 Tolstoy entertained an idea of a book (or, probably, books) about them in a planned series of cheap books for the common people. There is a revealing entry in Tolstoy's diary on 20 March 1909. First

19. That is, *The World as Will and as an Idea*, the main work of the German philosopher.

20. The word "Universe" in the brackets was written by Tolstoy in English.

Tolstoy mentioned in his talks with his associates, P.I. Biryukov and I.I. Gorbunov-Posadov, about compiling and publishing books for the common people. After that he recorded:

> All through this morning I have been reading the legend about Krishna. *And what I have rejected, having in mind our section of society, is superb for the common people* (emphasis mine – *S.D. S.*): a legend, similar to the Christian one, amidst another, alien people. We have decided [to compile the following books]: (1) an essay about India . . ., (2) the legend about Krishna, and (3) sayings of Krishna. Then possibly (4) sayings of the moderns — of Ramakrishna and Vivekananda . . . — *CW*, vol. 57, p. 40

In Tolstoy's notes and talks through 1909 there are some more references to Ramakrishna, and they are somewhat contradictory.

Thus on 7 May 1909 D.P. Makovitsky recorded that Tolstoy and Gorbunov-Posadov discussed their plans to bring out books for the common people and Tolstoy said that the first book should be about Krishna. Gorbunov-Posadov asked if Tolstoy meant Krishna or Ramakrishna. Tolstoy answered:

> No. Ramakrishna is modern, and he is weak. Among modern Indian thinkers the outstanding ones are Vivekananda — he will have to be abridged and published — and Abhedananda. — Mak., vol. 3, p. 404

But a month and a half later, on 24 June 1909, someone praised in Tolstoy's presence the *Vekhi* (Landmarks), the well known and controversial collection of philosophical and political articles by several Russian authors (published first in March 1909), and, according to D.P. Makovitsky's *Notes*,

> L.N. said that the *Vekhi* are not worth reading (their authors do not know what they want) when one can read

> Ramakrishna, the Buddha, Vivekananda, the Gospel, the Epistle of John. —Mak., vol. 3, p. 450

On 1 November 1909 Tolstoy made a short note in his diary:

> [I] read Ramakrishna. Weak. — *CW*, vol. 57, p. 163

But on 2 November 1909 D.P. Makovitsky recorded:

> He (i.e. Tolstoy – *S.D.S.*) has chosen from *The Sayings of Ramakrishna* 100 aphorisms and wants to add to them something from [Abhedananda's book] *My Master*.
>
> —Mak., vol. 4, p. 94

In those days Tolstoy must have talked much about Ramakrishna, because on 4 November 1909 D.P. Makovitsky recorded an exasperated remark by a lady guest (Mrs. S.A. Stakhovich, a close friend of Tolstoy's family) addressed to Tolstoy himself; "Please leave alone your confounded Ramakrishna!" (Mak., vol. 4, p. 96).

From the commentaries to the 57th volume of the *Complete Works* we learn that at the beginning of November 1909 Tolstoy read a book titled *The Sayings of Sri Ramakrishna Paramahamsa* and published in Madras in 1905[21] (*CW*, vol. 57, p. 381). It is in this book that Tolstoy marked about one hundred "sayings" to be translated and published in Russian. The book itself is reported to have been preserved at the library in Yasnaya Polyana, Tolstoy's estate (now Tolstoy's museum). According to D.P. Makovitsky's *Notes*, as late as 2 December 1909, less than a year before his death, Tolstoy again discussed with Gorbunov-Posadov the would-be book about Ramakrishna (Mak., vol. 4, p. 121). But, unfortunately, during Tolstoy's lifetime this book did not materialise.

It is only after Tolstoy's death, in 1913, that a "Tolstoyan," I.F. Nazhivin, translated into Russian and got

---

21. *The Sayings of Sri Ramakrishna Paramahamsa*, 2nd edn., Madras: Printed at the Brahmavadin Press, 1905.

published Max Müller's book on Ramakrishna, including a selection of Ramakrishna's "sayings."[22] It is worth noting that I.F. Nazhivin's translation was published in the series called "The Green Stick." When Tolstoy was a boy, his elder brother told him that there existed a miraculous "green stick" which could make happy the whole of mankind. The two boys tried to find this "green stick," but failed. And I.F. Nazhivin called his book series with the name of Tolstoy's childhood dream.

So, there is a certain ambivalence in Tolstoy's attitude towards Ramakrishna during 1909.[23] An indubitable interest, on the one hand, and rather harsh critical judgements, on the other. How shall we explain this? For the time being I would suggest the following tentative explanation. Before 1909 Tolstoy had known Ramakrishna only through the mediation either of the German theosophical journal or of P.A. Sergeyenko (who sent to Tolstoy *excerpts* from Max Müller's book, probably having chosen exactly what he thought might interest and please Tolstoy). But when in 1909 Tolstoy himself came to read

22. Max Müller, *Shri Ramakrishna Paramahamsa: His Life and Teaching*, tr. from English by I.F. Nazhivin, Moscow: "Green Stick" Publishers, 1913. It is worth noting that I. F. Nazhivin, in the preface to his translation of Max Müller's book on Ramakrishna, remarked that he had rejected, had not included in his edition, a number of Ramakrishna's sayings, because he considered them "weak." It would be interesting to compare the selections made by Tolstoy himself and by his "follower."

23. For the last year of Tolstoy's life, 1910, we seem to have only one reference to Ramakrishna: in D.P. Makovitsky's *Notes* for 3 April 1910 (Mak., vol. 4, p. 218). In Tolstoy's presence his friend P.A. Boulanger (a Russian with a French surname) praised Ramakrishna. But no remarks by Tolstoy himself are recorded in this case.

an Indian edition of Ramakrishna's "sayings," he was for the first time confronted with the whole gamut of Ramakrishna's feelings, thoughts, and expressions. And obviously some of them went against Tolstoy's own feelings and thoughts, conditioned as they were by modern Russian, i.e. European, culture. Hence the remarks about Ramakrishna's "weakness."

It may well be that sometimes Tolstoy just misunderstood Ramakrishna, because Tolstoy's knowledge of Indian culture was, after all, rather limited (which limitation he shared with the majority of his compatriots). Had Tolstoy understood Ramakrishna better, he might have found him not "weak." But sometimes Tolstoy liked Ramakrishna exactly because he misunderstood his deeds and his intents. For instance, D.P. Makovitsky in his *Notes* recorded that on 18 November 1909 there was a talk about sexual education and Tolstoy said:

> . . . I liked very much: Ramakrishna would dress as a woman and live among women in order to annihilate in himself the consciousness of sexual difference.
>
> — Mak., vol. 4, p. 108

But, as far as I understand, the reasons why Ramakrishna "would dress as a woman and live among women" were different from those surmised by Tolstoy. Tolstoy would have hardly understood or appreciated the real religious reasons of Ramakrishna in this case.

I won't try to further specify here my suggestion and to define what exactly Tolstoy must have disliked in Ramakrishna's "sayings," what he might have understood and what misunderstood. This must become a subject of a careful research. Among other things, one has to study closely the copy of *The Sayings of Sri Ramakrishna Paramahamsa* with Tolstoy's marks preserved in the museum of Yasnaya Polyana, to see what Tolstoy has chosen and what he has rejected. These and similar detailed observations must be included in the framework of a more comprehensive comparative study. There must be compared, on the one hand, Tolstoy's philosophical and religious outlook as a whole, in its evolution, and, on the other, Ramakrishna's religious world. Moreover, these two outstanding personalities should be studied and compared not just as unique thinkers or sages, but as representatives of their respective cultures, of their respective traditions. This is a huge task indeed.

Here and now I would like just to show that this kind of research is very promising and may bring interesting results.

The cultural situations in which Tolstoy and Ramakrishna lived were similar in many important respects. Both in Russia and in India traditional religious systems were strained in the process of modernisation and were confronted with other religions of mankind. Both in Russia and in India there were people who reacted to these challenges by trying to close themselves up in their orthodoxy, to reject any innovation, any search in the field of religion. But in both countries there were also such people who were ready to face the challenges of the time, to find new answers to new problems. Tolstoy and Ramakrishna belonged to this type of people.

Tolstoy first tried to reform the Orthodox Christianity which he had inherited as a Russian. Of course, he himself thought and said that he wanted to go back to the "real", "pristine" Christianity. In this respect he may be compared with certain Hindu reformers of the nineteenth century. But by the end of his life Tolstoy actually went beyond Christianity towards a kind of universal, if rather vaguely defined, religion. I suppose some modern Indian parallels to this may also be found.

Now I would like to quote some passages from Tolstoy, which will show his views on philosophical and religious synthesis, on philosophical and religious universalism.

On 16 May 1889 Tolstoy put down in his diary:

> [I] read an article about Lamenais [*sic*!][24] by Janet.[25] There is much that is good. How to obtain the certainty of knowledge? They always say: by reason? But everyone has his own reason. So an authority is needed: a revelation, confirmed with a miracle. What an awful rubbish. And what kind of sophistry! It is supposed that such a truth is needed with which all people would agree. But such a truth with which all people would agree there is not, not because there is no truth, but because not all agree. And the establishing of truth through revelation confirmed with a miracle does not lead to a greater agreement, on the contrary, it leads to a greater disagreement: a miracle against another miracle, a revelation against another revelation, one negates another. There is no truth, with which all people would agree, but there is a constant movement, both mine and of all people, to the truth with which all agree, cannot help agreeing. All people believe in such truth and go to it. And in the movement towards truth there is always agreement. Disagreement is there only in the imagined fixed truth. — *CW*, vol. 50, p. 82[26]

---

24. Hugues-Félicité Robert de Lamennais (alias de La Mennais, 1782–1854) was a French Catholic priest, and philosophical and political writer.
25. Paul Janet (1823–1899) was a very prolific French philosophical writer. It is difficult to say what paper by him Tolstoy read in 1889. But there is a book: *Paul Janet, La Philosophie de Lamennais*, Paris: Félix Alcan, 1890. In 2008 the book was republished as a paperback:

    http://www.thenile.com.au/ books/Paul-Janet/La-Philosophie-de-Lamennais/9780554781976/
26. Cf.http://az.lib.ru/t/tolstoj_lew_nikolaewich/text_1360.shtml

On 28 January 1891 Tolstoy wrote a letter to D.A. Khilkov,[27] who at that time considered himself a follower of Tolstoy's ideas and suggested that all such followers should meet and, probably, unite. In this letter Tolstoy wrote:

> You say: unity. But unity is possible only in truth. In order to obtain unity with people, we need not go towards each other, towards people, but we all must go towards God or truth. Only there unity is obtained, and not with him with whom I want or suppose that I have to get unity, but with him who has come to the same place where I have come.
>
> I imagine the world as a huge temple, in which light falls down from above towards the very middle. In order to come together, all people have to go towards this light, and it is there, in the middle, that we all, coming from different sides, will come all together — and will meet quite unexpected people. And this is exactly what will give joy. It is this kind of unity and by this kind of means that we can and must seek; but we cannot help each other with this. — *CW*, vol. 65, p. 230

When I first read an extract from this letter in R. Rolland's book on Tolstoy, I recalled right away Ramakrishna's well-known words: *jata mat, tata path* (There are as many ways as there are points of view). Indeed, the similarity here is striking.

And the last passage that I would like to quote is taken from Tolstoy's letter to another "follower" of his,

---

27. Prince Dmitriy Alexandrovich Khilkov (1858 1914) was a Russian military officer influenced by Tolstoy's ideas and persecuted for "Tolstoyism." Between 1887 and 1905 Tolstoy and Khilkov corresponded a lot. But after 1905 Khilkov was reconverted to Orthodox Christianity and Russian patriotism. He died at the front at the very beginning of First World War.

M.V. Alyokhin,[28] who had also suggested that all "Tolstoyans" should unite. Tolstoy wrote back to him in June 1892:

> Unity is possible only in truth, and in order to achieve truth only one thing is needed: to seek it with constant, incessant spiritual efforts. . . . One has to be humble, to get rid of pride, of the vanity of one's own separate opinion, and, above all, to get rid of all such considerations as, for instance, if I believe in this way, I will be with the government or with the people, or with holy fathers or the church, or, if I believe in this way, I may be justified before people and myself, or that it is customary to believe so. One has to get rid of all this and beforehand be ready to accept that the realisation of truth will be unprofitable for me, will humiliate me. Coming together won't help to know truth. There is only one salvation — in coming nearer to truth, and this is the only means of unity. An artificial unification may enfeeble the urge towards truth. . . . Besides, the unity that you seek, the unity in God, is effected at such a depth, where our sight often cannot penetrate. . . . So let us do that which leads to unity, i.e. draw ourselves nearer to God, and let us not trouble about unity. . . . You say it is easier to do things together. What sorts of things? Ploughing, mowing, driving piles into earth — yes, but drawing nearer to God is possible only alone. Only through God, as through a heart, there is a free communication of all parts of a body. And a direct communication, not through God, is but seeming. You must have experienced it. And I have experienced and experience. And what might seem strange: with those people with whom there is a real communication through God, there is nothing to talk about, there is no need to talk, there is no desire to talk, but there is a desire to talk, to argue about something and

28. Mitrofan Vasil'yevich Alyokhin (1857–1936) was a Russian painter, banished in 1900 to the town of Nalchik for his "Tolstoyism."

> define something only with those with whom there is not yet this godly communication; with such people you try to establish a blood-circuit without a heart, but it is impossible, a futile work. — *CW*, vol. 66, pp. 241-42

But at the very end of the same letter, switching, as it were, from the *pāramārthika* (supreme truth) to the *vyāvahārika* (practical existence) level of discourse, Tolstoy wrote:

> . . . Further steps I envisage right now . . . in doing exactly the opposite to what you want, i.e. to separate ourselves, to close our ranks; [we must] do the opposite: to find the best means of communication with the whole large world of all people, to find such a way of communication, which will enable us, without making any concessions, to communicate, to love and be loved. Farewell! — Ibid.

These "sayings" of "Maharshi" Tolstoy, if I am not mistaken, sound very Indian and very topical for all of us today.

Contributors

Androsov, Valeri, a main fellow of the Institute of Oriental Studies (Moscow); the author of: *Nagarjuna and His Teaching, The Buddha Shakyamuni and Indian Buddhism: Present-day Reading of Ancient Texts; Nagarjuna and His Teaching; Dictionary of Indian-Tibetan and Russian Buddhism; Nagarjuna's Buddhist Teaching: Religious-Philosophic Treatises.*

Bongard-Levin, Grigori (1933-2008), an academician of the Russian Academy of Sciences; Head & Professor, Center of Indian and Buddhist Studies at Moscow State University; editor of journals: *News on Ancient History* and *Ancient Civilizations: New Discoveries;* the author and editor of books on the history, culture and philosophy of India; Honorary member of several foreign academies and a recipient of Golden Medal of Asian Society of Bengal, St. Mark award of Venice, Padma Bhushan, etc.

Isaeva, Natalya, a former leading researcher at the Institute of Oriental Studies (Moscow); the author of *Sankara and Indian Philosophy; Word, Creating the World: From Early Vedanta to Kashmirian Saivism*; the main contributor on Vedanta in many Russian encyclopaedias.

Kanaeva, Natalya, a senior researcher at the Institute of Philosophy, Russian Academy of Sciences; main area of study is Indian epistemology and logic; translated and commented "Anumāna-parīkṣā" from *Tattvasaṁgraha* by Śantarakṣita with *Pañjika* of Kamalaśīla and *Nayakarṇikā* of Vinayavijaya; has been teaching philosophy and logic for more than twenty years in different Moscow universities and institutes.

Kostyuchenko, Vladislav, a former (now retired) Professor of Philosophy, Moscow State University; main area of study is Indian philosophy of the nineteenth-twentieth centuries; author of many articles and books like *Integral Vedanta, Classical Vedanta and Neovedantists.*

Litman, Alexei (1923-1992), a former leading researcher at the Institute of Oriental Studies (Moscow); main books: *Philosophical Thought of Independent India; Traditions of Philosophic Naturalism of India and Dev Atman's World-views; Contemporary Indian Philosophy.*

Lysenko, Victoria, main researcher at the Institute of Philosophy, Russian Academy of Sciences; main books: *"Philosophy on Nature" in India: The Atomistic Theory of the Vaiśeśika; Early Buddhist Philosophy; Universe of Vaiśeśika; Buddhism: Religion and Philosophy*; translated and commented in Russian *Praśastapādabhāśya* and *Nyāyakandali by Sridhāra*; teaches Indian philosophy at a number of universities in Moscow.

Ostrovskaya, Yelena, a leading researcher at the Institute of Oriental Studies (St. Petersburg); UNESCO professor; principal works: translation, commentaries and studies of *Abhidharmakośa* by Vasubandhu and *Yogasutra* by Vyāsa (co-author); main area of study: Buddhist philosophy and its practices.

Pimenov, Alexei, a former assistant professor at the Physics-Engineering University in Moscow; main area of studies: Mimāmsā, Indian culture.

Pskhu, Ruzana, PhD, assistant professor, Department of History of Philosophy at the Peoples' Friendship University (Moscow). Author of *Vedārthasaṁgraha of Rāmānuja and Formation of Viśiṣṭādvaita.*

Rudoy, Valeri (1940 - 2009), a leading researcher and head of division on Buddhist studies at the Institute of Oriental Studies (St. Petersburg); principal works: translation, commentaries and studies of *Abhidharmakośa* by Vasubandhu and *Yogasūtra* by Vyāsa (co-author); main area of study: history of philosophy, religion and culture of Asia and Far East.

Sementsov, Vsevolod (1941-1986), a former senior researcher at the Institute of Philosophy, USSR Academy of Sciences; main works: *Problems of the Interpretation of Brahmanic Prose, Bhagavadgita in Tradition and Modern Academic Commentaries;* poetry translation of Bhagavadgita in Russian.

Serebriany, Sergei, Director, Institute for Advanced Studies in the Humanities, Russian State University for the Humanities, Moscow; the fields of research work: Indian languages and literatures (Sanskrit, Hindi, Bengali), Indian philosophy; comparative studies; publications include: *Vidyāpati; Vidyāpati's "Puruṣa-parīkṣā"* (translation from Sanskrit), *The Novel in Modern Indian Culture.*

Shokhin, Vladimir, Head, Department of Philosophy of Religion, Institute of Philosophy, Russian Academy of Sciences; Head & Professor, Chair of Metaphysics and Theology, State University of Humanities; principal books: *Ancient India in Russian Culture: XI –XV centuries; Brahmanic Philosophy: Formative and Early Classical Periods; Moon Light of Samkhya: The Samkhyakarika of*

Isvarakrisna with the Commentaries by Gaudapadacharia and Sri Vachaspati Misra; The Tatwa Samasa, the Samkhya Sutra Vriti; The First Indian Philosophers; Nyayasutras with their commentaries, *Nyayabhasya, Indian Philosophy of Sraman Period.*

Stepanyants, Marietta, the Director of the Center for Oriental Philosophies' Studies at the Institute of Philosophy, Russian Academy of Sciences; Head & Professor, UNESCO Chair "Philosophy in Dialogue of Cultures"; main works: *Islamic Philosophy and Social Thought (19th – 20th Centuries), Sufi Wisdom; Introduction to Eastern Thought; Comparative Ethics in a Global Age.* (Ed.); the 1st Vice-President of the World Federation of Philosophical Societies; initiated the establishment of Mahatma Gandhi Chair on Indian philosophy in Moscow of which she has been the Head and Professor since its foundation.

Terentyev, Andrey, a former research fellow at the Institute of Oriental Studies (St. Petersburg); main area of studies: Jainism and Buddhism; translation of Sanskrit and Tibetan texts; publisher & editor of the journal *Buddhism in Russia.*

Index